TIME AFTER

Studies in Continental Thought

John Sallis, EDITOR

Time After Time

David Wood

Indiana University Press

Bloomington and Indianapolis

This book is a publication of

Indiana University Press
601 North Morton Street
Bloomington, IN 47404-3797 USA

http://iupress.indiana.edu

Telephone orders   800-842-6796
Fax orders   812-855-7931
Orders by e-mail   iuporder@indiana.edu

Library of Congress Cataloging-in-Publication Data

Wood, David (David C.)
Time after time / David Wood.
p. cm. — (Studies in continental thought)
Includes bibliographical references and index.
ISBN 978-0-253-34896-8 (cloth : alk. paper) — ISBN 978-0-253-21909-1 (pbk. : alk. paper) 1. Time. 2. Heidegger, Martin, 1889–1976. 3. Derrida, Jacques. I. Title.
BD638.W6545 2007
115—dc22
2006039401
1 2 3 4 5 12 11 10 09 08 07

To my mother
Mary Elizabeth Wood

Contents

Preface   ix
Acknowledgments   xi

Introduction   1

PART I. WHY TIME BREAKS DOWN

1. Interruptions, Regressions, Discontinuities:
   Why Time Breaks Down   9
2. Time-Shelters: An Essay in the Poetics
   of Time   24
3. Economies of Time: Beyond Activity and
   Passivity   37

PART II. HEIDEGGER'S STRUGGLE WITH TIME

4. Reiterating the Temporal: Toward a
   Rethinking of Heidegger on Time   59
5. From Representation to Engagement   84
6. Glimpses of Being in Dasein's Development:
   Reading and Writing after Heidegger   102

PART III. THE EVENT OF TIME

7. The Event of Philosophy: Heidegger,
   Foucault, Deleuze   119
8. Political Openings: Heidegger 1933–34   131
9. Following Derrida   144

PART IV. ART AND TIME

10. The Dark Side of Narrative   163
11. Thinking Eccentrically about Time:
    The Strange Loops of Escher and Calvino   170
12. Art as Event   182

Notes   203
Selected Bibliography   231
Index   241

Preface

In *The Deconstruction of Time* (2nd ed., 2001), I set aside the surface quar-
rels between phenomenology and deconstruction to pursue a key common concern—rethinking our traditional "metaphysical" understanding
of time and indeed many of our commonsense views. In pursuit of this
aim, I engaged with that other tradition of Nietzsche, Husserl, Heidegger,
and Derrida, demonstrating that Derrida's declaration that there can be
"no non-metaphysical concept of time" blinds us to the fact that our age
is one of unprecedented flourishing for alternative ways of understanding and inhabiting time.

In *Time After Time*, this project is extended and deepened by wider
and more sustained considerations of our experience of the breakdown
of narrative continuity and integrity, by more specific engagements with
Heidegger and Derrida, and by forays into both art and literature. *Time
After Time* echoes the idea that "The king is dead; long live the king." A
certain sense of time has broken at the knees, but time and the temporal
have never been more conspicuously central to contemporary experience. In particular, the horizon of the future seems to have fractured.
The end of the cold war seemed to open up unlimited possibilities for
human progress. And yet globalization and free trade seem to bring
more poverty and conflict, and to put into terminal doubt the very idea
of progress. Global warming opens up the prospect that background
conditions we took to be constant may be shifting in ways that threaten
the sustainability of life on the planet. And yet the political will to respond effectively seems to be missing, putting into question our most
cherished political institutions. This book does not focus explicitly on

ix

these shifts in the tectonic plates of history but on the experiential, conceptual, theoretical, and philosophical shifts in which they are undoubtedly reflected.

Acknowledgments

I have dedicated individual chapters in this book to the memory of Paul Ricoeur and Jacques Derrida, a very small token of the gratitude I owe to each of them and of my boundless admiration for both. This book has gestated over many years and conversations, and I am grateful to many other interlocutors: Robert Bernasconi, Jay Bernstein, Walter Brogan, Jack Caputo, Ed Casey, Tina Chanter, Paul Davies, Joanna Hodge, Len Lawlor, John Llewelyn, Antje Kapust, Richard Kearney, Catherine Keller, Irene Klaver, Rick Lee, David Levin, John McCumber, Michael Naas, Kelly Oliver, Morag Patrick, John Protevi, John Sallis, Dennis Schmidt, Charles Scott, François Raffoul, Jonathan Rée; my Warwick ex-colleagues, especially Keith Ansell-Pearson, Andrew Benjamin, the late Cyril Barrett, Christine Battersby, and Miguel de Beistegui; and my Vanderbilt colleagues, especially Michael Bess, Beth Conklin, Volney Gay, Michael Hodges, Gregg Horowitz, José Medina, and Diane Perpich. I have profited immensely from discussions with my (many now ex-) Ph.D. students on this topic, especially Robin Ambrose, Joel Beaupré, Bret Davis, Jonathan Dronsfield, Darren Hutchinson, Apple Igrek, Zbizek Kotowitz, John Mullarkey, Aaron Simmons, James Williams, and Jason Winfree. Finally, I owe my initiation into the phenomenology of internal time-consciousness as an undergraduate at Manchester to Wolfe Mays (1912–2005). His memory too is dear.

I would like to thank Janet Rabinowitch and Dee Mortensen of Indiana University Press, as well as John Sallis, the general editor of Studies in Continental Thought, for their support and interest in my work over the years. Thanks too to Carolyn Cusick for a first-rate index.

I am grateful for permission to draw on all or part of the following publications in preparing this volume.

Chapter 2: revised version of "Time-shelters: an essay in the poetics of time," in *Time and the Instant,* edited by Robin Durie and David Webb (Manchester: Clinamen Press, 2000).

Chapter 4: revised version of "Reiterating the Temporal: Heidegger and Destiny," in *Reading Heidegger: Commemorations,* edited by John Sallis (Bloomington: Indiana, 1992).

Chapter 8: revised version of "Political Openings: Heidegger 1933–34," in *Graduate Faculty Philosophy Journal,* New School for Social Research, 1991.

Chapter 9: revised version of "Following Derrida" in *Deconstruction and Philosophy: The Texts of Jacques Derrida,* edited by John Sallis (Chicago: University of Chicago Press, 1986).

Chapter 10: incorporates material from "Double Trouble: Narrative Imagination as a Carnival Dragon," in *Transversing the Imaginary,* edited by Peter Gratton and John Manoussakis (Evanston: Northwestern University Press, 2005).

Chapter 11: revised version of "Escher and Calvino: Thinking Eccentrically about Time," in *Journal of Philosophy and the Visual Arts,* edited by A. E. Benjamin (London: Academy Editions, 1989).

Permission to use the following images is gratefully acknowledged:

1. M. C. Escher's "Ascending and Descending," © 2006 The M. C. Escher Company-Holland. All rights reserved. www.mcescher.com.

2. Thomas Cole, *Voyage of Life: Youth* (1840), © Munson-Williams-Proctor Arts Institute.

3. Robert Smithson, Yucatan Mirror Displacements (seventh), 1969. Nine original slides © Estate of Robert Smithson / licensed by VAGA, New York, N.Y. Image courtesy James Cohan Gallery, New York.

TIME AFTER TIME

Introduction

It is certain to me that the world exists anew every moment; that the existence of things every moment ceases and is every moment renewed.
—Jonathan Edwards

The eternal hourglass of existence is turned upside down again and again, and you with it, speck of dust! Would you not throw yourself down and gnash your teeth and curse the demon who spoke thus? Or have you once experienced a tremendous moment when you would have answered him:—"You are a god and never have I heard anything more divine."—If this thought gained possession of you, it would change you as you are or perhaps crush you. [. . .] How well disposed would you have to become to yourself and to life to crave nothing more fervently than this ultimate eternal confirmation and seal?
—Nietzsche

The time is out of joint.
—Shakespeare, *Hamlet*

Arriving at the title of this book was an exercise in humility, the kind of humility that borders on humiliation, the kind that only trawling Amazon (or Google) can deliver to a prospective author. I had been toying with "Time and Time Again," a suggestive phrase that could be lifted out of vernacular speech and be dignified as the name of a book. It turns out some fourteen other people have had the same idea. Ever flexible, I thought I might anyway prefer *Time After Time*. (Was I just replaying Aesop's fox's reaction to high-reach grapes?) But this fair lady too had danced with many other suitors—more than danced, in fact. After this chastening experience, it took me a while to realize that most of these authors (and their publishers) had been perfectly happy, unless they were bone ignorant, to re-use a good title. Why should I be so picky? And they were writing romantic fiction, sci-fi, mysteries—not "philosophy." I realized too that, right under my nose, this reluctant student was being taught a valuable lesson about time, history, repetition, and originality—the very subject of the book. I seem to have wanted some

1

virginal opportunity to teach some innocent young phrase the delights of civilized subtlety for the first time. Instead, I discovered what I "knew"—the "always already," that I am not the first, that the norm of creativity is (re-)interpretation, transformation, productive inheritance.

At first glance, this seems like a comedown, the recognition that our desire for the truly original is a chimera of worldly innocence. But this deflationary verdict may be premature. Perhaps we should not oppose originality and repetition at all. What if a certain repetition were a condition of originality rather than an obstacle to it? The premise of using a title like *Time After Time* was (of course) that this is a well-known phrase whose redeployment as the title of an academic book generates a certain effect of semantic (and genre and voice) dislocation. The fact that it has been used as the title of other books from popular culture—not to mention CDs—in a sense extends or redoubles the semantic plane that is being productively dislocated.[1] It is perhaps an oversimplistic formulation, but the central tenet of the dislocating redeployment here is the movement from an unconscious associative level of significance to one in which the phrase is explicitly offering itself as the object of multilayered reflective interpretation.

And there is no need to understand this remark in an elitist way—claiming that the philosophical deployment of this term is superior to its everyday senses. It is certainly different in that it encourages the (re-)articulation of the mysteries of repetition. But these mysteries are in so many ways the stuff of life itself—waking up each morning, falling in love (again), the birth of a child, daily habit—which we both negotiate and indeed marvel at before formal philosophizing ever enters the scene.

There is a delightful passage in *Of Grammatology* in which Derrida cites Saussure's outrage at the historical corruption of the surname Lefèbvre (into Lefebure) by a typographical error.[2] Derrida responds by embracing the unloved "bastard" word. And we can do the same with the heterogeneous history of our title in the world of books and music.

Nonetheless, it is hard to accept the idea that there is nothing new under the sun, that everything is just some form or other of continuity. This, however, would be another mistake—an important mistake and not unconnected to the lesson of Borges's story about Pierre Menard, who rewrote part of Cervantes's *Don Quixote* word for word, but produced a completely different text:

"Cervantes' text and Menard's are verbally identical, but the second is almost infinitely richer. (More ambiguous, his detractors will say, but ambiguity is richness.)"[3]

The point of these thought (or writing) experiments is that originality does not have to do with the surface content of the phenomenon in question, but rather with its relation to history, context, cultural setting, and so forth. There is a wholly *formal* way of elucidating a paradox of originality—that most banal repetition fails as repetition because if the original event was not a case of repetition, the subsequent case (or repetition) will fail to capture the salient feature of the first, namely, its originality. To truly repeat, one would have to repeat its originality, which is impossible. One can at best be original in a new way. Nietzsche's concern (in *Thus Spoke Zarathustra*) with mere followers takes up this issue, as does Heidegger's understanding of a productive reading of an illustrious predecessor. (This question is taken up at greater length in chapter 6, "Glimpses of Being in Dasein's Development.") One has to bring *one's own guiding idea* to the reading to engage at a sufficiently deep level.

The formal paradox suggests two possible solutions to our negotiation of repetition. First, that where repetition grasps the nettle and sets itself to rework the inaugural power of an earlier event, it can be affirmed, not as an exact repetition of a content, but as a newly situated transformation of the power of the original. Second, mere repetition, surface imitation, properly speaking, fails even as repetition—as Kierkegaard well understood—because it does not understand the event status of the original.[4] To compound the puzzle one more step: it has to be admitted that (even) the "pale imitation" case of repetition cannot wholly be characterized negatively. In all its historical exhaustion, it may yet do something it did not intend. And here again, there is another opening. Years of empty ritual conformity may preserve a symbolic practice for subsequent reanimation.

But is there not a residual sense in which the ragtag jostling marketplace from which the phrase "Time after time" emerges is a threat to my authorial control, and hence to the integrity with which I chose *this* title rather than *that*? I cannot surely rule out the misunderstandings that this thick entanglement of cultural connections carry with them, and I cannot claim credit for all the rich associations that readers will bring to their understanding of this phrase. But such hesitations are foolish. These concerns can be raised about any word to which one gives the promise of new life. The issues of blame and credit are really not to the point. One (re-)launches words and phrases thoughtfully, reflectively, but finally with a hope and a prayer. We can only do so much. After that they are on their own.

My recovery from disappointment over the title of this book echoes what I went through when Northwestern refused to allow me to revise *The Deconstruction of Time* on the occasion of its republication (2001). I was upset and frustrated until I realized what an impossible and unending task that would have proved to be. Instead, they invited me to add a new Preface, which gave me all the freedom I could possibly have wanted and little of the responsibility.

In these two cases, I have highlighted the affective dimension of a repetition, exploring how, in each case, its significance and value changed when it was affectively reframed. These accounts generalize the import of the Nietzschean epigraph hung over the gate to this introduction.[5] Nietzsche was writing about the idea of eternal return, that everything would get repeated exactly and infinitely, and he imagines two completely different existential responses to this thought. Despair seems obvious enough. But affirmation? How could one view the eternal return as a source of exhilaration? The secret, perhaps, lies in the precise way he puts the question: "How well disposed would you have to become to yourself and to life to crave nothing more fervently than this ultimate eternal confirmation and seal?" What seems to be at stake is the possibility of taking up a radically different attitude to oneself and to life, from which a different attitude toward repetition will flow. We can call this an affective transformation, but it is more than that. It is a matter of cognitive restructuring too. Consider the experience of waking up to a new day. Obviously, one can just stumble semiconsciously into the day. But what is it like to face the repetition of a "new day" in a clear-sighted way? How can one avoid the horror that nothing much has changed, "here we are again," and that this will happen over and over again for the foreseeable future? The sense of horror seems justified. But it rests on a certain synthesis of present and past (and future) in which one stands outside the present and compares this moment with past and future ones. One discovers that these moments are substantially the same, and one can feel trapped in empty repetition. But this thought only works if one is willing to privilege the detached comparative attitude. And there is a ready alternative available—to affirm the singularity of this moment, or this opening onto the day, and come to enjoy its sensuous (and in other ways living) actuality. At the extreme, one comes to appreciate even what presents itself as an exact repetition for its *this-timeness*. Eating a delicious peach would give no new pleasure if the pleasure of the last delicious peach were still fully available. The sheer renewal of sensation, recognizing the need for this renewal—that pleasure remembered is not pleasure sustained—is one source of an affirmative transformation of the condition of repetition. But there are clearly others just as powerful, especially if we abandon the high desert of Nietzsche's exact repetitions, as Deleuze insists we must.

In the various discussions of the *event* that follow, I talk about ways in which particular events, or eventuations, creative openings like those offered by thinking or by art, can mirror what is at least a central dimension of the structure of time as such—its openness to the future, its surging forward, leaving behind "what has been." And yet this "central dimension" is clearly not the whole truth about time, for we also find regressive repetition, an inability to break out of destructive cycles, as well as many healthy ways of keeping the past alive, resisting the impulse to start all over again. Moreover, instead of thinking that we need to contrast ways of transforming the past with true creativity; we have come to see that the two may be inseparable. When it comes to art, this general truth can nonetheless get specified in quite different ways, from Barnett Newman's sublime witness to the moment, to Robert Smithson's proposed remedial transformations of abandoned mine-workings, and his responsiveness to ruin and devastation.

This book repeatedly takes up in various ways the theme of the breakdown of Time, or more cautiously, of our traditional models of time. As much as we have come to appreciate the pervasiveness of narrative, we have lost faith in its capacity to supply the big picture, to the point at which one could almost recycle Hegel's verdict on art and say that "narrative, considered in its highest vocation, is a thing of the past"—that it can no longer provide the deep assurance that it once could, even though local narrativity runs riot. I show how the novels of Italo Calvino and M. C. Escher's lithographs each "deconstruct" the illusion of narrative continuity even as they hang their integrity as works of literature or art on that very illusion. And in a broad assessment of Richard Kearney's commitment to the narrative imagination, I try to show how it actually operates in counterpoint to disruptive tendencies (such as the "double") that it cannot tame, what I call the "dark side" of narrative.

There is perhaps a broader pathology of temporal connectivity, symptoms of which are to be found in the relative attenuation, if not collapse, both of social memory and of the capacity to project a shared future for our community, whatever that might be. Our destiny is less and less manifest, and our fate more and more troubling. This breakdown is not just happening "out there" in culture—I argue that individual human development from childhood onward delivers to us, as adults, a package of incompletely worked-through ways of being, crudely lashed together. What Heidegger calls *Angst* can be understood as our flickering access to earlier ways of being in the world. This implies that our temporally and historically engaged existence will *standardly* involve negotiation with our layered temporal multiplicity.

The broadly existential trajectory that this sets up explains in part my continuing sympathy with the project of *Being and Time* and its various successive echoes in the 1920s, even as I have come to appreciate much of what he attempts in his later writings. Heidegger's tragic political engagements in 1933–34 have everything to do with the possibility of projecting a future for one's community, while his writings from the mid-1930s onward (*Contributions to Philosophy; Nietzsche*) are in part attempts to deal with the breakdown of the capacity to actively project and envision such a future (having had his eyes opened to the madness of the Third Reich). His solution? A withdrawal from the temptations of philosophical prescription and legislation into a certain reticence, preparing the way, calling on the gods to return. But again, what suffered breakdown was the narrative of restructuring, of revolutionary transformation, of implementation. And Heidegger's whole new manner of writing bears awkward witness to this change and presents us with the challenge of reading him, coming after him. Can we understand him better than he understood himself? This may seem presumptuous, but it is precisely what he claims with respect to Kant, and what Kant claims with respect to Plato.

This is my entry point to a time-driven re-reading of Heidegger himself that brings out the significance of our incomplete human development, as we have just seen. It is also the issue driving the chapter "Following Derrida," originally a conference paper immediately preceding a major presentation by Derrida, which attempts to deal with the problem that can be variously identified as Nietzsche's refusal of followers, Bloom's anxiety of influence, and the general problem of how one extracts oneself from the transferential grip of a powerful philosophical mentor. "Following Derrida" dramatizes in a singular way the struggle between the desire for originality and the recognition that one is overwhelmingly indebted to the other, even for the terms in which originality might be measured.

If this book has a methodological integrity, it rests on the repeated invocation of the idea that the task of philosophy is to create and recreate the space of tension and struggle within which received wisdom insecurely basks. "Time after time" points both to repetition as the site of so many of these struggles and to the emerging field of complex, stratified, nonlinear temporality that becomes visible after a more innocent sense of time has become a thing of the past.

PART I. WHY TIME BREAKS DOWN

1

Interruptions, Regressions, Discontinuities
Why Time Breaks Down

The dimension of time has been shattered—we cannot love or
think except in fragments of time.
—Calvino

Nietzsche said that we had not got rid of God if we still believed in grammar. The same could be said of time. For Time, too, is dead—the great
river has dried up, the great dam has burst, and the turbines of grand
design have ceased turning. What remains are the little creeks, the
tributaries, the rhizomal springs, the seasonal flood and droughts. Time
has become fractured, dispersed, irregular . . . plural.

For a brief period—perhaps only as long as the Enlightenment—time
was on our side. That "we" even constituted a side had everything to do
with the great river called progress, emancipation, equality, and justice.
For most of us, such secular theodicy has been shattered by the horrors
of war, genocidal extermination, and now the prospect of environmental
meltdown. If the model of time as a great river has any purchase on our
reason or imagination, it is now quite as likely to be as a subterranean
flow that threatens to wash away the foundations of the city, and indeed,
of nature. But this apocalyptic vision is arguably just an inversion of
what came before.

There are those who would lament this state of affairs, who would
mourn the demise of this myth. I propose to celebrate it, and to discuss
its positive consequences. This breakdown has two different implications. First, the historical delimitation of the idea that time has some sort
of substantial unity spawns not just the apocalyptic substitution of a
rather different unified fate, but also a concern for a differential set of
finite temporalities, of which any temporal unity would be a *product*,
rather than a presupposition. We might tentatively call this an ontic
treatment of time, in which what is revealed is structural complexity.
Second, the linear continuity of time can be seen, not as a necessary

9

truth, but as a quite specific structural presupposition, which can itself be historically delimited. Such delimitation releases us, as we shall see, into time as an essential openness. This might equally tentatively be thought of ontologically. Our thinking about time is transformed if we allow ourselves to make these moves.

Preliminary Itching and Scratching

In his book *Einstein's Dream*, Alan Lightman begins to recount the reverie of May 20, 1905:

> A glance along the crowded booths on Spitalgasse tells the story. The shoppers walk hesitantly from one stall to the next, discovering what each shop sells. . . . These are not tourists in Berne on their first visit. These are the citizens of Berne. Many walk with maps, directing the map-holders from one arcade to the next in the city they have lived in all their lives. . . . Many walk with notebooks, to read what they have learned while it is briefly in their heads. For in this world, people have no memories.

Such imaginative experiments with time are becoming increasingly common. I started listing movies (*Last Year at Marienbad, Back to the Future, Hiroshima Mon Amour*), and writers—Joyce, Proust, V. Woolf, Calvino, Marquez—until it became clear how redundant it is to give examples of what we meet around every corner. Modern culture bears pervasive witness to the breakdown in the traditional lived experience of time. We may not, literally, have lost our memories, but loss still attaches itself to memory—and not just to specific items of the past, but to the whole framework in which past, present, and future are coherently connected.

It would be tempting to try to construct the story of this breakdown, a story that would speak of the development of accurate clocks, of the industrialization of the day (hourly wages, timetables, schedules, etc.), of the development of capital and its accompanying institutions, of insurance, and more recently of broadcasting and the Internet—introducing global simultaneity.[1] These historical ingredients would, of course, be part of the story. So too would be their various impacts on our experiences of our bodies, our relations to each other, our identity, and of the passage of time itself. Yet at the brink of such a narrative, we hesitate. Not out of the complexity of the task, which would be cause enough; we hesitate over the very project of narrativity—whether we still have confidence in the fundamental grounds of intelligibility that narrative presupposes. Who, you may wonder, is hesitating here? Just the fastidious philosopher? Perhaps, but such hesitation is an opportunity for all of us to reflect on where we stand with regard to time. For Augustine, it is thinking about time that initiates the perplexity, that begins to scratch where it had never itched. But in this age, when time is in so many ways out of joint, there is plenty of itching and scratching before ever the philosopher comes on the scene.

I attempt here to explain why it seems to us that time is out of joint, why it *is* out of joint, and how we might respond to this situation.[2] I begin with a minimal account of the structure of our human temporality against which I hope to be able to illuminate the inadequacies and failures of the options currently available to us. Hesitating turns to trembling here when I think of how presumptuous this schematic account is, but here goes.

1. We cannot understand ourselves—our experiences, our actions, our lives—simply in terms of our position on one or more temporal series, ordered in terms of before and after. We cannot avoid understanding ourselves in terms of past, present, and future.
2. We need an account of the dynamic quality of our insertion into this framework, for the relation between past, present, and future is a complex and constantly moving feast.
3. We need to acknowledge the ways in which this dynamism is both intimately tied to representation and subject to various forms of representational sclerosis, leading to empty repetition.
4. We need to recognize the importance of what could be called affective horizonality as well as the interplay between our capacity to project a future and the health of our grand narratives about time and history. This affective horizonality is perhaps most visible when the closing down of our time-horizon coincides with a practical and affective disengagement.
5. We need to acknowledge the impossibility of settling our accounts with the past.
6. We need to keep open a sense of what I will call the infinite possibilities of the moment, which would constitute a point of radical disruption to the imagined linearity of time.

Time Is Not Just a Philosopher's Invention

Oscar Wilde once returned from France, declaring that "reports of my death have been greatly exaggerated." When we philosophers say that something is dead, does not exist, or has ended—this has been said of God, of art, of the subject, of the author, and of philosophy itself—an adaptation of Wilde's remark seems appropriate. The humor of this remark lies in the fact that Wilde is playing off an all-or-nothing alternative (between life and death) against a judgment of degree, where "exaggeration" might be an appropriate comment. It is just this tension that fuels much philosophical reflection.

Time is dead in the sense that models of its overarching unity no longer convince us. It would be easy to reply that they were never anything more than philosophical fictions. For example, to claim that Hegel's model of time as the form in which Spirit unfurls its inexorable developmental path is at best limping to a sorry end is to say something that might upset some of the philosophical faithful, but would not worry those who never bought into this idea in the first place.

The moral of these examples might well be a generalization of the logic of "The king is dead, long live the king"—that all that has proved itself unworkable is a form, or a formulation, or a version of a certain idea. Not the idea itself. And that, of course, is itself a formulation of another general law of time—the cycle of life: birth, growth, decline, death, rebirth.

But this response is too sanguine, too complacent. And not just because, as Derrida once claimed, time is essentially a metaphysical concept and every reformulation would turn in this same circle. The bubbles that philosophers blow often burst without too much fallout. But the idea of time as a single, intelligible, coherent continuity is not just a philosopher's invention, not just a representation, as we might say. It operates, or has operated, in some form or other at the basis of the Enlightenment idea of progress, the Christian idea of providential history and salvation; and indeed, it seems to have transmuted itself into the basic tenet of capitalist expansionism. And to be quite clear about this—I am not talking just about theoretical constructions, but about the deep backdrops of our everyday experience. It still might be replied that these stories are not really stories of continuity at all: Christianity involves an initial fall and a subsequent redemption, the Enlightenment explicitly arises out of the dark ages, capitalism is self-consciously contrasted with feudalism, and so on. But this only forces a necessary clarification—that continuity does not imply that there is no change, even serious change. It can even accommodate "setbacks," decline, recovery. Perhaps, then, continuity should be thought of as suspended from a principle of intelligibility, not built on some more primitive principle of succession. The unity-through-continuity (or otherwise) of an individual human life, for example, is not assured just by temporal succession, but by the possibility of experiential and reflective integration—the story one can tell of one's life. And what this all suggests is that the difficulties on whose door we are knocking are not to do with time as *constitutive* of human experience, as Kant would say, but rather its *regulative* employment. Time, understood as the successive orderability of all experience, might, in some sense, be an a priori condition of experience. But nothing guarantees that such formal assurances will add up to intelligibility at the human level. The question then becomes—if we understand these grand narratives of time as "regulative ideas," that is, as ways we need to believe that time and history can be organized, as umbrellas of intelligibility— what if these umbrellas have holes in them? Could such regulative ideas decay and become unusable? For Kant, regulative principles only "offer rules according to which a unity of experience may arise from perception."[3] To suppose otherwise is to fall into illusion, as he says in his "Transcendental Dialectic."

Interestingly, it is just this word *illusion* that Freud repeats when he locates the source of the religious illusion in our attempt to provide assurances of safety to our infantile sense of our own helplessness. And if anything like Freud's argument holds up, the "end" of Time offers a powerful example of the withering away of a regulative umbrella.

I will delay unfurling a discussion of this umbrella function just for a moment. First, I need to establish something only so far hinted at— that the overarching accounts of time that we draw from science and from our own practices of measurement do not begin to meet the kind of need we are discussing. It may well be that everything that ever happens can, more or less, be located within the calendar system, the series of dates and times that, at least in principle, opens indefinitely in both directions from the birth of Christ. Such a system employs the principles of counting, succession, and divisibility to ensure that every event, in principle, can be temporally tagged. But this holism of temporal accountancy does not supply significance. If anything, it mocks our desire for significance.[4] We fare little better when we consider what physics teaches us—at least when it allows that time can be detached from space—namely, that it does indeed have a direction, one supplied by the thermodynamic law that tells us that the universe tends toward the maximizing of entropy, as Clausius put it (1865). In other words, the law of the increase of disorder. Now it would be wrong to refuse to connect this with human experience. Anyone with a kitchen can bear witness to the local power of entropy. But human experience is precisely that of resistance to entropy, trying to create order out of chaos, to cultivate gardens on the edge of the jungle, to create shapes and symmetries out of the messy stuff of the world, to slow down our own drift into death and decay. So if anything, thermodynamics provides not so much a backdrop of intelligibility as the stage on which we humans continually shout our defiance: Do not go gently into that good night. . . .[5]

Here, perhaps, we rejoin Freud's discussion of religion, which begins from our helplessness as infants but testifies to the fact that insofar as we are living beings seeking to preserve our life and strength, we struggle even as adults with overwhelming powers.[6] We only ever win the "life and death" struggle temporarily.

The Enlightenment and Christianity share a teleological structure, whether it is truth, freedom, and prosperity or salvation that is promised. For the thinkers I grew up reading—the gang of iconoclasts from Kierkegaard and Nietzsche to Heidegger, Foucault, and Derrida—these visions lie in ruins. As Francis Fukuyama puts it, "The twentieth century has made all of us into deep historical pessimists." But one does not need to have had iconoclasts for teachers. The twentieth century had its own ways of making us doubt. The idea of providence never claimed that the road would be straight and smooth. But in the slaughter of the world wars, in Hiroshima, and in Auschwitz, the python of providential history has found pigs even it could not swallow. Even Fukuyama's *The End of History*, a book touted for its triumphalism, written after the fall of the Berlin Wall but before Bosnia, ends with more cautious remarks such as, "It is possible that if events continue to unfold as they have done over the past few decades, that the idea of a universal and directional history leading up to liberal democracy may become more plausible to people." The evidence for there having been, in the end, "one journey and one destination . . . must remain provisionally inconclusive," he says, and adds that even if we all arrive at that place, we may subsequently "set [our] eyes on a new and more distant journey."[7]

I quote these remarks, not just to show that Fukuyama's triumphalism is more muted than some have suggested, but to bring into sharper focus the very status of the claims being contested. The struggle, as he presents it, is between relativism and liberal democratic progressivism. Fukuyama suggests that if things carry on (getting better) as now, the "idea of universal history may become more plausible to people," though "the evidence must remain inconclusive."

Fukuyama's book is in many ways a brilliant tour-de-force, but even leaving aside Derrida's devastating demolition job in *Specters of Marx*,[8] what is clear from these last pages is that the "idea of a universal history" can at best be a provisional hope; it can never again be a compelling principle of reason. Fukuyama's account of how people might come to find it "plausible"—the experience of a few good years—is exactly the sort that leads people cultivating the potash-rich soil under a volcano to believe it will not erupt again.[9] The idea of a providential history, and more generally, of a universal and directional history, has been broken.[10] That is not to say it cannot be put back together again, but it will not then have the same status. This is as it should be. And we may expect that the conflict between "relativists" and "universalists" might come to take a more productive form.

An interim gloss on why time breaks down would be this: Whether we are concerned with cosmic time, the history of the world, or our own lifetime, or our daily experience of time, whether we are theorists or not, "Time" is essentially tied to questions of coherence, connectivity, significance—to what we might call horizonality: frameworks of experience, understanding, expectation, interpretation. We see the germs of this connection to meaning when an uncanny coincidence occurs—a repetition, a memory, a chance meeting—and a small umbrella starts to sprout. "It was destiny!" "It was meant to be!" "Accident" doesn't stand a chance. To say that time breaks down is to say that in many ways, at many levels, the expectations, desires, and demands we make of the world for its intelligibility are not met. The fact that the regulative is not constitutive breaks through our hull like an iceberg.

Time, Identity, and
Fragmentary Social Practices

It became fashionable in the 1970s to discover ruptures, breaks, and discontinuities where before we had imagined continuities, identity, smooth transitions. In the academy, this often degenerated into polemics in which listening to the other side ceased, and genuine rifts appeared! And yet much of what was going on consisted of mock battles, confusions over the nature of the struggle, and over the level at which concepts like break, continuity, and rupture operate. I will argue that these mock battles provide an opportunity for us to refigure our understanding of time. But despite the methodological difficulties attendant on the production of another grand narrative, I will show that these time-wars and identity-wars do not come out of thin air.

The simplest, most general kind of model I have in mind when I think about discontinuity, regression, and interruption would be this: that many of the entities, the systems, the situations we come across, which it might be tempting to understand in terms of the development of some inner principle (like subject or substance), need instead to be understood in terms of the simultaneous cooperation of a number of distinct "economies," or subsystems, or guiding desires, or interests. Our failure to make the intellectual shift from what we could call a metaphysical postulate of substantialist identity to a grasp of identity as an achievement of cooperation (often fragile and unstable), means that certain problems become insoluble. Or they become soluble only by pathological means, as when a nation understands itself in terms of racial purity and then implements measures to effect this purity, so avoiding the need to confront the more complex problems of cooperation. The recognition of multiplicity amidst apparent unity illustrates the importance of models in guiding interpretation but does not tell us anything specific about time. Suppose, however, that within political systems based on justice a claim to injustice arises, and that this is tied to a historic failure of recognition—a description that could have been taken from Aristotle's account of the grounds for revolution. This description fits, for example, the Civil Rights Movement, numerous European peasant revolts, and various demands for ethnic recognition and self-determination the world over. The demand for recognition is not just the demand for fairness of distribution. It may be a demand for historic compensation (as with the Native Americans over the expropriation of their land)—which is one form such an eruption can take, or it may be a demand for acknowledgement, even apology. The need for recognition seems to be irreducible to material compensation (though there are points of connection). Political systems that fail to address both may be taken aback by the unassuaged anger of the unrecognized. Moreover, the variant—misrecognition—can provoke the same reaction. And once we admit that the symbolic dimension of social and historical existence operates according to different laws than those that focus on our material prosperity, we not only find ourselves entering into the "incalculable" dimension of (for example) social trauma (e.g., the history of slavery) but also into the intersection between social history and individual psychology. The difficulty of effecting a successful apology or offering of recognition may well be bound up with the economies and investments of individual psyches. What we think of as a mature adult human is not a being who has entirely left behind his childish ways, but rather a being who has orchestrated a generally successful balancing act between instinctual desires, infantile anxieties, and adjustment to "reality."

It has been a common complaint that the deconstruction of the subject, of identity in all its forms, is a species of intellectual irresponsibility, on the grounds that it takes an integrated or integral "I" both to act and to take responsibility.[11] Promoting deconstruction is thought to weaken the moral fiber. Of course it can easily be argued that precisely the reverse is true—that although it may weaken the dogmatism of true-believer essentialism, this is a theater of cruelty we can do without. It can be argued that responsibility requires a kind of *phronesis* that does not so much massage the boundaries of self as acknowledge their historicity, multiplicity, and so forth.[12] But I offer these counterarguments only as a prelude to a more serious claim—that these disputes are, at least in part, based on what Ryle called a category mistake.[13]

As human agents and subjects we find ourselves immersed in, regulated by, and variously constituted by many different orders or "economies," to each of which is attached a certain schema of time and identity. Simply as embodied beings, for example, we are caught up in diurnal metabolic cycles, cycles of sleeping and waking, menstrual cycles (for over half of us), and processes of maturation and aging. These interwoven cycles sustain various economies of self-maintenance, reproduction, and death. We are also symbolic beings engaged in certain social practices—of recognition, witnessing, taking and attributing responsibility, making promises, saying "I" and "you"—in which, by and large, we take part as unanalyzed identities. And parallel practices of the management of time arise in the way we find ourselves locked into various legal, financial, and political practices in which our names and signatures play central roles. Or more accurately, the practices by which we manage deviations from the present (contracts, debts, credit cards, etc.) are where we need to look to understand the boundaries and norms attached to our names. So we find that even having a name is a many-layered phenomenon, as are the opportunities and constraints, the constitutive norms that surround and permeate it, which begin in families and friendships, and become increasingly circumscribed by legal and financial systems.

Nietzsche described Christianity as a hangman's metaphysics. Perhaps we could add that modern liberalism is a debt-collector's metaphysics. The deep claim in each case is that if identities are tied up with the management of boundaries, the values by which such management is achieved are derived from the complex social practices of which they form a part. And these social practices may not be obviously human in any traditional sense; rather, they are exhausted by certain accountancy algorithms. The "I" that is a complex of body rhythms, and by virtue of having a name belongs to so many systems of identification and recognition, and as a number has a distinct status on all kinds of legal and financial (and medical and employment) records—this "I" is also utterly fragmented in its interface with the world of commodity consumption. As consumers, our identity is utterly redundant. For this part of the economy to work, we could each be simply a collection of mutable temporary desires and identifications. Consumerism encourages what Marcuse once called repressive desublimation, the dissolution of a complexly integrated self into one committed to the satisfaction of its desires, with little residual capacity for discerning, except by trial and error, what its true desires might be.[14] To understand capitalism as an economic system in the strong sense is to understand it as a machine, and as essentially invasive, by which I mean that it operates by the blind and ruthless disregard and penetration of every boundary generated by a different or earlier distribution of "things." It is only at a particular phase of its development that capitalism has anything to do with individualism.

Capitalism is the most creative destructive force the world has ever seen. Traditional symbolic boundaries such as self, body, family, life and death, nation, even species, are all being probed and questioned, not by nihilistic postmodernists, but by the force of capital itself. Some examples: corporate raiders who buy a company, analyze it into profit components, and realize its assets by breaking it up; commuter marriages, in which partners live in different states, even different countries, maintaining bonds by e-mail and air travel; the medicalization of health and pregnancy, in which our bodies become the sites of small business partnerships with hospitals and drug companies, and death becomes an accounting question; multinational companies more powerful than states that can in effect buy the legal system, the tax system, the financial institutions they need; the imminent creation of trans-species or designer species for commercial purposes; the creation of cloned organ reserves—farms for living spare parts that fit exactly our year and model number. If we feel anxiety, even revulsion at any of these thoughts, which only stray a little into the future, we could perhaps understand that feeling as the marking of a boundary, like the bump when we drive over the curb.

Consequences for Our Experience of Time

We can keep our heads in the sand, or we can, to use an image of Husserl's, shine our light into the dark corners, even though we may fear what we see. I want now to explain why and how all this has consequences for our experience of time.

Freud used to think of himself as an archaeologist of the mind, digging up buried memories. But the analogy quickens when we imagine a desert storm uncovering long-hidden remains, or a high tide washing ashore relics from a sunken wreck. Freud offers us a picture of the human being as the product of what I will call incomplete development.[15] In different books he argues for and speculates upon human development on at least three distinct levels:

1. As complex living beings, with a continuing relation to primitive forms of life and even inorganic existence;
2. As civilized humans, bearing residues of social formations present at the dawn of man;
3. As adults, trailing around a complex history of our development and maturation from infancy that we never quite leave behind.

The implication of each of these stories is profound and cuts right across any suggestion of a genetic fallacy. For they each tell us, not just how we have got to where we are today, but what it is for us to be where we are today. They tell us that where we have been continues to be part of where we are, who we are. As Heidegger puts it in *Being and Time*, "Dasein is its past."[16] How can this be? Surely our past is . . . past—over? Of course, various backdated propositions are true of me—that I was born on this or that day. And clearly I am the product of all the causal influences on me. What more is there to say?

The really interesting claim implicit in Freud's work is that we are the products of a series of incomplete transformations from one mode of psychic organization to another, which correspond to different modalities of intersubjectivity—from self-blind dependency to self-conscious autonomy.

What I mean by incomplete transformation is this: that we never wholly leave behind previous structures of organization, that even in our adult maturity, we are driven by interests only partly sublimated, we are inhabited by infantile longings that erupt unexpectedly, and so on. These are not just individual memories, but structures or economies of selfhood. And what we call maturity, sanity, and so on are more or less well-managed strategies of cooperation between these different economies. If Freud is right, one of the commonest places at which time breaks down is in dreams. The unconscious has no use for the linearity characteristic of what we ordinarily understand by time. As such, dreaming is a break in the shape of our experience. And if, as he believed for the most part, dreams are wish-fulfillments, then of course even if the sequentiality of dreams is hard to pin down, they are themselves expressions of a regressive temporality, a displacement of action in the real world onto an imaginary scene. Moreover, if he is right about the death-drive, this too is a symptom of a fundamentally regressive tendency of the organic—to return to a more archaic state. Finally, of course, we must mention his account of *Nachtraglichkeit*,[17] usually translated as "belatedness," or deferred action, which is more than simple delay, but rather involves the translation or recoding of an earlier event onto a later one. Such an idea not only effects a break with any simple continuist model of ideality, but it also proposes what one might call a dimension of action prior to the distinction between space and time, one whose economy consists of signifiers and psychic forces.

I have mentioned Freud not to champion his position, but to give an illustration of a model of an identity composed of a set of distinct layers of psychic economy, whose "unity," insofar as it is achieved, is a product of luck and good management, as well as struggle. This stratified identity makes it easier to see how a variety of interruptions could occur.

So far I have gestured in various ways at how even within an entity that is relatively self-contained, something like interruption can occur, juxtaposing what could be loosely called a "return of the repressed" to some kind of *aufhebung*, in which time would be figured progressively as a sequence of immanent exhibitions. The claim is both that the appearance of unity needs to be thought of as a multiplicity and that these various dimensions have their own rhythms, economies, or logics. I have suggested that different ways of inhabiting time are bound up with different ways of managing boundaries of the Self. We can see this in the way in which, as Freud describes it, the Reality Principle serves to moderate and (by delay) to fulfill the strivings of the Pleasure Principle, and we can each testify to the experience of shifting from one economy to another, risking serious danger for intense and immediate pleasure, or deferring present satisfaction for a greater chance of future pleasure. We have each witnessed in ourselves and others the switch from what one could call a negotiating stance, where the boundaries of possibility are elastic, to a rigid, even paranoid stance, where boundaries are staked out and defended "to the death." Our understanding of temporal continuity follows the same lines of cleavage—"That's it, it's over. I never want to see you again" *versus* "We need time to work this out."

More broadly, the same could be said of the distinction between constitutive and regulative ways of organizing time. We might suggest, for example, that when Kierkegaard talks about "despairingly willing to be oneself," he is talking about escaping our subjectively constituted desperation by suspending it within a regulative framework of hope. The movement from one frame to another brings a dramatic—even life-saving—interruption. In Kierkegaard's case, we should recall, the possibility of this form of existential salvation followed what Kierkegaard himself called an "earthquake," a conversation in which his father confessed to him such severe improprieties as would bring about the classic Freudian displacement onto an ideal father.[18] Kierkegaard's conversion of the father principle produces a kind of reaffirmation of a certain affectivity of time, an umbrella of hope.

Conclusion

The breakdown of Time is one of the most thought-provoking aspects of the present age. It calls for a sophisticated response—not just at the level of theoretical representation, but also at the level of experience, interpretation, reading. The implication of the previous section is that while there may well be many regressive, infantile, primary-process-type sources of anxiety that pitch us back into rigid traditional ways of inhabiting time, this very insight opens up the very complexity of our temporal dwelling that can release us from those regressive modalities. It is characteristic of what we could call the rigid personality to insist on black/white, yes/no, binary choices. "You are either with us, or with the terrorists." Merleau-Ponty describes a fascinating experiment in which people are shown a sequence of images of a dog morphing into a cat. Some notice the process, others insist that the dog stays a dog or that the cat was always a cat. This suggests, rather nicely, that category rigidity has a direct temporal correlate—the inability to accept transition, change.

This either/or logic precisely infects our affective relation to time. It is not difficult to interpret attacks on the absence of ultimate grounds as attacks on intelligibility as such. While this conclusion may not be rational, it does adhere to a certain (rigid) affective logic. We can see

the practical impact of the erosion of the middle ground of temporal fa-
cility in the growth of depression and addiction. Depression could be
said to be a pathological disabling of the horizonality of time in which
the past does not function as a resource, and the future is not available as a projective ground. If we are right, the subjective horizonality
of time is intimately tied to the broader symbolic apparatuses available
and the interpersonal nexus. Addiction, in this respect, is peculiarly
symptomatic—especially where the vehicle itself gives pleasure and a
certain vacation from the real. For as repetition of the same activity,
addiction could be seen as a form of the synthesis of time that overrides
the contingency of the everyday and that guarantees a minimal sense of
projectable identity. Whatever the future will bring, I (and my habit)
will remain intact. But this "solution" is captive to a rigid logic that insists that only guaranteed continuity, only the appearance at least of an
autonomous identity, will do. And if the grand umbrellas have broken,
then the smallest intact identity shelter is an oasis in the desert of time.

We have something to learn—as philosophers, theorists, thinkers—
from these pathological expressions of horizonlessness. And it is precisely in avoiding the temptation of all-or-nothing, either/or, absolute
guarantees or despair, that we can begin again, as Heidegger put it, to
think. So the final question I want to pose is, What would a thinking be
like (and a comportment) that would expect the unexpected, not rob it
in advance of its powers, but in some way welcome it?

Nietzsche's response to this question is unavoidable. For him, the
death of God meant very precisely the end of all absolute grounds or
underpinnings, and in particular, the collapse of cosmic or human teleology. And Nietzsche saw as the most urgent need an antidote to the
pessimism that might ensue. Although he called it his most scientific
hypothesis, the idea of eternal return is also a litmus test of the success
of our affective transformation, of whether we have weaned ourselves
from the absolutist dependency. The question he asks is, Can we affirm
(not just accept) the idea that everything that ever has been, is, and ever
shall be, has already occurred (and will again) an infinite number of
times?

We could discuss the literal claim Nietzsche is making here, but his
point is to leave no more room for a providential teleology than does the
myth of Sisyphus.[19] Eternal return is not itself the answer. It is a supposition just as crazy as the one it displaces. It *needed* to be! Its power lies
in that although it purports to be a representation of time, it also *explodes*
representability, for there is no discernible difference between any event
and its identical repetition. The central idea of affirmation is a kind of
conversion of this unrepresentability of time, but it remains essentially
abstract. The task Nietzsche bequeaths to us is to let it concretely inform
our thinking.

I would like to outline, schematically, something of what an affirmation of the end of Time might look like. First, there was something right about Lyotard's welcoming of the variety and the wealth of local small-scale narrative activity—in the wake of the demise of grand narrative.[20] The restoration of a limited legitimacy to the fairy tale, to songs, to the testimony of the dispossessed, to diaries, to confessions, is a form of resistance to what we might call the "tall stories" of the West. And I would link this recognition of a power of proliferating narrativity to Ricoeur's attempt at a resolution of the various aporias of time through a general account of narrative as a reworking of Kant's productive imagination.[21]

Narrative links together history, literature, and biography with the fragments of self-understanding by which we come to understand ourselves and our lives in conversation with our friends. Narrativity is a democratic, elastic, sense-making activity that also enacts a resistance to the infinite dispersion of our commodified lives. In narrative, we may find powerful resources for filling out our existential historicity, resources that bear witness to our finitude and mortality, on which, as Heidegger claims, any access to history as a discipline ultimately rests.

It would be wrong to think of narrative solely in terms of representation. It has a dynamic and a pathos that exceeds representation. And most importantly, it takes us time and again to the brink of representability, when, for example, someone who is asked to "tell their story" cannot speak, or cannot be heard.

When Heidegger says that what is most thought-provoking in this most thought-provoking of ages is that we are still not thinking, he is not saying that we cannot tell stories.[22] What he is trying to reopen is the horizon of response, or openness within which any synthetic or productive activity takes place. Thinking is not just a doing, but (as he puts it) a thanking, and tied to memory, or what we might call responsiveness. And in his later writings, he comes to speak of the possibility of (an) event: *Ereignis*.[23]

With Heidegger, and also with Levinas, Derrida, Lyotard, Benjamin, we have come to hear many voices of the Event, in which the fate of philosophy itself, or whatever needs to succeed it, is tied up with a certain fundamental reorientation to time. At great risk of obscuring vital differences, we could say that understanding time as Event in this way restores to the Moment the possibility of inaugurating a radical renewal. This can be expressed in terms of Being, the infinite, the Other, even the messiah.[24] Radical renewal does not mean beginning linear time again. It is a relaunching of time itself as intensity, possibility, as open.

What are we to do with this? Or make of this? We could add these stories of the Event to our compendium, but this would miss the point. While they may appear as claims about the Moment, about the Now, about the nature of temporality, they are best seen as ways of interrupting even our most exciting narrative play, giving us reason to hesitate, to ponder, to invite, to welcome something of a different order. The messiah, the *ubermensch* and their like, would not, in fact, be other beings, but precisely our developing capacity, which perhaps cannot be realized in an instant, to allow that all representations draw on what exceeds them and open onto possibilities they cannot envisage: productive dependency.[25]

Afterword

Academic life can be wonderful, and it can at times be discouraging. I recall a discussion at the Robert Penn Warren Humanities Center at Vanderbilt, at which one of my colleagues (a chemist, as it happens) spoke up for the Real World in the most unproblematic tone of voice, in the course of a conversation that seemed to him to have got away from it. And he was right; some of my other colleagues had got lost in word games. But the truth is that both parties had hopelessly lost touch with that fragile space of detached engagement that is the privilege of the university. To speak of the Real World without a trace of hesitation betrays a lack of education. Equally, to think that Reality is just another concept that we use is to have hopelessly lost touch—not just with "the Real," but with the ongoing task of thinking. Such thinking is a reflective practice, a practice that indeed has an object but that operates with a historically determined discourse, that deploys its concepts rhetorically, that does not just describe but produces knowledge, that is engaged in a necessary idealization from which questions of relevance, applicability, even "truth," inevitably flow.

What I called hesitation is not a real-time event. I am speaking of a certain practical recognition that our theories rest on schemes and that between schemes and things there are not just inevitable gaps, but an abyss of difference. He who does not hesitate is lost. It is my bet that the "negative capability"[26] required to function effectively in this abyss is to be found in all that work in the sciences and the humanities that can remember well enough (which often means recognizing the impossibility of adequate memory) to be able to welcome the event of time. Then Einstein's dream of a town without memory will no longer be an allegory of our contemporary existence.

2

Time-Shelters
An Essay in the Poetics of Time

> And the source of coming to be for existing beings is that into
> which destruction, too, happens, according to necessity, for they
> pay penalty and retribution to each other for their injustice
> according to the assessment of Time.
> —(Anaximander)[1]

The greatest thinkers, from Anaximander onward, have known that time is not merely a diverting topic but a pervasive and hydra-headed problem. Indeed, much philosophy reads like the construction of sea-walls against it. For time is the destroyer of all that we are proud of, including pride itself, and it even threatens the realization of philosophy's highest ideals.[2] Time is the possibility of corruption at the deepest level. And yet, without time's synthetic powers, without organized temporal extension, there would be nothing to be corrupted. Time makes as well as breaks. Time giveth and it taketh away.*

However, the pervasiveness of time in philosophy does not arise simply at the level of intuition—that all things are finite, and all experiences are in time. Its shadowy form lurks beneath the surface of most of the central problems of philosophy, and it has a major impact on how we think of identity, of truth, meaning, reason, freedom, language, existence, and of the self; the list is endless. Even talking of a major impact on these problems is too weak a verdict. It would be wrong to imagine there being happy, respectable problems only subsequently visited by the scourge of time. Without time, these would not be the problems that they are at all. How a person stays the same person over time may be a problem. But would we be persons at all without the challenge this problem presents? In brief, time is not just a special problem, not just the proper object of research on the philosophy of time.

---

* This meditation on time-shelters is dedicated to the memory of Paul Ricoeur (1913–2005).

Yet the ubiquity and pervasiveness of time does not, as tidy minds might hope, make it discountable. If everything, in addition to its natural color, were tinted by a peculiar shade of pink, we *could* discount the fact, because we could neither detect the color nor understand the meaning of this condition. But time is not the name of a simple predicate or homogenous condition. Nor is it simply the name of a neutral dimension on which independently identifiable things can be ranged, like birds on a telephone wire.

Is there then any overarching way in which we can start to think of time? If we followed Anaximander, we could say that time is the economy of being.

Anaximander's fragment has stimulated many different translations and readings, and I do not intend to enter into these matters here.[3] But it is clear that there are a number of different *levels* at which it could be read. It is a vision of cosmic pathos: everything comes and goes. It allows us to focus on the very phenomena of emergence into presence, lingering persistence, and withdrawal. And it points to a radical *heterogeneity* in time. Time involves not just a sequence of identical now-points but a plurality of *beings* whose being is dramatized temporally.

This latter perspective is the one I wish to pursue here. And I can begin to explain the title of this chapter by recalling the title of an eccentric and delightful book by Gaston Bachelard: *The Poetics of Space,* a study of intimate spaces.[4] Bachelard combined, in the most remarkable way, a scientific and a poetic mind, and this book is dedicated to the description of a whole range of worldly enclosures—shells, cupboards, nests, houses, boxes. It makes a powerful contribution to the project of providing alternative models to that of a single neutral geometrical Space, a project being pursued in so many ways—from Merleau-Ponty's phenomenology of embodiment, to the recent renewal of interest in architecture.[5] But what would a poetics of time look like? And what use would it be?

The Poetics of Time could title a work celebrating the literary, existential, and artistic variety of temporal forms. I will not be doing that directly here, but what I propose will bring it closer. Allow me to offer for your contemplation two principles, each with powerful consequences for our philosophical practice:

1. Critique, deconstruction, revisionary metaphysics (however different from one another), each presuppose a prior level of philosophical engagement with phenomena that we will here call *interpretation*. They are not *substitutes* for it, though they may demonstrate its limits or set up a backwash of new considerations for further interpretation. But they *do* presuppose it.

2. Such interpretation itself presupposes typically unthematized *schemata* of space and time. And these schemas have a crucial role in determining even the limited adequacy of our interpretations.

I am concerned here with pursuing a particular reading of the Anaximander fragment—one in which time appears plurally in beings whose being is dramatized temporally. I will be providing a framework for the way in which time enters into the constitution of beings, not just Being—of things, events, complexes of relationships, institutions, persons, and so on. With a glance back at Bachelard, in this poetics of time I will call all such beings *time-shelters,* even if I have to concede that the distinction between space and time is if anything even more fragile than the boundaries that mark out beings from one another. Consider, for example, the ear, its labyrinthine complexity dedicated to the requirements of sound and its transmission, or those shapes for charming time that we call musical instruments.

Time-shelters could be described as local economies of time. The word *economy* here responds to two exigencies: to preserve a metaphysical neutrality of the sort that Husserl's phenomenology attempted to sustain— in particular, to belong to the pole of neither the object nor the subject; and to capture the possibility of formally describing the modes of constitutive and regulative management of the boundaries of things of all sorts, by which their being and identity is created and preserved. The language of economy is as suitable a discourse as any in which to pursue ontological neutrality (a theme developed in the next chapter, "Economies of Time"). Where what we call natural phenomena are being discussed, the claim is being made that they exhibit general properties that transcend their natural domain.

What is a time-shelter? Let me offer an account in a somewhat queer key: the universe as a whole is entropic. Human beings, however— indeed, all living beings—are essentially negentropic. In the midst of growing disorganization, we find creatures that consume and manufacture organization and complexity, whether at the molecular level or that of information. These frames generate internal boundaries within the world, ones that both establish and mediate the relationship of inner and outer. No model of the world as a homogeneous unity survives a moment's scrutiny. And the presumption of a higher-order synthesis of these lower-level orders (as for example in Leibniz's *Monadology*) will here be suspended for want of plausibility. The implications of this for our thinking about time are profound. If there are semi-autonomous local economies that relate in each case to various "outsides," then the boundary between inside and outside will function much as what has been described as an event-horizon at the "rim" of the astronomer's black hole. A boundary is not a thing but a cluster of procedures for the management of otherness. Crossing the boundary brings about a discontinuity of both spatial and temporal relationality. Such discontinuities provide what we could call shelters for the growth of more luxuriant forms of spatial and temporal organization.

This phenomenon of sheltering has enormously wide ramifications, but I would like to clarify its significance before offering some illustrations. Shelters are persistent forms of event-discontinuity in the world. They manage the boundaries of inside and outside by representing the outside within; by translating, buffering, and anticipating that which impinges; by resistance, accommodation, expansion, and exchange; and by establishing for these purposes rhythms, rules, and regularities. But they are not, and cannot be, sealed to the outside, nor are they immune to total transformation or destruction. The boundaries of shelters are essentially permeable in ways that allow interruption—invasion, infection, corruption. It may always be possible—I take no view on this—to give a location in world time to sheltered events. What is distinctive about shelters and their event-horizons is that such external correlation is often as tortuous as translation between languages.[6]

The implication of all this is not that there are absolute boundaries sheltering local temporalities (as there may be with black holes), but that such boundaries, at which are negotiated and managed the literal transactions across them and which pose difficulties even for the virtual penetrations of description and calculation, are nonetheless real. The language of flux is not enough. Or at least there are orders of flux.

Husserl's account of the phenomenology of inner time-consciousness begins innocently enough, we might think, by a methodological bracketing-out of the world and of objective time so as to focus on the indisputable temporality of inner time-consciousness—which would seem to survive even the destruction of all we know—as long as we can still dream, remember, or imagine. My initial appeal is no less intuitive, and indeed arguably allows us to step back even more effectively. Most of the "things" we see around us are shelters of the sort I have described—from football matches to musical performances, from chemical reactions to trees, from states to universities. What they have in common is that they each exhibit semi-autonomous temporal organization—not just organization in time, but of time.

But how are we to think of temporal structure and organization? Time is distinct from any appearance. It is not in itself anything we can have in front of us, present to us. When we do think about it, it is easy to identify it with the passage of time. We can witness the flowing of the stream, the rising of the sun, the movement of the hand on the clock. If we think of time simply as change, then clearly we have some direct experience of it. And some such object or content of consciousness is essential. Sheer empty consciousness, were it imaginable, would be an eternal present. Temporal structure is, however, available to us more indirectly—through music, for example, which provides us with powerful intuitive access to the idea of temporal structure.

Music, we could say, is the dramatization of time in all its variety. And that very variety, ranging from fugue to Cage, gives us some intuitive access to times and temporal structures in the plural. The awareness we have of our own bodily rhythms—pulse, breathing, sleeping and waking, hunger and satiation—undoubtedly functions as something like a clock, as the metronome that each of us is, a primitive somatic synthesizing of time. It is surely such rhythmic interlacings that a phenomenological theory of temporal constitution takes for granted, so that we always arise and find ourselves, not just as heavy sacks of skin set off against the world, but in rhythm. If music is, in this sense, a derived experience of time, dependent on the temporal organization of our embodiment, it allows us for the first time a glimpse of these structures, precisely through the operation of aesthetic distance. I hear the music; I am not identical with it as I am with my own rhythmic jungle. For Plato, art directs us to timeless forms, but music directs us to the forms of time. For all the importance of tone, timbre, and other intrinsic qualities of sound, music also exemplifies a radical reduction of the real, sensory reduction, selectivity, separation from objects, even persons. Music is perhaps the best intuitive source we have of temporal structure. It exhibits variation, development, coordination, interference, interweaving, and recapitulation as well as all the psychological dimensions associated with memory and expectation. It combines the operation of rules, rhythms, and repetition to occupy in an exemplary way that middle ground in which subject and object are intimately entangled. And if this is so, we find in the structure of music the same phenomenon of double mapping that characterizes the traditional concept of the person as a being subject both to rules and rhythms and to principles and passions. Although I shall not pursue the matter here, it is clear that the interference patterns between these two types of temporal structure generate many of the problematic self-understandings we find in traditional reflections on the self. More generally, openness to the entanglement of distinct and conflicting times, plots, and even logics is a powerful hermeneutic principle when thinking about people, texts, history, and natural phenomena (e.g., disease, atmospheric changes such as global warming, economic cycles).[7]

It is important to clarify the status of this account of time-shelters. It operates primarily at what I would call the ontic, rather than ontological level. And I believe it conforms to powerful intuitions about what entities in general are—relatively autonomous local economies of time (and, it has to be said, space).[8] Identity, on this model, has a great deal to do with this relative autonomy or semi-permeability to what is external; it is something sustained rather than given. This very account of identity exhibits the same property of having to be sustained and developed. I take it not merely to be a description of the way things are, but to have hermeneutic power, the results of which will confirm its value as a model.

I did not begin with Anaximander for nothing, and in this account of time-shelters, there is clearly an adumbration of the ontological as well, for it offers a very general account of what it is for anything at all to be. But to talk about the ontological is not necessarily to talk about totality. What does this account of time-shelters do for the traditional problem of whether time is one or many? To pursue the project of articulating local temporal economies, we have to suspend the thesis of the unity of time, to put it out of action, as Husserl would say, just as one has to suspend one's ordinary visual relation to the world when looking through the microscope, and one's ambient auditory awareness when listening to music. We suspend the thesis of the unity of time in the following sense: we no longer take for granted that all times will line up in a single series, that all series have the same form, and even that all time is serial. It may be argued that this thesis nonetheless has a regulative value—I think it does—but the recognition of such a regulative value is squandered if it remains an a priori reassurance.[9] It is far more productive to interpret the unity of time as a principle of boundary permeability, which could be expressed in the following way:

All beings are realms in which a certain more or less powerful order holds sway. Each order constitutes a boundary, hence an inside and an outside, or a laminated set or entangled matrix of such insides and outsides. These boundaries are not, however, primarily spatial, but economic. And insofar as economy is concerned not just with permanence and continuity but also with destiny, transformation, dehiscence, and conflagration, then what is at stake is always time. If, as I am claiming, local economies generate discrete temporal interiorities, then the thesis of the unity of time would change its modality. It would become a claim about the permeability, corruptibility, and fragility of any autonomous time. Not all that is fragile breaks, and the vulnerability of all boundaries to breaching does not license temporal totalization.[10] The pianist always *may* collapse in the middle of a live performance, but most often, human mortality allows the concert its own time.[11]

All this is offered as a contribution to a hermeneutics, not just ontology. There is, however, a great gap in this whole account, a massive lacuna. I have claimed that beings of all sorts are time-shelters, that they exhibit, contain, and are constituted by, local temporal orders, between which there can be both allergy and respect. So far I have given little idea of how these responses arise, or how they are possible.

The language of economy allows a certain ontological *neutrality,* which licensed our putting to one side the question of the origin of time-shelters or the extent of our contribution to their emergence, maintenance, and disappearance. That we could successfully even begin without considering such matters does, of course, betray a certain concealed ontological commitment—that these local economies that we call beings have a certain autonomy in relation to individual human beings.

Let me be explicit: I am not considering the universe as it might somehow be in-itself, in its noumenal reality. Nor am I considering it in the idiosyncratic light in which it appears to this or that subject. Our account of time-shelters can, for the most part, be understood as an account of a dimension of our thrownness, what we find ourselves already in, confronted with, surrounded by; ways in which the real is already constituted, determined, articulated; ways we take over and adopt as our own, and in so doing come to be subjects in the first place. Time-shelters are not just *subjective* phenomena, but describe the umbrella forms of what *we* take to be real.

What is it, then, that is so resoundingly mute in our account? The name we commonly give to that field of meaningful structures in which we find ourselves is language. To draw language successfully into the temporal constitution of beings is something I cannot begin to tackle here in any general way. Even in individual words, language names, honors, creates, protects, holds open, and preserves the beings we have described as sheltering and being sheltered by local time. Through *poetry*, language can bring these realms to presence, can make manifest the fragility of their lingering between coming into being and passing away. And in what Aristotle called his *Poetics*, it is through those dramatic constructions of language that we call tragedy that man's own finitude is taken hold of and worked through. Language as *poesis*, as making and constituting, is inseparable from the appearance of such time-shelters.

There is, however, a particular way of pursuing this connection between time and language that I would like to discuss briefly here—one in which it is the being of "man" himself that is in question—that remarkable intellectual adventure which Paul Ricoeur offered us in *Time and Narrative*.[12]

The site of Augustine's perplexity about time was that of reflection. And in view of the subsequent efforts of philosophers, one might think that there was something about reflection that doomed our thinking about time not just to initial confusion but to final failure. In this book Ricoeur takes up the challenge and singles out as the persistent difficulty in the history of philosophy that of reconciling, of doing equal justice to, both phenomenological and cosmological time. In the story he tells, Aristotle's understanding of time as "the number of movement with respect of the 'before' and 'after'" gives us no way of thinking about time as experienced, even if an apprehending subject is actually required on

Aristotle's model. Augustine's account of the distention of the soul, while it addresses that problem, does not offer us any basis on which to think of objective time. And he needs to be able to account for this, because he wants to say that time began at the point at which the world was created. Kant, Ricoeur suggests, may give to the mind the role of being the condition of worldly time, but gives us no phenomenology of experience; while Husserl, for his part, has great difficulty in reconstituting objective time after the *epoché*. Finally, Heidegger's attempt to think of world-time as a leveled-off, authentic time is a failure, because even this world-time, Ricoeur claims, is tied to individual Daseins.

I will not, at the moment, comment on the details of this story. What it indicates is the scope of Ricoeur's concern about time. His suggestion seems to be not merely that time is pervasive, as I have claimed, but that Augustine's perplexity about time reflects a deeper failure to think time: not just Augustine's failure, but the failure of a tradition.

Time and Narrative is structured around a hypothesis—which in mock-Heideggerian idiom Ricoeur sums up at one point as the claim that narrative is the guardian of time. More carefully expressed, it is the claim that the phenomenology of time, found, for example, in Husserl's *Phenomenology of Internal Time-Consciousness,* "the most exemplary attempt to express the lived experience of time," leads to the multiplication of aporias. And these tangles only get unraveled through "the mediation of the indirect discourse of narrative."[13] One can hear Kant's claim that intuitions without concepts are blind in Ricoeur's insistence that phenomenology must embrace the conceptual resources of language. But he is going further and saying that what Kant called schematism in his Analytic of Principles, the application of a concept to an instance by a productive rule-governed imagination, need not be thought of as "an art concealed in the depths of the human soul whose real modes of activity nature is hardly likely ever to allow us to discover and to have open to our gaze."[14] It can be found "writ large" in narrative.[15] Through narrative, successive events are subjected to *configuration,* a concept that generalizes Aristotle's account of plot in his *Poetics.* Narrative heals aporia.

But Ricoeur's extraordinary power and virtues as a thinker emerge most strongly in the final chapter of *Time and Narrative III.* Here he reviews the argument of the book, and as if the ravages of time and reviews could not be relied on to do it for him, he begins to unravel his own knitting. The hypothesis that narrative relieves us of the aporetics of time is seen to have limits. One of the central products of narrative is to allow us to construct a narrative identity—both at the level of history (and, for example, the identity of a nation),[16] and at the level of the individual life. This represents a considerable advance over accounts based on substance, or bodily continuity, or memory. Ricoeur had approached this idea earlier in his book on Freud, in which psychoanalytical treat-

ment, which Freud himself had called "the talking cure," is seen to cul-
minate not in psychic readjustments but in the construction of a story
that makes sense of one's own life, or especially those parts of one's own
life that would otherwise be unthinkable.[17] Narrative draws in and allows mediation between causal and intentional time; it encompasses
both events that happen to me and actions I perform. In this way it deploys our most powerful synthesizing abilities in constituting an identity.
And insofar as it deals with both events and actions, it could be said to
transcend the aporetic opposition between cosmological and phenomenological time.

In our idiom, Ricoeur's account of narrative, when applied to the
constitution of personal identity, manages the boundary of the self—
excluding what will not fit, articulating what will. A person is not just
a body, but surely the need to maintain boundaries is presupposed by
any concept of personal identity—the idea of an individual substance
would be only a magical solution. But it is open to the objection that it
makes identity somewhat unstable, insofar as many stories can be woven
from the same material. Ricoeur treats this, not as an objection, but as
a limitation—a distinction to which I shall return. We might equally
regard it as an advantage to have a model that can accommodate the
contingency and revisability of identity, a model that is not an all-or-
nothing solution.

Ricoeur also admits another, perhaps more worrying problem. Narrative identity *stresses the intelligible organization of events* at the expense of
the will, the ethical moment, the moment of decision, of impetus. (He
alludes to Levinas on promising, but he could equally have cited Heidegger.) In each of these examples, narrative does not just heal, it opens
new rifts—first, the irresolvable plurality of stories, and then the opposition between the organizing power of imagination, on the one hand,
and the will on the other. Ricoeur's account of the significance of these
difficulties is classic. Narrative does not *resolve* aporias, it makes them
productive, which suggests that a formal or logical solution to our problems (for example, McTaggart's proof of the dependence of the B-series
[cosmic time] on the A-series [lived time]) may not be required even if
it were possible. His further, Kantian, gloss on these difficulties is to say
that the limits of his account of narrative can be seen not as a defect but
as "circumscribing its domain of validity."[18] But another reading of the
appearance of these limits is possible: that they represent the return of
the repressed, the re-emergence of the aporetic dimension that narrative
was hired to keep under control. Limits of validity mean: beyond this
point, unintelligibility, contradiction, aporia. Is not Ricoeur putting a
brave face on time's reassertion of its power to disrupt all attempts at
conceptual domestication?

As if this were not bad enough, Ricoeur discovers that the aporia generated by the gulf between cosmic and phenomenological time, a gulf bridged by narrative, the aporia that occupies center stage in *Time and Narrative*, is in fact only one of many aporias to which our thinking about time is subject. The second is precisely that of time as one and as many, not in the sense of local time-frames that we discussed earlier, but rather, that we think of time as one and yet as divided between past, present, and future. Without rehearsing the argument here—he makes a subtle deployment of the idea of the unity of history—suffice it to say that Ricoeur finds narrative even less able to deal with this difficulty. The third and last aporia he designates is the inscrutability of time, by which he refers to the various ways in which time continually breaks through our attempts to constitute it, to clarify its meaning, to show us its deep archaic enveloping mystery:

> What fails is not thinking, in any acceptation of this term, but the impulse—or to put it a better way, the *hubris*—that impels our thinking to posit itself as the master of meaning. . . . [T]ime, escaping our will to mastery, surges forth on the side of what . . . is the true master of meaning.[19]

Now the true master here is Ricoeur himself, who, after the fact, and after Augustine, has recast the plot of *Time and Narrative* as a confession, in which the presumption of synthesizing thought is confronted by a power that exceeds it. If time ever seems to be acquiescing in our configuring plots, you can be sure it is silently gathering its forces for revenge. Of course, the oddest paradox now arises. For we have made time into the hero of a story of confinement and release. Has not narrative finally closed the trap and triumphed?

In the account we have given so far, we have sketched the path of Ricoeur's own reflections on his attempt to both bind and illuminate time through narrative. But the third aporia he discusses—the inscrutability of time, its power to reassert its envelopment—surely opens another front: the wider relation between time and language. One response to the breakdown, or the coming up against limits, of the power of narrative to tame time might be to reassess the specific theory of language to which Ricoeur is committed in discussing narrative. To put it very simply, might it not be that narrative is committed to the possibility of a *certain closure of meaning*, which will inexorably be breached? In other words, narrative selects from but does not exhaust the power of language to resolve the aporias of time; its particular forte is synthesis. But it has no monopoly on linguistic synthesis, and more particularly, it may be just such a strength that is its weakness. If time is not essentially captured by the effects of closure facilitated by narrative, then we must either find time showing through in the very pathos of narrative's failure, or we must look elsewhere. We might expect that resources for such an expansion could be found in metaphor and metonymy, which seem to allow us to think the nonlinear, creative interruption of that articulation of sense through time that we call narrative. We recall that the study of metaphor and narrative are, for Ricoeur, integral parts of a general poetics, "one vast poetic sphere," and both are instances of the productive imagination. We have already seen him describe narrative in terms of production; we know that Ricoeur, following Aristotle, who thought of plot as the mimesis of an action, allows the poetic a role in the narrative refiguring of action; we know that Ricoeur ultimately seeks to harness the poetic for speculative and eventually practical ends. Without undertaking here a full-scale review of *The Rule of Metaphor*, it would not misrepresent Ricoeur to conclude that his deployment of metaphor and narrative separately and in harness is subordinated to a law of productivity, in which the moment of synthesis has the last word. If this is right, then we will not be able to find in metaphor a countervailing force that would interrupt narrative or set up different trails of connectedness. Resources for such interruption can be found in the work of Derrida, Heidegger, Blanchot, Levinas, and others.[20]

My discussion of narrative has been framed by the problem of the aporias of time. Ricoeur introduced narrative poetics as an antidote to the multiplication of aporias in a pure phenomenology of time divested of these resources of linguistic synthesis. But as if by a process of selective mutation, new aporias continued to erupt. Should we not treat Ricoeur's analysis, and his extraordinary confession, as evidence of time's recursive power of interruption of our best-laid plots and plans?

Ricoeur hoped that narrative time would heal the aporias of time, in particular its diremption into phenomenological and cosmological time, in which the subject/object opposition flourishes unhindered. Elsewhere I have argued from a somewhat different direction for a convergence of these two limbs of time.[21] I claim that the radical difficulty of thinking of phenomenological and cosmic time together is a consequence of the misplaced thesis of the unity and linearity of time. This is an a priori assumption that neither the natural nor the interpretive sciences bear out. I argue that the complexity of the temporal structures that arise from the ashes of the thesis of unity takes us a long way toward convergence. The first part of this chapter, dealing with time-shelters, rests on and exemplifies such a convergence. And the second part, focusing on Ricoeur's account of *Time and Narrative*, confirms such an approach, even as it runs up against limits. I too would now like to turn to the question of limits, to take up again the way Ricoeur presents the issue, and to attempt a somewhat different formulation.

The thesis of the inevitable return of aporia, which Ricoeur does not formulate but which is not too difficult to erect on the evidence of his work, might be thought to have a simple explanation. If references to phenomenological and cosmic time are not just to partial models of the real, but to discrete and autonomous dimensions of the real, then any *being* subject to double mapping, subject to constitution by both of these forms of time, would face not just an intellectual difficulty in reconciling two partial descriptions of the same thing—like the Evening Star and the Morning Star. Such a being would suffer diremption, and the wound could never finally be healed. Such a being, it might be said, is man. The quest for reconciliation following, most notably, Kant, typically involves the subordination of causality (cosmological time) to self-legislation (phenomenological time), or at least the establishment of the independence of the latter from the former. If I am right, however, this account of diremption rests on an opposition that the setting aside of the unity of time thesis would dramatically weaken. My account, however, makes things worse, not better.

I have tried to suggest that in various complex ways we think of time plurally and structurally. But this entire approach, even if valid, is itself limited. The accounts we have given of the economy of local time-shelters, and Ricoeur's accounts of narrative and of narrative identity, as we have relayed them, are analytical, neutral, and involve a certain "distance."

The stage for the re-emergence of such a split can be found, amazingly enough, in Book VIII of Aristotle's *Poetics*. He wrote: "Unity of plot does not . . . consist in the unity of the hero. For infinitely various are the incidents in one man's life, which cannot be reduced to unity. . . . That is the error of all poets who imagine . . . that as Heracles was one man the story of Heracles must also be a unity. Homer . . . seems happily to have discerned the truth. . . . In composing the Odyssey . . . and likewise the Iliad [he made them] center around an *action* that . . . is one" (my emphasis).[22]

The construction of a narrative is an aesthetic unity, whether of a human life or a nation. If Aristotle is right, then even the supple connective resources of narrativity may be doomed to a certain failure, because there will always be bits that belong but do not fit and never will. We may even conclude that the narrative quest for identity is a dangerous one, exhibiting at a more plausible level the same rigidities of self-understanding as we left behind when we left behind the idea of substance.[23] But we might equally conclude that the demand for some sort of temporal intelligibility is unavoidable for humans, even as we recognize it to be unfulfillable. Earlier, when describing the order that holds sway in all beings, I claimed that each order constitutes a boundary, hence an inside and an outside, or a laminated set or entangled matrix of such insides and outsides. Our survival, day to day, does not usually depend on narrative intelligibility being successfully maintained. What we call our embodiment, the maintenance of our corporeal integrity, not to mention our struggles for truth, or for minimal control over the forces that surround us—all these are conjoined and entangled with narrative in an economy that intermingles a multiplicity of times and rhythms. It would be my hope that such a description, for all its complexity, would actually make interpretation if not easier, at least less liable to over-simplifying. But might it not be that, again, this whole account can be circumscribed within a fatal limitation?

In the account we have been offering, Time has, on the whole, been presented positively, constructively, economically; and some such account as this seems indispensable. But what does it tell us about what it is *to be* a being described in this way—one that manages the maintenance of fragile and permeable boundaries? Can we reduce madness and mortality to questions of economy? They are surely not *theories*, but neither are they simple conditions we must endure. The language of economy is no attempt at their theoretical evaporation, but this language might, however, be indispensable for us to get any handle at all on such mortal issues. Ricoeur's last aporia centered on the inscrutability of time. We should perhaps remember here that time is not just a beyond, enveloping all our little bubbles of order. For all our ability to breed domestic forms of time, it also holds in reserve the apocalyptic possibility of dissolving any and all of the horizons of significance we have created for ourselves.[24]

What, then, after all this, of the ethical? If Anaximander spoke of "injustice," surely, as Theophrastus first complained, this is a misplaced poetic metaphor. What we have here is a cosmology—a cool, detached ontology. And do we not fall foul of Levinas's critique of the neutrality of ontology?

A discourse becomes ethical, not simply by speaking of the other, but in the ways it offers itself to appropriation. It is precisely the understanding of the fragility and vulnerability of all beings that both opens the space of ethics and prevents its premature humanistic closure. The best appropriation of this text would be one that enhanced respect for the miracle of diverse beings, including oneself, and for the variety of forms of survival and expenditure. At this point, poetics would become ethics.

3

Economies of Time
Beyond Activity and Passivity

Time and the Subject

For a philosophical neophyte languishing in Augustinian innocence about time, there is nothing quite like Kant's *Critique of Pure Reason* for opening up the idea that time might play an "active" role in organizing our knowledge and experience. Time occupies a central place in his Copernican revolution, moving from being an external dimension to being an inner condition. And yet it does not take long to wonder whether time can be restricted—and it soon seems like a restriction—to *inner* intuition and to the function of confirming the contours of the world of objective knowledge. At this point, Husserl's phenomenology can seem to lift the restrictions; human temporalizing is no longer simply in the business of exploring what already exists but is a productive and potentially creative force.[1] Music, literature—indeed, experience more broadly—do not just *take place in time;* they are each temporally knitted together. Time is dramatized *as* music, *as* passion, *as* film, *as* literature. Time is not just the necessary backdrop enabling these phenomena to occur; time is integrally tied in to these activities. And it is precisely as activity that it is to be understood, as bound up with the intentional life of a subject.

And yet what we might call the creative liberation of time as an active temporalization is surely fatally compromised by what has come to be thought of as the deconstruction of the subject. Was that liberation simply a false trail? Must we now abandon those heady prospects?

37

In the wake of the moribund "subject," do we have to revert to a pre-critical objectivism in thinking about time? In this chapter, I show how the thought of the gift, developed both by Heidegger and Derrida, opens onto a new terrain, that of the economy(-ies) of time, and a renewed promise.

The connection between temporality and activity can seem important to hold on to. Is it not precisely through human activity—whether mental or physical—that so much of what makes this a distinctively human world has come into being? And is it not phenomenology that supplies the key by which to escape so many naïve philosophical positions? But things are not so simple. First of all, talk about activity here quickly becomes problematic. If activity means something that takes place in time, then temporalizing cannot be an activity in any ordinary sense. And indeed, Husserl insists that intentional acts are not to be understood psychologically. They do not take place at the level of constituted things; instead, they serve to make such a realm possible. Ultimately, the point is made by insisting on the autonomy of the transcendental. The second complication arises through the recognition of an ineliminably passive dimension even within intentional life, in language, our historical determination, culture, and so on. I am thinking here of Husserl's discussion of passive synthesis.[2] Our acts find themselves following contours they themselves have not invented. And even the subject of such acts turns out to have a history, or perhaps even to *be* a history. So the connection between activity and temporality is not as simple as had been thought.

However, if we suppose Heidegger to have inherited, albeit obliquely, the mantle of phenomenology from Husserl, the implication of the title of his magnum opus and of his continuing concerns in various forms is not that this essential contamination of the purity of activity requires that time be set aside as one of the central concerns of philosophy. Quite the opposite. The fundamental question of *Being and Time*—that of the meaning of Being—is to be answered by two investigations: (1) "the interpretation of Dasein in terms of temporality," and (2) "the explication of time as the transcendental horizon for the question of Being" (p. 37 [H41]). As is well known, *Being and Time* offers us a version of the first and leaves the second as an open question.

What I would like to do now is to show how the idea of *economy* slowly imposes itself on us from this point on through developments within Heidegger's own thought and subsequently in Derrida's writing. I will try to show how—in *Counterfeit Money* and then in the *Gift of Death*—Derrida continues to pursue these questions, and I will offer some assessment of the kinds of relations Derrida is crystallizing for us. Finally, I will discuss where that leaves time. And where *that* leaves us.

From the Subject to Economy

It is not difficult to see the opposition between passivity and activity as limited in its power to illuminate. That activity acts on something might suggest a "passivity" on the part of that which is acted upon, an acquiescence, showing that activity presupposes some cooperation, some relation—not least, for example, material on which to act. Here passivity would not be opposed to activity but would complement it. Activity that is appropriate to the circumstances, that conforms to rules, that is tailored to certain objectives could be said to display a certain passivity in allowing its positive determination by something other than itself. Again, if this can be called passivity, it serves to enhance, direct, and specify the activity in question, rather than being opposed to it. To attempt to stage an opposition between activity and passivity, one would have to work with a naïve, unchanging subject at the most unproductive psychological level. This is not entirely uncommon. Those manuals for worldly success basically require the subject to decide its own priorities and goals and then work clear-sightedly and instrumentally to achieve them, as if (a) it could be sure it really had decided its *own* priorities, and (b) those goals might not be affected by further reflection, for example, on the kind of person one would have to become to achieve them.

In *Being and Time,* Heidegger undermines any naïve sense of activity in many ways. I will be schematic. The most fundamental shape of this move is to argue that Dasein is essentially "outside" itself in a multiplicity of dimensions and that this sets up a whole series of possibilities of relational alignment and misalignment, discussed under the heading of *Eigentlichkeit* (authenticity). *Eigentlichkeit* is critical for determining whether it is I who acts, or just *das Man* (one, the They), and from there it is not difficult to ask whether *das Man* truly acts at all. Moreover, the possibilities of realignment may be thought of as acts or activities in their own right, what might once have been called the activities of the soul. When Heidegger writes about hearing the call of conscience, accepting our own guilt, and about taking up a relation to one's own death, it is not a fully authentic subject that is addressed or that takes up such a relation. Such a subject is brought about in and through such a response or such a "decision."

It might seem that in his critique of the Cartesian concept of the world and man's relation to it, Heidegger is merely undoing an academic prejudice. When he talks about attempts at proving the existence of the external world as a scandal of philosophy, it certainly is an academic prejudice that he has in his sights. But the combined effect of his existential analytic and the various sections directed against Descartes is to re-educate the reader, to teach us to think and talk in a different way, to open up new possibilities of experience. When he says, for example, that *das Man* is not something from which for the most part we can separate ourselves, but something to which we belong, he is trying to reposition our sense of agency—not, one might say, as a given, but as an achievement—except that this *achievement* is not the product of will, but precisely of a complex renegotiation of the very site of self and will. This complex renegotiation is even more clearly what is required by what I am calling the realignment with temporality.

We have to extract ourselves from the illusion of a temporal version of commodity fetishism, one that fails to grasp the calendar we live by as our own creation, or at least our own calculative hypostatization of natural cycles. That in itself involves a number of activity/passivity switchbacks. But we also have to grasp the possibility of authentic temporalizing, taking on board the historical opportunities open to us, recognizing that some of these are only possible for us as members of a community who recognize they are engaged in a common struggle,[3] recognizing that my individual mortality is not so much a limitation as a condition for that passion without which nothing great ever happens.[4] That condition only operates, however, when grasped as *Entschlossenheit* (resoluteness). To take up an attitude to my own death is in itself what we could call a self-constitutive action. It brings about a realignment of the subject with a new conception of self. But what is death? Heidegger calls it "the possibility of [my] absolute impossibility."[5] To relate to my own death is to grasp the impossibility of that relation, not in the trivial sense that I cannot survive to complete it, but because "my death" is an abyssal, nonthematizable condition. And, yes, it is one that I do not choose, but neither do I simply suffer it.

Agency in *Being and Time* is deeply problematized, because the subject of agency is essentially displaced and because one of the central issues of agency then becomes the recovery of the possibility of agency by a (re-)alignment with conditions of possibility with which one had lost touch.[6] If it needed special reinforcement, the example of my being-toward-death makes it clear that something troubling has happened to the relationship between time and the subject that had seemed so positive and productive in Husserl. But actually it is precisely because the relation has remained so close that we need to follow our thinking about time down such dark alleys. Particularly when we look at Derrida's discussion of some of these matters (gift, sacrifice, secret), we will have to ask whether this connection *should* be preserved.

Let me explain more generally about the dark alleys first. What I mean is this: if we suppose that the connection between time and the subject is, if not the only illuminating one for time, at least one that has prospered in the last two centuries (with Kant, Hegel, Nietzsche, Husserl, Bergson, and others), then we might expect that the twists and turns undertaken by the subject—or whatever comes after the subject—might give birth to more complex ways of thinking (about) time. This path we will now pursue, though for the record it is worth considering the alternative possibility—that the connection between time and the subject was predicated on a coincidence of errors about each, which once lifted would free them from their relationship. We should not forget that each has been separately considered to be an essentially metaphysical concept, united only in their relation to presence: the subject being a privileged form of self-presence to which other things and people could be made present, and time being understood either as a series of presents (nows) or as having a direction toward or away from some sort of apotheosis of presence (the origin or end of time). We might think that if it is folly to try to come up with a nonmetaphysical conception of time, it would equally be folly to presume that the connection between time and the subject would survive deconstruction. The evidence, however, shows that if anything, the way the deconstructive transformation of both time and the subject get developed is marked out by their mutual dependency. *On Time and Being* [1962] offers us another phase in the development of this relationship, one that will take us much closer to Derrida's discussion of the gift and to the more widespread use of the idea of economy.[7] I will also make some use of the summary report of the seminar that took place some eight months after the lecture, which, not for the first time, charts some of the distance between *Being and Time* and *On Time and Being,* and shows just how explicitly *On Time and Being* is directed to charting that movement.

Heidegger begins this lecture with a disorienting challenge. We do not expect immediate intelligibility from great works of art (Klee), great poetry (Trakl), or theoretical physics (Heisenberg), and yet we expect directly useful worldly wisdom from philosophy. Heidegger makes it discretely clear that whatever once was the case, this account is no longer satisfactory:

1. "It might be that a kind of thinking *has become* necessary . . ."
2. "The attempt to think Being without beings *becomes* necessary because otherwise . . . there is *no longer* any possibility of explicitly bringing into view the Being of *what is today* all over the earth, let alone of adequately determining the relation of man to what *has been called 'Being' up to now.*"

There is something especially problematic about "today"—we might suppose this has something to do with the pervasiveness of technology. But Heidegger also sets out a general view of history: "From the dawn of Western-European thinking until today, being means the same as presencing." He will approach the difficulty of thinking, of philosophical thinking, through the difficulty of thinking the relation between time and Being. Our problem, a most serious problem—and one that is clearly not a local or topical problem, but the problem of philosophy—can be put succinctly:

> Every attempt to think adequately the relation of Being and time with the help of the current and imprecise representations of time and Being immediately becomes ensnared in a hopeless tangle of relations that have hardly been thought out.[8]

For example, we suppose that Being is some sort of thing, hence "temporal" by virtue of being "in time." But it is clearly not a thing at all. Time, like things, seems to be constantly "passing away," but it is not a thing either.

Heidegger exploits the confusion and embarrassment we have in trying to think of Being or time as if they belonged to the domain of things in order to get us to take seriously the idiomatic expression "there is Being," "there is time"—*es gibt Sein, es gibt Zeit.* This is not the first time he has made this move (cf. *Letter on Humanism,* where he says the *es* is Being and the *gibt* "indicates the giving nature of Being granting its truth").[9] But I would like to take this opportunity to think through what is going on here. Heidegger has declared bankrupt the resources provided by the verb *to be,* even with its range of allied tenses and moods, for thinking Being, time, and the connection between them. Much of *Being and Time* was precisely an attempt to exploit those resources to delineate the complexity of Dasein's ecstatic temporality. And clearly some progress can be made on the structure of that complexity in this way. But Heidegger is convinced that the great army of expressions linked to the verb *to be* has been largely infiltrated by those whose allegiance is to things—beings that are—rather than to what it means for them to be. The verb has been taken over by its common deployment, by the objects in its train. But there is also something deficient, I believe, in the neutrality of the verb *to be.* It is my sense that he comes to see such neutrality as a legacy of Cartesian subjectivism, for which *what is* is just *there,* available for interpretation, consumption, by an active subject. (I admit, it is not entirely fair of me to attribute this position to Descartes, for whom it is quite crucial that there be something for which he is not responsible—namely, the idea of perfection.)

This is a very live issue in *Being and Time.* In his introduction, Heidegger uses very active language to talk about the way in which we can overcome "the naiveté of a haphazard, 'immediate,' and unreflective 'beholding' [*Schauen*]."[10] "The way in which Being and its structures are encountered in the mode of phenomenon is one which must first of all be wrested [*Abgewonnen*] from the objects of phenomenology." And there are a number of references of this sort in *Being and Time,* wherever what is at stake is overcoming a structure of concealment (for example, one in which "Dasein . . . falls back upon its world . . . and interpret[s] itself in terms of that world by its reflected light . . . fall[ing] prey to the tradition of which it has more or less explicitly taken hold," p. 18 [H21]). Where Dasein has fallen into error, some sort of action is needed to restore the situation. But the language of giving, of the *es gibt,* of the recognition of what we might call an independent source, is at the very least prepared for in *Being and Time.* We need look no further than the early discussion of the concept of *phenomenon* as that which shows-itself-in-itself, or of *logos* as a letting-something-be-seen.

Heidegger, of course, recognizes the distinctness of these expressions when he talks of the verb *phanesthai* as middle-voiced, neither active nor passive.[11] What I believe will turn out to be crucial is the logic of interaction, the forms of relation that such middle-voiced sites generate. They resist relational incorporation by a presumed preexisting subject, and recognizing that resistance, that autonomy of site, allows us to develop precisely the complexities of our relationship to them. If, returning now to *On Time and Being,* Being is to be thought through the *es gibt,* through the expression *es gibt Sein,* what is gained is a site for relational development, one independent both from the subject—there is nothing *else* doing the giving, certainly not me, not obviously God—and from things in the world, from entities, from beings. But it is also a site with a certain specific character, one carefully set against the presumed activities of a grasping subject, one that will allow us to think through the possibility of other powers and that will allow us eventually to connect with various logics or economies of relation. The possibility of such a destiny makes it all the more important to focus on the strategic grounds for *giving* having been minted for us in the first place.

Early on in the first section of *Being and Time,* Heidegger lays out one of his most fundamental problems. We may not think that Being is a problem, because it seems self-evident. Everyone understands "The sky is blue," "I am merry." But these utterances exhibit only what he calls an average kind of intelligibility. The implication of what he is saying is that, as Augustine said about time, as long as we do not think about it, we understand it. The meaning of Being is veiled, if you like, by its "self-evidence." Heidegger very quickly talks about our behavior toward things embodying an enigma, an intelligibility that is unintelligible, and so on. He concludes from all this that the question of Being is still obscure and still needs adequate formulation. When we read these lines, however, it is not difficult to oscillate between agreeing with Heidegger, on the one hand, and supposing, on the other, that there is only an enigma if you begin with a problem, that the "is" in "the sky is blue" will not bear the weight he wishes to place on it. If I say "the sky darkens," I am equally making a truth claim about the color of the sky, but the *is* seems to have evaporated.

Now we could say this shows just how sneaky Being can be, we could talk about a double withdrawal, and so on. But in fact, there is nothing that requires that this or that way of speaking should be able to deliver the insight Heidegger seeks. And instead of offering us two ways of thinking about a common phrase, it might be more productive to find grammatically connected forms of the same words to make the same point. Something like this happens with presence and presencing, and then with giving and gift. Instead of supposing that the commonplaceness of the "is" hides its deep significance, it is much easier to see that a product can disguise the process by which it is produced, or a state can conceal the event through which it came into being, or that an outcome can hide its conditions of possibility. I have suggested the analogy here with Marx's critique of commodity fetishism. And of course the gamble that Heidegger takes here is that the words he privileges to dramatize what in theatrical terms we might call the action of Being are able to make a virtue of their specificity. To be blunt, to think Being in terms of giving looks like subordinating a general to a regional ontology, to use Husserlian language, or thinking the ontological in terms of the ontic. My question will be this: What motivates this choice of language, and what possibilities (and limitations) for thought does it entail?

From Being to Giving

I would like first to quote two short passages from *On Time and Being* that spell out the work that giving will be expected to perform, and then to locate its emergence as a relation within a developing sequence of thought. These two passages continue Heidegger's explication of what is involved in *experiencing* the *es gibt*. I will cut into the exposition:

> In this way, [it] . . . must become clear how there is/ It gives Being and how there is/ It gives time. In this giving, it becomes apparent how that giving is to be determined which as a relation, first holds the two toward each other and brings them into being.[12]

This tells us little more than the shape of the relation of Being and time and the role that giving will play in it. The next passage will show the point at which giving is located in the action:

> Being, by which all things are marked, Being means presencing. Thought with regard to what presences, presencing shows itself as letting-presence. But now we must try to think this letting-presence explicitly insofar as presencing is admitted. Letting shows its character in bringing into unconcealment. To let presence means: to unconceal, to bring into openness. In un-

concealing prevails a giving, the giving that gives presencing, that is, Being, in letting-presence.[13]

Heidegger is doing a number of things here: (1) He is taking for granted the distinction between presence and presencing. This begins to help us detach Being from those things that are merely present, by associating Being, rather, with presencing. (2) He is adding a certain determination to presencing—letting—one that seems at first undecidable between activity and passivity. (3) He links this letting to unconcealment; this is what "letting-presence" means. (4) He then interprets such unconcealing as (a) giving.

This giving is said to give presencing. What he means is not that there is something beneath presencing, but rather that we can best think of presencing, which itself makes what is present possible, by and through the grammar and logic of giving, through the kinds of distinctive relations that it sets up. What are these relations? It is clear that Heidegger knows he has not given us much help so far. So he sets the scene again for another practice session, exploring these relationships by offering the thought of the "giving concealed in unconcealment" as the proper alternative to thinking Being as the ground of beings. Allow me one more short citation:

> As the gift of this *It gives*, being belongs to giving. As a gift, Being is not expelled from giving. Being, presencing is transmuted. As allowing-to-presence, it belongs to unconcealing; as the gift of unconcealing it is retained in the giving. Being *is* not. There is, It gives Being as the unconcealing; as the gift of unconcealing it is retained in the giving. Being *is* not. There is, *It gives* Being as the unconcealing of presencing.[14]

Heidegger is providing us here with another workout. The aim is to show that the wealth of the transformations possible in this thinking of the gift can more adequately develop our thinking of Being than can the word *being* itself. Central to this is the gift/giving distinction and the way in which unconcealment and letting-presencing can be thought in these terms. It must be something of an accident that in German "there is" is captured by *es gibt*. What is not an accident is that Heidegger invests in this word.

In *Given Time,* Derrida launches a certain "simplifying representation" of the logic of the gift as he has found it in Heidegger: that where time is understood as a circle, the gift is impossible. It could only take place "at the instant of an effraction."

> There would be a gift only at the instant when the paradoxical instant (in the sense in which Kierkegaard says of the paradoxical instant of decision that it is madness) tears time apart. In this sense one would never have the time of a gift. In any case, time, the "present" of the gift, is no longer thinkable as a now, that is as a present bound up in the temporal synthesis.[15]

Derrida then goes on to show how the gift itself shares in this impossibility. (What is true of its relation to time is true of its relation to logic, or relation.) He writes of a subject identical to itself trying to constitute its own unity through the gesture of the gift.[16] Derrida is drawing on the paradoxes of (auto-)constitution. I would like to explore these questions with regard to a text Derrida does not, to my knowledge, discuss in *Given Time:* Heidegger's *What Is Called Thinking?*[17] which is devoted to expanding our sense of what it is to think, drawing on the Old English word *thanc.*

When Heidegger develops the idea of the thanc, it is both in connection with, and at times by distinction from, the heart.[18] Thus:

> [Such] thinking . . . is almost closer to the origins than that thinking of the heart which Pascal, centuries later and even then in conscious opposition to mathematical thinking, tried to retrieve. [139]

> But the word "the thanc" does not mean only what we call a man's disposition or heart, and whose essential nature we can hardly fathom. [140]

> The original word "thanc" is imbued with the original nature of memory: the gathering of the constant intention of everything that the heart holds in present being. Intention here is understood in this sense: the inclination with which the inmost meditation of the heart turns toward all that is in being— the inclination that is not within its own control and therefore also need not necessarily be first enacted as such. [141]

Heidegger here uses the language of debt ("Original thinking is the thanks owed for being." [151]), but he distances this relation from one of conventional recompense (which he links to business). And then he asks whether thanc, memory, and thanks derive from thinking or vice versa, and again insists, not on the words, but on what is happening "in substance," distinguishing the richer language of thinking from the common usage of thanc, thought, memory, and so on. Heidegger clearly marks a constitutional paradox in a way somewhat different from Derrida.[19]

The Return of the Ontic?

Let us pause here for a moment. Through the *es gibt* and then through *Ereignis*—appropriation, or the event of appropriation, as he develops these terms in *On Time and Being*—Heidegger is contriving to get a handle on an originary sense of time and to think Being more satisfactorily. It is not, of course, that *Ereignis* is a new general concept "under which Being and time could be subsumed." "Logical classifications mean nothing here."

For as we think Being itself and follow what is its own, Being proves to be destiny's gift of presence, the gift granted by the giving of time. The gift of presence is the property of *Ereignis*.[20]

We may ask here whether the language of gift/giving—which seems to run the risk of trying to elucidate the ontological via the ontic—doesn't fall foul of that difficulty. Recall that it is in *On Time and Being* that Heidegger says he wants to think Being without reference to beings. We surely cannot use the word(s) gift/giving without opening ourselves to whatever this colorful family of terms will throw at us. How is that compatible with the quest for the originary?

But there is another question. In *Being and Time*[21] Heidegger traces the metaphysical residue of Hegel's treatment of time by the way in which he has swallowed, not just the ordinary sense of time as a series of nows, but also the importance of the figure of the circle, both found in Aristotle's *Physics*.

Leaving aside Heidegger's insistence elsewhere on good and bad circles, Derrida argues that Heidegger's introduction of the language of giving/gift further entangles him with the problematics of the circle, and to be quick about it, a certain logic. This logic is ultimately that of identity, which, distributed in time, takes the form of restitution, of return, of completion.

As always, Derrida has an ambivalent attitude to this verdict, as he has to words such as *thinking* and *experience* (where actually he shows guarded approval), as well as to such a word as *event*. In "Choreographies" he had spoken of "the thought of the gift [as] disturbing without reversing the order of ontology."[22]

Derrida in effect receives the *es gibt* from Heidegger as a gift, but he treats it, not with gratitude, but with a certain irreverence. Just as Heidegger's talk of the destiny of Being ends up being subverted by entanglement in the postal system, so the gift is shown to be embedded in an aporetic logic, a logic of paradox, one which shows the gift to be impossible. On Marcel Mauss's account (in *The Gift*), the gift is linked with the requirement to repay in an economy of exchange, which destroys the very meaning of "gift." But even without straying into such a theoretical discourse, the mere intention to give, to be generous, draws giving into a logic of self-satisfaction, which undermines the premise of selflessness. And should the gift be recognized or acknowledged as a gift, let alone occasion gratitude, its purity, and hence its essence as a gift, will be compromised. Derrida is not wholly critical of Mauss's position. Indeed, he understands Mauss's observation that it is essential that the gift not be returned immediately, as requiring a delay, as evidence of the way in which the gift "gives time," and it is in this way that the gift—in various symbolic ways—can indeed contribute to explaining the "total social fact" as Mauss thought it could. Derrida argues that Mauss's attempts to found modern systems of economic exchange on gift systems (showing that "credit," for example, is original and not a late product of the development of the economy) fail, and that Mauss gets caught up in a kind of madness. Let us look briefly at this.

Derrida focuses on the point at which Mauss is talking about those cases of potlatch (beloved of Bataille) in which, for the Indian tribes in question, one has to *expend* all one has, keeping nothing back (e.g., destroying 1000 blankets)—an act that brings honor and nobility. Derrida's argument is that Mauss's attempt to hold fast to the words "gift" and "exchange" shows him caught up in a kind of madness: "It ruins everything that claims to know what gift and non-gift mean." Derrida's claim is that the word "gift" is caught up in a logic that destroys it (and by implication undermines Heidegger's optimism about the language of the "gift").

There is undoubtedly more to be said about the potlatch example— nobility might be rationally bestowed on a mass blanket destroyer if that act were interpreted as the power to produce more—which would bring in the whole economy of production. But interestingly, Derrida's point is not to undermine Heidegger's use of the gift, but first to demonstrate its aporetic consequences and then to embrace them. The fact that the logic of the gift disrupts or undermines the very possibility of the gift only shows that the gift is not a thing governed by the logic of identity but is bound up with signs subject to dissemination and governed by no stable semantic foundation.

There is not space here to deal in depth with Derrida's discussion of Baudelaire's short story "Counterfeit Money." It is an extraordinary tale, one that embodies innumerable Derridean themes. A man gives a "counterfeit coin" to a beggar. His friend imagines the innocent speculative possibilities this might open up for the beggar until he realizes that the man's aim was also prudential—to save money—and this he cannot forgive. The tale takes place after the "friends" have left the tobacconist's shop; and the ambiguous "economy" of tobacco supplies a reservoir of resonant parallel meanings. The basic issues have to do with the way the impossible logic of the gift is (or is not) overcome by giving something that is not what it seems (a false coin), and by the various layers at which this story can be analyzed. If the narrator cannot forgive his friend for his calculative approach, is he too not operating according to the very same logic (could he not have been more generous—not least to a friend)? Is that what Baudelaire is saying?

All this goes to show that the "gift"—which even in Baudelaire's story is thought to be capable of "giving the beggar a good time (albeit speculatively)"—is always caught up in a complex logic that it cannot control. Interestingly, the narrator's disappointment comes at the point at which he realizes his friend was not wholly attuned to the possibility of the "coin" as an (unpredictable) event. More of this shortly. What are we to conclude about time?

Let us make a distinction between problems and questions. Problems are dealt with successfully by being solved. Questions are dealt with successfully by being properly addressed and taken up into thought. Vienna positivist Rudolf Carnap claimed (in the 1920s) to have solved the problem of time by eliminating temporal predicates from his logical notation. He had solved a problem by eliminating the possibility of even posing the question! There are many ways of thinking about time that generate paradoxes or contradictions, and we might suppose that success would consist in eliminating them. Derrida is in effect saying that the issue is not to eliminate paradox but to locate it properly and understand its significance.

My general response to this issue[23] is (1) that time cannot be wholly conceptualized, formally captured in concepts, because (2) the very idea of a concept is of something that orders phenomena according to a rule, that treats singularities as particulars, that is, as instances of something general, that is committed to a certain model of time (linear, continuist, unitary, etc.), and (3) experience moves in and out of conceptualizability, and never more significantly than when what is in play are the layers or dimensions of time.

Essentially Temporal Experiences: Some Working Examples

I will now offer some *examples* of essentially temporal experiences, examples that are personal but not idiosyncratic, examples that are each capable of interminable analysis. Some raise questions to which there are no proper answers—especially those involving memory. Memory can often seem like a temporal version of Escher's architectural drawings: there is no space in which all these planes can be resolved. (See chapter 11, below.) Others make clear the complexity of my (our) insertion in time and ways in which—through ecstasy or boredom—time seems to break out into visibility.

1. I am looking at an old photograph of a woman in her twenties. It is faded and badly composed—a snapshot. She is pretty, with dark eyes, long hair tied back. In the background, large rocks and a beach, with a hint of sea. I am told it is a photograph of my mother. I wonder who took the picture. Had she met my father then? I know that this scene predates my existence on earth—indeed, just to be clear, my

existence anywhere. I was not even a possibility. I am looking at her. She seems to be looking at me. But we are worlds apart.

2. I am looking at an old photograph of myself as a boy. I had white hair—is that really me? I never noticed my hair changing color. This is *a picture* of me, not *me*. Where is that person now? Am I that person? What did he dream of being, of doing? Would he have acknowledged, respected, imagined this me? What has happened between then and now? Can that have been so real, given how much "it" has changed? And this moment—as I write (or you read), listen, see, think—how "real" is it? We know it will soon pass. Does that contribute to its "reality" (as does the flowing of a river) or detract from it?

3. I talk to someone I once loved. She is still as wonderful as ever. I still love her. I remember now having felt before, dreadfully, "This is so wonderful—it cannot last." I remember praying I would never look into her eyes and see but the ashes of passion. I remember the layers of pain with which we have wrapped each other. I tell myself that one can forgive but not forget, one cannot just undo scars even if one wants to. And yet I imagine, I wonder, if things couldn't, impossibly, be restored, or perhaps another form of the magic be revived.

4. I visit my grandfather, lying in hospital alone. He recognizes me through his tears, and we talk about the roses in his garden, the need to keep the grass cut. It was he who had paid me to learn the Greek alphabet as a young child and who had learned Hebrew to read the Bible in the original so he could promote his atheism on a sounder scholarly basis. I remember rumors of his successes as a textile chemist—inventing the first drip-dry shirt, the sock that wouldn't lump—and his failure to attain recognition. I say good-bye to him and to the grapes beside his bed.

5. I am sitting in an Oxford cloister, hearing an unbelievable choir singing a Bach chorale. I do not know whether I give myself to the music or whether it comes and takes me away, but I find myself held, suspended in a timeless time, caressed by patterns of sound, (re-)crystallized into another kind of being. I note that one could not possibly die while listening to Bach.

6. I am waiting for a plane. I have read *The Independent* from cover to cover. I have even re-read some of the letters to the editor. I have counted the number of acoustic tiles in the ceiling. I have calculated the percent of men, women, and children in the waiting room. I have tried to guess which are the Brits returning to the UK, and which are American visitors. I have gone through various checklists in my mind. An announcement is made—the plane will be delayed a further 45 minutes—unforeseen technical difficulties. I am pleased that these problems have emerged sooner rather than later, and annoyed

that they emerged now rather than earlier. But the overwhelming truth is that I am unutterably bored. At that moment, Time, in one of its incarnations, appears to me—the sheer, tedious, empty, awful passage of time. A child, confused, hungry, lost . . . begins to cry. . . . The apparition begins to fade.

7. I am on the island of Majorca—a summer resort at Christmas—almost everything is closed except, strangely, a couple of Irish bars. I walk along the beach, kicking the new sand washed by the tide. Something comes to me on the breeze. The fragrance of a complex and highly distinct pine resin. I am instantly transported to another island, thirty years before, and an utterly different mode of being in the world—one whose subtlety and wealth of possibilities is witnessed by the melodic tonality of the pine resin fragrance. I am reminded . . . of Proust.

I offer these examples to remind us, in case we could ever forget, of the fleshy texture of time, of the human and inhuman time(s) by which we find ourselves seized. In these examples, typically at least, no decision seems to have been made about the economy of time, and as far as I can tell, no decision is required. The issue of restitution, of some sort of "return to self" is always there, but only as an impossibility, a puzzle that precisely "gives us pause," "gives us something to think about." The photographs expose any sense of "I" to the winds. My mother and I, once so close, have occupied wholly different worlds. I even have a photo of her world before I existed. (Imagine seeing a photo of the world as it is after you have died!) The experience of the death of love, of the dying of a family member—these do not simply close a circle, they dig great abysses in the soul. And the last three examples—of musical ecstasy, of dangling in boredom, and of Proustian memory (all tied up with being transported)—rip away any allegiance to the time of the clock or the calendar. All these examples show that the idea of temporal synthesis within a horizon of possibility is a severe idealization, one destroyed by . . . the experience of time.

And these, I stress, are ordinary experiences. What if they were *really* good examples, not by being extreme and unusual, but by capturing "writ large" the undecidable fate of every instant?

There is no ordinary or vulgar concept of time, or if there is—it is actually a model of time held by (some) *philosophers* since Aristotle, or perhaps one of many strands of our ordinary temporal understanding, Our actual pluri-dimensional, polyphonic temporalization is neither a concept nor adequately conceptualizable. This is not simply because "time itself" escapes conceptualization, but because various modes of the "subject's" insertion into experience are constantly competing for dominance—from light-footed agency to having language speak through me—and because various logics or economies of time are in dynamic tension, not just at the level of theoretical reflection, but in practice.

Time and the Event of the Other

Much of Derrida's later work was devoted in various ways to delimiting the economy of restitution and promoting the economy of interruption, of event, of chance. And in one formulation he suggests that the only possibility of the "pure gift" would be "out of time" "at an instant"—in other words, entirely beyond the economy of restitution, which is just that of identity deferred.

Derrida defines *event* as "a name for the aspect of what happens that we will never manage either to eliminate or to deny." "It is another name for experience," he continues, "which is always the experience of the other. The event is what does not allow itself to be subsumed under any concept, not even that of being. The happening of the event is what cannot and should not be prevented; it is another name for the future itself." He speaks here of "the impossible concept of messianic arrival," and how justice and revolution are at stake.[24]

It is in this context that Derrida writes of a "messianicity without messianism," and of a democracy-to-come.

> What I call messianicity without messianism is a call, a promise of an independent future for what is to come, and which comes like every messiah in the shape of peace and justice, a promise independent of religion, that is to say universal.[25]

Derrida is arguing, not for some utopian future, but for a certain anticipation of openness to the other, of justice, an imminent possibility. One might say that time itself has an ethical structure or that my words, in particular, carry with them the promise implied simply by being addressed to the other, that they welcome the other, whether construed as someone or something. What Abrahamic religions understand as a future present, an event that could actually occur, Derrida understands as a structure of anticipation that cannot ever arrive or be completed. Following Blanchot, he imagines a man meeting the messiah at the city gates and asking him only, "When will you come?"—suggesting that the actual appearance of a messiah would ruin everything, as does the belief that democracy has been accomplished. What Derrida had once recognized as a structure of deferment (*différance*) is now being proposed as a permanent open anticipation of the possibility of a certain justice. The privilege of the future that Heidegger had promoted in *Being and Time* is not being drawn into a broader ecstatic dimensionality as it is in

On Time and Being. Rather, the very significance of time is being recast in economic and ethical terms. The to-come (*a-venir*) makes the future into a hope and a promise built into the present. Symmetrically, the true "event" is not grasped in advance.

What is particularly revealing for phenomenology is the way Derrida describes the event as arriving in the absence of any horizon of expectation or anticipation—something, he admits, that is almost impossible to think. Such a horizon of expectation "anticipates the future and deadens it in advance. If I am sure that something will happen, it will not be an event."[26]

Interestingly, it is clear from what Derrida says that the "event" is in some sense an ideal possibility, but one we cannot rule out. It is also very problematic, because although it may prove to be a new origin, it will thereby set up those dreaded horizons of expectation. And if not, it will surely get appropriated. The question, as always, is how to facilitate non-assimilatory forms of recognition and relation.

To return to the gift: the thought of the gift is not a substitute for thinking of time. It does have certain virtues with regard to thinking time and the other, for example (allowing extensions to the social, even geopolitical—such as the burden of national debt). Part of what is political about Derrida is the way he allows, even encourages such connections. In the course of this, the absoluteness of the distinction between ontological and ontic, between the language (or thought) of being and that of beings, begins to be dissolved.[27]

But the question remains: If the gift is "impossible," how can there *be* generosity? If we supposed that our actual experience could be analyzed exhaustively in terms of logics or economies, we would have fallen back into precisely that logocentrism that Derrida and others have so long fought to expose. To take an example: it has been suggested that there is no pure gift because the anticipation of the pleasure of the recipient would be a reward, undermining the "generosity" required for the gift. This is a *symbolic* reward (it could, for example, consist in the anticipation of the recipient's pleasure after my death). There is no doubting the reality of the gift of food to a starving child. It could have been withheld, but it was not. The child lived. Nothing required the gift. The internal symbolic equation is no impediment to the act or even to part of its meaning.[28]

Many of my "examples" were impure cases—in which restitution and event were mingled ambiguously, without disrupting the texture of the experience. This makes clear both the ethical significance of the *economy* of the event and, less obviously, how we should understand Derrida's recent writings as solutions to a special problem of memory. These two thoughts are linked.

Openness to the "event" is, and Derrida clearly means it to be, openness to the singularity of the other. He talks about "absolute arrivals," about "unconditional hospitality," and so forth. "This absolute hospitality is offered to the outsider, the stranger, the new arrival." "Absolute arrivals must not be required to state their identity." Here there seems to be little to separate Derrida and Levinas. Insofar as the other is a person, what is interrupted by this economy of the event is every rule-bound economy, all recognition of instances of the moral law. And we have found here another way of formulating a sense of responsibility that requires us to go through the undecidable, to see beyond our existing categories and logics in order to decide responsibly.[29]

Memory and Responsibility

This reference to responsibility can be tied back to Heidegger and to what I have called a special problem of memory. Listen to Derrida for a moment:

> What I suffer from inconsolably always has the form, not only of loss, which is often!—but of the loss of memory: that what I am living not be kept, thus repeated, and—how to put it?—decipherable, as if an appeal for a witness had no witness. This for me is the very experience of death, of catastrophe. . . . The experience of cinders is the experience not only of forgetting, but of the forgetting of forgetting.[30]

One of the most intimate and intractable problems of philosophy is that of how not to betray what one knows, how not to be "too old for one's victories,"[31] we might say, how to remember what one knows, how to bring insight to bear on one's daily (as well as scholarly) practices. How to "bear something in mind"—not just repeating an idea like a mantra, but how, dare we say it, to appropriate it.

Here we would need to spend some time with Heidegger's haunting remarks in *What Is Called Thinking?* where he speaks of memory precisely as "a constant concentrated abiding with something."[32] In this formulation every word counts!

Heidegger speaks of original thanking as "the thanks owed for being," and then wriggles to escape from the vulgar sense of repayment that seems to thrust itself upon us at that point. The original sense of *thanc* was "the gathering of the constant intention of everything that the heart holds in present being" (141), while intention is understood as "the inclination with which the innermost meditation of the heart turns towards all that is in being" (140). These formulations are important. They suspend the active subject—memory is not just me trying hard to act in a certain way. Abiding, gathering, and holding are the words used for the essentially nonvoluntaristic relationship involved.

But a crucial problem remains. If the issue in question is time, are we going to be happy with even this language and with these references to "the present"? Here I think Derrida has a "solution" to the problem of "bearing in mind"—it is to pursue the aporetic dimensions of texts impurely or indirectly concerned with time. The word that then begins to emerge, for what starts to emerge, is *experience,* which he defines as "a non-passive endurance of aporia"—a willingness not just to tolerate but to generate and explore those contradictory tensions in our experience that give it its texture, complexity, and interest. Our delineation of the economies of restitution, of messianicity, of the to-come, and of event are (just) some of the most powerful strands of such tension, working as they do both between competing conceptualizations of time and within any experience of time.

A Worked Example: Abraham and Isaac

Kierkegaard's treatment of the story of Abraham and Isaac in *Fear and Trembling* is well known. In *The Gift of Death* Derrida offers an interpretation in which the conflict between Abraham's relationship to God (obedience) and his relationship to Isaac (duty, morality) is used to dramatize the way an adequate response to a singularity (here God) may be at the price of any and every other responsibility—the impossibility of an ethics without aporia. There is much to be said about this story— the resurrection of the self by risking the death of the other brings to mind Hegel's account of the life-and-death struggle in which it is my conspicuous willingness to die, to sacrifice my life, that brings about the Other's recognition and a transformation in my self-relatedness.

We can read in the story of Abraham and Isaac an analogous transformation of the self—a recognition of one's own singular responsibility. And we may speak of a gift of death in that it is coming face to face with death that gives me this new sense of my own being. Here we have dramatized something not unlike Heidegger's account of my grasping my own being toward death, my finitude. God is simply the name required by such dramatizations for the *other* in relation to which I grasp my own singularity. But I would like to propose a different interpretation of the Abraham and Isaac story.[33] Chronos devours his sons, those who will continue the line, the name legitimately—and yet they are returned (regurgitated). The father here is the principle of generation, legitimacy, conformity. To devour one's sons is to subsume them, appropriate them within the given order. And we can understand this as a fable of lived time itself; we may live, think we can live, as if each moment—each son—can be contained within horizons of expectation, "conformity to rule." But what we need to be brought to recognize either as a truth or as an imperative is that the future is essentially a power of disruption, not just continuity. Without that grasp, life becomes death; the future is just swallowed by our projective structures; nothing happens. To allow the future to happen is to be willing to kill that projective will. The contestability of all narratives of legitimate inheritance, in which precisely that will is at work, is at the heart of Derrida's *Specters of Marx*.[34]

Isaac is the product of the greatest expectation and faith beyond any justification. His original appearance was a miracle. Without Isaac, Abraham's seed would not continue (not legitimately).[35] To truly possess Isaac, Abraham has to renounce restitutive desire. This is an allegory not perhaps of "time itself" but of a certain economy of time.

Heidegger's discussion of the gift offers a way of continuing to think otherwise, venturing into a lexicon with unpredictable consequences; Derrida helps Heidegger to begin to live more dangerously.

Conclusion

If there is no concept of time other than "the vulgar," it is because the elaboration and exploration of the experience of time does not supply another concept, but shows precisely the limits of conceptuality. Derrida does not so much offer a critique of Heidegger on time as a way of emancipating Heidegger (and us) from a pervasive economy of restitution. Insofar as such a logic functions by the suppression of divergence (difference)—and the texture of experience is surely misconstrued without that dimension—Derrida is contributing to a new economy of experience. And through it, Heidegger's concern with memory (and thanking) is taken up and given new life as a practice of reading and interpretation, one that maintains an irrepressible openness to what may come and to the permanent possibility of justice.

PART II. HEIDEGGER'S STRUGGLE WITH TIME

4

Reiterating the Temporal
Toward a Rethinking of
Heidegger on Time

Would it be shameless ingratitude to share Heidegger's sense of the scope and importance of the time question and yet be unhappy at the course of his development of that question, especially after the 1920s? Time is of central importance to philosophy because very many philosophical questions can be reformulated as questions about time, because the various forms of philosophical questioning can be distinguished by their general orientation toward time, and finally, because both what we call *life* (or *existence*) and what we think of as the *time of the world* can be dramatically illuminated by the ongoing project of analyzing temporal structures.[1]

Yet although it is Heidegger who has most powerfully formulated such a critical place for time (both for understanding the philosophical tradition and in our continuing to *think*), I have shared with Derrida the sense that there is a lingering commitment to something like the privilege of presence in his thought, particularly exhibited in the continuing quest for the primordial. My project is to try to pursue the task of articulating the temporal that Heidegger frames in terms of the transcendental horizon for the question of Being, while at the same time dismantling these very terms and the trajectory they supply to Heidegger's thought.[2]

This chapter has something of the shape of a spider's web after the struggle with the fly—there are some ragged holes and many signs of disturbance. When Hegel writes, "A mended sock is better than a torn one. Not so with self-consciousness,"[3] I would like to think that the same can be claimed for writing.

Heidegger's effective subtitle for *Being and Time*[4] was "The Interpretation of Dasein in Terms of Temporality, and the Explication of Time as the Transcendental Horizon for the Question of Being."[5] I am not alone in having been captivated by these words and their promise. And yet the book that opened with the big question ends with questions that one would think it ought to have answered: "How is the [ecstatic] temporalizing of temporality to be interpreted? Is there a way which leads from primordial *time* to the meaning of *Being*? Does *time* itself manifest itself as the horizon of *Being*?" Three and a half years later, in *Kant and the Problem of Metaphysics*,[6] and particularly in section 4, the project of fundamental ontology is restated, repeated, perhaps for the last time. After that, with one or two notable exceptions, the problem of time and temporality *as such, in so many words,* recedes.[7] When time reappears, in *On Time and Being* (1962), it is virtually unrecognizable.

I cannot attempt here a reconstruction of Heidegger's whole path, but I would like nonetheless to venture a few remarks on what we could call a temporal repetition of Heidegger's project. The complexity of the issues involved is formidable, and I cannot claim to have even begun to address them all, let alone to have an adequate articulation of them. But I hope at least to indicate a certain direction of thought.

I begin from three senses of unease. First, that Heidegger's thinking about time and temporality in the 1920s opened up paths not taken, and that we might come to find these paths compelling. Second, that there are some very general philosophical dangers attached to the path Heidegger did take in pursuing the question of Being. Third, and more specifically, when a key temporal concept does emerge—with the *Geschick des Seins*—we need to give it the most cautious welcome. My attitude toward Heidegger is, at least superficially, not unlike Heidegger's toward Husserl, when he continued to read his *Logical Investigations* long after Husserl had moved on. I will try to present these sources of unease as at least plausible grounds for a return to Heidegger's thought of the 1920s. The scope of this chapter is not limited to a redirecting of our reading of Heidegger. But the breathtaking scope and depth of his own attempts to rethink the major philosophers of time—particularly Aristotle, Augustine, Kant and Hegel—as well as the rest of the tradition, make him *indépassable*.

Finally, and most difficult, I want to suggest ways in which it might be possible to think of Being, the a priori, transcendence, the ontological difference, primordiality—all the values that drive Heidegger forward after 1929, and drive him away from time and the temporal—in a very different way. This last part is the most speculative and the least complete. It represents a preparedness to take what one might call the heroic (perhaps suicidal) course of trying to accommodate and fold back into a new temporality all of Heidegger's "ontological" concerns, rather than simply treating them as symptoms of some sort of folly. It would involve saying of these what Heidegger says of the traits of the common conception of time, that "they are not simply arbitrary fabrications and inventions. The essence of time must itself make these kinds of conceptions possible and even plausible."[8]

The Project of *Being and Time*

I began by referring to the very brief period in which the project of *Being and Time* flowered and faded. In fact, we could push this back to the summer of 1924 and his lecture "The Concept of Time,"[9] or to his lecture course on *The History of the Concept of Time*[10] in the summer of 1925, which has been called his "proto-SZ."[11] The published version of this course prepares us for the care Heidegger takes to prepare the way for the project and also for his subsequent repeated failure to complete the outline of his course. Here he manages only a final fifteen pages dealing with "The Exposition of Time Itself," after three hundred pages closely corresponding to the first half of *Being and Time* as we know it. He discusses particularly the relation between death, authenticity, and Dasein's being a whole.

This relation sets the theme for much of the second division of *Being and Time*,[12] which is heavily structured by the search for a way of understanding Dasein as a whole, by the distinctions between authentic and inauthentic temporality, between *Geschehen* (Historizing) and *Geschichtlichkeit* (Historicality), and by the need both to describe and account for the ordinary concept of time, and to contrast it to an ecstatic-horizonal one. But there is a wider frame to these discussions, which Heidegger describes as follows: "Our aim is . . . to work out the question of the meaning of *Being* and to do so concretely. Our *provisional* [*vorlaufiges*] aim [my emphasis] is the interpretation of *time* as the possible horizon for any understanding whatsoever of Being." The place of time in the text is, from the very beginning, subservient to the question of the meaning of Being. If time were not seen as the key to the meaning of Being, it would not be entertained. The term that bears the weight here is *vorlaufiges*, which means *provisional*, but also *temporary, for the present*, and (even more amusingly in English), *for the time being*. What does this tell us? Let us leave aside that he understands his own text as a treatise with a purpose and a path, in which, we might suppose, the discussion of time is to be subordinated to the question of Being according to a quite traditional temporal schema. The important thing is that Heidegger is introducing the relation between Being and Time in terms of priority, difference, and deferment. And his treatment of time in his subsequent three lecture courses consistently bears out this subordination.

The most obvious thing to learn from this is how misplaced it would be to complain when Heidegger turns away from time and the temporal in pursuit of the question of the meaning of Being. For not only at the beginning of *Being and Time* but in many other places, he repeatedly insists on the ontological interest he has in time, and how this cannot be in the ordinary sense of *being extended in time,* which would not distinguish us from rocks. If that is so, the restricted nature of Heidegger's interest in time is hardly one we could challenge. But there is one possibility that this intimate link of priority, deferment, and difference between Being and Time occludes. It is the possibility that Being might, in the end, be nothing other than Time. As a guiding proposition, this would caution against the turning away from time in pursuit of the question of Being. It might enforce a kind of discipline on what one thought it possible to say about Being. For the implication would be that everything that one previously thought one could build *on* ecstatic temporality, one would have to think *through* it. One would have to develop ways of thinking in which mappings, overlayings, interweavings, readings, harmonic coordination would substitute for foundational ones. Be-*ing* would be nothing but a way of tim*ing.*

The distinction between *Zeitlichkeit* and *Temporalität,* for example, which is fundamental to the working of *Being and Time,* is presented in terms of an "as" relation. Heidegger writes that *"Temporalität* means *Zeitlichkeit* insofar as *Zeitlichkeit* itself is made into a theme as a condition of the possibility of the understanding of being and of ontology as such."[13] These two terms do not, as Heidegger puts it, quite coincide. And in 1936, in a rare return to such language, this slippage turns into a gulf, and he links *Temporalität* and *Ereignis.*[14] My point is: what would it be to think in temporal terms this very *as*-relation between *Zeitlichkeit* and *Temporalität?* What would it be like to fold back time onto itself, to thicken and stratify it rather than depart the scene?

But let us return to *Being and Time,* Part 1, which ends, as we have said, with the question of whether "time itself manifest[s] itself as the horizon of Being" that the book sets itself to answer. In *The Basic Problems of Phenomenology* (1927), we find a phenomenological working through of mediaeval ontology in relation to Kant, and (in chapter 4) he addresses the fundamental ontological presuppositions of logic. In Part 2, we move from "traditional discussions" back to fundamental ontology, but more particularly, Heidegger immediately broaches the problem of the ontological difference through Time, *Zeitlichkeit* and *Temporalität.* At the end of this Part 2, Heidegger's tone is very different from *Being and Time.* For, having taken this time the route through Kant's conception of the transcendental, he feels he can now claim to have shown that "time is the primary horizon of transcendental science, of ontology, or in short, it is the transcendental horizon. It is for this reason," he goes on, "that the title of the first part of the investigation of *Being and Time* reads 'The Interpretation of Dasein in Terms of Temporality, and the Explication of Time as the Transcendental Horizon for the Question of Being.'"[15] The very last section seems to sum things up most satisfactorily. He describes phenomenology as "Temporal or transcendental science" (contrasted with positive science), and he begins to link the transcendental temporality required to think the "a priori" to the Platonic conception of anamnesis.

Aristotle makes an appearance in *The Metaphysical Foundations of Logic,* but this time the central figure is Leibniz, and again it is the problem of Transcendence that ushers in the discussions of time. Now famously, Heidegger affirms the essential neutrality—prior to any concrete, including sexual factuality—of Dasein in *Being and Time,* and he describes Dasein as essentially dispersed. More importantly, and though some have wished to underplay this, Heidegger again thinks through the idea of fundamental ontology and argues for "a special problematic which has for its theme beings as a whole . . . [and which would deal with] the metaphysics of existence . . . [and even] the question of an ethics" (*MAL,* 199; *MFL,* 157). This he calls *metontology.* He describes it as arising within "the essence of ontology itself and is the result of its overturning [*Umschlag*], its *metabole*" (*MAL,* 199; *MFL,* 157). Heidegger does not to my knowledge explicitly come back to this, though the transformation of the fundamental question in *An Introduction to Metaphysics* ("Why is there anything at all, rather than nothing?"[16]) seems to reflect this increasingly ontic orientation. But one way of reading it would be as a sign of what is to come, namely, the breakdown of the very project of fundamental ontology, which runs parallel to the move away from time and the transcendental.[17]

There are, I believe, other seeds of the move away from time in the last sections of this book. But I ought to make explicit what I mean by *moving away from time and temporal,* because it reflects my whole orientation toward Heidegger. In the difference between *Zeitlichkeit* and *Temporalität* there is the beginning of a fascinating lexical movement that one might almost call Hegelian. *Temporalität* is *Zeitlichkeit* insofar as . . . (as we have suggested above). The Hegelian version would be that *Temporalität* is the truth of *Zeitlichkeit.* When I talk of moving away from time and the temporal, I mean moving away from the continued reference back to *Zeitlichkeit,* and the increasing preparedness to discuss *Temporalität* on its own and finally to abandon it in favor of, at times, overtly atemporal language.[18] But what would it be to be faithful to the complexities of the *existentiell* and *Zeitlichkeit*?

Let us look at one of the seeds of this development, bearing in mind that Heidegger thinks he has now *shown* that time is the transcendental horizon for the question of Being, that he has answered the last question in *Being and Time.* In section 12 ("Transcendence and temporality"), Heidegger confronts what he sees as a danger, namely, that we may come to see the three temporal ecstases—making-present, coming-toward, and having-been—as having a unity that after all has some kind of presentness itself, so that one could finally say that this ecstatic unity is what time *is*. He has previously countered this by saying that *time temporalizes (itself)*, which in its linguistic expression avoids suggesting a reduction of time to identity.[19] Here—and he is specifically trying to differentiate his position from Bergson and his *élan vital*—he suggests that "the unity of the ecstases is itself ecstatic." Again, trying to capture this, he writes: "Temporalization is the free oscillation of the whole of primordial temporality; time reaches and contracts itself." Heidegger also tries to transcendentalize, one might say, the idea of *horizon* (as when it is said that time is the horizon for the question of Being). Each *ecstasis* is both a being-carried-away, an overcoming of barriers, and produces a kind of closure, or horizon. Heidegger suggests we think of there being a primordial horizonal unity corresponding to the unity of the *ecstases*. He calls this horizonal unity *ecstematic*. I must now quote the paragraph that follows in full:

> This ecstematic unity of the horizon of temporality is nothing other than the temporal condition for the possibility of *world* and the world's essential belonging to transcendence. For transcendence has its possibility in the unity of ecstatic momentum. This oscillation [*Schwingung*] of the self-temporalizing ecstases is, as such, the upswing [*Uberschwung*] regarded as [swinging] toward all possible beings that can factically enter there into a world. The ecstematic temporalizes itself, oscillating as a worlding [*Welten*]. *World entry* happens only insofar as something like ecstatic oscillation temporalizes itself as a particular temporality.[20]

Difficult though it is, this passage is seminal in connecting the work of the 1920s to the later concerns, particularly the return to the question of Time in *On Time and Being*. In the word "oscillation" there are strong anticipations of the later discussion of the *Zuspiel*, the interplay between the three dimensions of time, which he calls "the true extending, playing in the very heart of time" (*OTB*, 15). This would give us a stronger sense of the continuity of Heidegger's project. So too would the parallels between this upswing and the *es gibt* and *Geschick*. Heidegger's discussion of the way an ecstatic horizon opens up a certain space could be said to presage his remarks about freedom and about destiny and fate.

What this suggests, at least, is that these texts of the late 1920s are working within a problematic that is about to be shattered, and that they already prepare the way for this shattering. This preparation is accomplished by certain very specific moves that Heidegger makes—one hesitates to say *almost without thinking*, but certainly repeatedly—and without accompanying justification. What I am talking about is the announcement of the requirement of *unity* of a differentiated set that he has already analyzed transcendentally. This unity cannot, however, be ontic, nor can it be transcendental in any sense that would carry the burden of a deeper sense of presence. So it has to be understood in a way that would not have these drawbacks. Heidegger hits on *free oscillation* as a way of describing this new, deeper nonobjective unity. This, then, allows the parallel construction of a corresponding horizonal (ecstematic) unity. And the celebratory paragraph we quoted is the result.

Now I confess to lingering Kantian worries about this language. Opposing a *way of thinking* to philosophical method is not without risk. We *could* say that Heidegger assumes not just the value but the fact of *unity* here, and that by doing so, he evinces a metaphysical prejudice in favor of the simple and the stable, and we could argue that this in itself is a reason to treat much of his later work with suspicion. But equally we could say that this is not simple prejudice; it is a way of justifying the march of a certain reflexive, syntactic intensification, in which simples get divided, divided things get opened out, what is opened up gets drawn together into a unity, and that unity then divides (oscillates) and moves (swings). And if we graft onto this the *Geschick des Seins,* we would find a rhythmic approaching and withdrawal of what oscillates and swings.

Heidegger has a defense against the charge of mere metaphor,[21] which claims that the ontic meaning (of *house,* for example) that we might think is proper is actually only fully grasped through a kind of meditative thinking. In this case, the fact that the regions and movements addressed by this discourse cannot be found within what we call space and time, within the world, is a confirmation, not a refutation, of their sense, for it is the possibility of space, time, and world that is the issue. However, this only opens a *logical* space; it does not tell us how to understand what is being said. We can undoubtedly link Heidegger's discourse to the limit discourse of other philosophers (think of Husserl on time as an Absolute Flux) and, if one thinks of oscillation, swinging, and vibration, there are undoubtedly echoes of Christian mysticism.

I have elsewhere charged that tapestry that we call the philosophical tradition with a lack of interest in the complexity of time. My general project could be described as a persistence in the attempt to translate the transcendental into the temporal by dropping assumptions about linearity, unidimensionality, and so on. Nietzsche's account of the eternal recurrence could be said to stand as a model. What this would mean for Heidegger's own quasi-transcendental discourse about temporality is highly contentious, but basically it would mean treating each of his moves as pointing to, and indeed exemplifying, the possibility of levels of intensification (and dispersion) of ontic time. To give one concrete example: the relation between the unity of the three ecstases and the three ecstases themselves would be no different in kind from the relationship between a chord and the three notes from which it was composed—or perhaps better, a tune and its notes. Again, the relation between *Zeit-lichkeit* and *Temporalität* would be no different in kind from the relation between a sound and its being repeated as a note. This is what was meant above by *folding back*. Heidegger's whole discourse is, however unwillingly, a conceptual construction that points away from the temporal toward its conditions of possibility.

My question is whether a complex account of existential time might not be able to accommodate all that Heidegger wants to say. Might it not be that Heidegger begins with *the everyday (or philosophically commonplace) view of everyday time,* to which he then opposes alternatives? What if everyday time were actually multi-stranded (not just entangled[22] in some negative sense); what if the units and styles of its measurement were not only not unifiable, but never thought to exhaust our everyday understanding? What if there were a fundamental problem of escaping from our models of time that needs to be resolved before we describe authentic time and primordial time?

I will not attempt to summarize the last major volume in this series of reworkings of *Being and Time,* but suffice it to say that Heidegger's 1929 *Kant and the Problem of Metaphysics* continues to pursue the intimate connection between time and fundamental ontology through a reading of Kant. His assessment of the importance of the transcendental imagination in the first critique and its fate in the second edition is such as to suggest that Kant's defense of reason here meets an abyss from which he turns away—the essential finitude of man. Heidegger tries to show the inherently temporal character of Kant's laying of the foundation of metaphysics (i.e., transcendence). Heidegger treats the transcendental imagination as a ground for the unity of sensibility and understanding, which is "also the root of both stems." This "root" grows out of primordial time. And this primordial time can be seen to unify the three modes of pure synthesis—pure apprehension, pure reproduction, and pure recognition—as the temporalizing of time. "Ontological knowledge," he writes, "is made up of 'transcendental determinations of time' because transcendence is temporalized in primordial time" (*KPM,* 203).

Heidegger later offers us a succinct review of *Being and Time,* focused on the problem of philosophy as forgetting. He very much gives the impression that this treatment of Kant does not so much advance the course of fundamental ontology, to which he is still here committed, as demonstrate his ability to translate Kant into his own terms, hence the remark of Cassirer[23] that he reads Kant as a usurper. The three pages of questions with which he ends the book (and which ask about the way forward from Kant to Hegel that would restate "Logic as the system of Pure Reason") raise in sharpened form the limitations posed by Dasein's finitude and rework the primacy of the question of Being as that of our friendship toward "the essential, the simple, and the stable" (*KPM*, 255). *Basic Problems* ended with a long quote from Kant defending philosophy against the philosophy of feeling; the *Metaphysical Foundations of Logic* takes us back from Leibniz to Plato with a quotation from the *Republic* linking transcendence and Being; and the Kant book ends with a quotation from Aristotle—to the effect that what we have always sought and has always eluded us is Being. Heidegger, in other words, demonstrates an extraordinary persistence in maintaining the focus on the question of Being and on the question of time as a necessary path to pondering that question.

In articulating these doubts about the later course of his thinking, I asked whether or not the very intimacy Heidegger insists on between time and Being was not a subtle exclusion of the possibility that they might be one and the same (by which I do *not* mean that they belong together). In this light, and in the light of the course of his later development, consider this final quotation from *Kant and the Problem of Metaphysics:*

> If the problematic of metaphysics is designated as that of Being and Time [*Sein und Zeit*] the explication which has been given concerning the idea of a fundamental ontology makes it clear that it is the conjunction "and" in the above title which expresses the central problem. (*KPM*, 251)

If, in fact, he had already resolved this problem in crucial ways, as one of the subordination of Time to Being at the very beginning of *Being and Time*, what could this question mean? He concludes:

> Neither Being nor time need be deprived of the meanings which they have until now, but a more primordial explication of these terms must establish their justification and limits. (*KPM*, 251)

This sits most uneasily with the claim made in a number of places in these books that the words *time* and *temporal* no longer have their ordinary meanings. Heidegger's central move, which appears in the Kant book (*KPM*, 249) and elsewhere, is to argue that the a priority of Being is a temporal determination requiring a different sense of time to be thought. What we have to ask is whether the engine of primordiality that generates these other times is not itself questionable. This, surely, is the point of Derrida's claim that no alternative conception of time will escape from being metaphysical.[24] To dig deeper, to find an even earlier *earlier* may indeed attract these difficulties. My question would be whether we are still operating, not with models of everyday time, but with everyday models of time that need radical revision.[25]

It is this possibility that I hope to have opened up by an all-too-brief review of the way Heidegger continued to pursue the project laid out in *Being and Time*. After this period, Heidegger finds other horses to ride in pursuit of the question of Being and allows the gap between time and its ontological appropriation to grow to the point at which the latter separates off and takes on a life of its own. I, on the other hand, at least imagine another way forward, in which we do not so much supplement the ordinary concept of time with authentic and primordial additions as explore further the structural complexities of the temporal in the hope that the question of Being might be, if not solved, at least dissolved in the process. Furthermore, I am not convinced by the necessity or the propriety of the release of the Being question from the horizon of Time, and I would like in the second section to explain why.

Turning away from Time

I am, of course, not the first to want to rethink the path that leads from *Being and Time*.[26] More than anyone else, Heidegger himself did that. Indeed, the very path he took was the product of such continuing reflection. In his *Letter on Humanism* he answers the question of whether *Being and Time* was a blind alley with a powerful and indignant affirmation of its problematic: the truth of Being. But the only references to time in this response are in the importance of persistence, patience, and warning against illusory measures of progress. In "The End of Philosophy and the Task of Thinking,"[27] he says he has been trying "again and again since 1930 to shape the question of *Being and Time* in a more primordial fashion . . . to subject the point of departure in *Being and Time* to an immanent criticism."[28] He floats the idea of substituting the title "Opening and Presence" for *Being and Time*, but such a translation would not free us from questioning. We would still have to ask: "But where does the opening come from and how is it given?" The book, he seems to be saying, is or has a destiny. His fidelity to its *Sache*, the matter of thinking, is unchanged. But again, there is no reference here to time or temporality, and a great deal of talk of the open, the free open, lighting, *Präsenz*, and so on. It is as if the reference to the *transcendental horizon* in the original formulation of the project of *Being and Time* has not simply been dropped, but in its death has spawned a productive *space* of questioning that has entirely displaced time and temporality. If this is so, it is because time as it is dealt with in *Being and Time* has become inessential—a possible solution to a problem that remains, unsolved. Time, the kept woman of philosophers down the ages, has been ditched when found wanting.

Of course, this is not quite true. Time has been displaced only in the sense that its place has shifted. It remains wedded as ever to ontological duties, and it appears in the form of destiny. But as Heidegger will explain in *On Time and Being*, time now means something very different. I shall argue that this new determination of time in terms of the thinking that comes to a head in *On Time and Being* represents a loss as much as a gain.

To do this, I will first nibble away at some of the assumptions behind Heidegger's later thought and argue that this renders the move away from *Zeitlichkeit* open to renewed scrutiny. I shall be attempting, against the tide, to take up a certain distance from Heidegger. The general form of this distance is to say that the central thrust of Heidegger's later thought is problematic: there is an *unthought* in his texts that yet sustains them. But this unthought may not be quite the gift one might have hoped for.

There are two aspects or dimensions to what I am calling problematic here. In each case, we are concerned with a feature of *thinking* that importantly compromises its purity. This forces us, I believe, to reassess what is undertaken in its name and what it excludes. For it is hard to accept that it can exclude at one level what already taints it at another. The two dimensions I have chosen to discuss here are ontic discourse and the "logic" of Heidegger's thought. I will argue that the ontic roots of Heidegger's language from *Sorge* to *es Gibt* fatally injure attempts at a thinking that would, in his words, think "Being without reference to beings." And I will argue that it is possible to begin to give an account of the hidden law of Heidegger's thought, of which he says he is not in command.[29] The combined consequence of these considerations is in effect to pose a series of questions: Does not the attempt to ask the question of Being rest on the possibility of a privileged language, or at least a language privileged in its relation to language? Do the lexical associations that join ownness to appropriation, to property, to belonging, to hearing, to giving, to the gift, and so on really give continuity to the matter of thinking? And what ground can there be for the privilege accorded to *this particular chain*? These questions are not gratuitous. If it is the lure of this discourse (together with the luminotopological discourse of opening, clearing, and lighting) that permits the displacement of time and the temporal, then a certain abrasion of that lure might draw us back to the point at which time would have a different future.

I will begin with some doubts about Heidegger's ontic discourse. By ontic discourse I mean particularly the chain of terms associated with property and dwelling: giving, sending, granting, bestowing, preserving, withholding, belonging, withdrawing, nearness, abiding opening, spacing. We need, perhaps, a certain exteriority in reading Heidegger, even if one cannot simply go around him, and even if the very idea of exteriority to such a thinker is essentially problematic. For if, one by one, or in small clusters, we can learn to follow and perhaps operate with each of these terms, there comes a time when we begin to notice the common space they occupy—which we could call the space of a primitive economy—an economy prior to mediated exchange, prior to money, prior to representation, and so on.[30] Heidegger only ever pauses over this language, he never questions or thinks it as a whole. But I do not see how *we* can avoid thinking it more critically.

What is it to reflect like this on Heidegger's language? What kind of event is it to come to hear another refrain amidst the notes? This question, I would claim, is absolutely central to understanding what is and what is not happening, for example, in his *On the Way to Language,* and in a curiously redoubled way. Heidegger announces at the beginning of "The Nature of Language" his aim "to bring us face to face with the possibility of undergoing an experience with language," an experience in which our usual unthinking use of language is disturbed.[31] Does the dawning sense that a certain discourse is wedded to a particular unspoken economy count as such an experience? I will return to this question a little later in my discussion of Heidegger's machinery.

The archaic quality of this discourse is not thematic for Heidegger for the simple reason that it is through what we could almost call its gift of certain possibilities of syntactic transformation that he can pursue his speculative dehiscence of the *is.* The word Being (*Sein*) itself offers certain possibilities—more in German than in English, while the verbal form of the *is* suggests a much greater wealth of expansion, especially through the wealth of articulation of tenses. And the two divisions of *Being and Time* could be said to be structured, first, by an articulation of Being, and second, by an expansion of the *is* through the complexities of tense. The capacity to position oneself through the use of complex tense is an extraordinarily fruitful field for philosophical inquiry. The diverse possibilities that languages provide for this would suggest different kinds of temporal openness. Heidegger is clearly also concerned with *mood,* both in *Being and Time* and later in his discussions of activity and passivity. We may suppose that the possibility of dehiscence of the *is* in directions other than tense is part of what drives the turn after the 1920s. The interpretation of the other *is*—of identity—as belonging-together points in the same direction.

Heidegger is working his way through the manifold meanings of Being by pursuing tense and mood in the *is* of existence and predication, and by a kind of relational deconstruction of the *is* of identity. The moment of translation (especially of Parmenides, Heraclitus, and Anaximander) is the point of maximum vulnerability to such a dehiscence. It is not clear to me that Heidegger always made the distinctions I am making here, but the project of the dual dehiscent articulation of the *is* is clear.

The tension between the articulation of these two *is*'s affects the internal organization of *Being and Time*—especially the subjection of *Zeitlichkeit* to considerations of identity through authenticity—and the struggle between *Zeitlichkeit* and *Temporalität*, between *Gegenwartigkeit* and *Anwesenheit*, and more broadly between the Heidegger of the 1920s and the later Heidegger.

The dehiscence of the *is* of identity into questions of belonging, possession, gift, and so on is a double gesture. Introducing the relationality of belonging into identity involves difference, irreducible division. This difference is contained, first by its articulation within the static lexicon of primitive (premercantile) economy in which the relationship between the self and what Kierkegaard called the constituting Power is articulated in terms of primitive economic relations, and second, by its subjection to a time ultimately determined by considerations of identity. This primitive relational lexicon derives its positive power from the thought that it could reverse the condensation effects locked into identity, or presence. But the caged creature is only released into a pen in which the bars are stronger and the locks bigger.

What is put into play in this lexicon of giving, belonging, bestowing are various contained forms of identity constituting and generating relationships. But their containment is assured from the outset. It is assured by the economy that frames this lexicon, which essentially excludes representation, signs, structure, and, we might add, writing; it excludes the outside, and in particular it excludes, in an important respect, time. When Heidegger returns to time (in *On Time and Being*), it is to bind it to space, to displace it, to emasculate its possibilities.

The containment of this economy is assured, in the sense that the law of enchainment, which would add terms to the series, holds that no new term shall introduce dispersion or representation; no new term shall introduce alien currency into the economy.

Heidegger, on the occasion of his refusal of the Berlin chair in March 1934, in what is undoubtedly a political statement too, wrote of his work "being intimately rooted in the life of the peasants."[32] It is here, too, that he talks of the fundamental way in which he is not in command of the hidden law of his own work and of peasant existence wanting to be left to its own law.[33]

Enormous questions open up here. We would have to work through Heidegger's relation to Dilthey's *Weltanschauung-philosophie* and the whole refusal of psychologism, anthropologism, and so on. But the question has to be asked: What is the hidden law of his work, and what is the law of the peasants' existence, and what connection can we make between the law of this *dwelling* and the lexicon of primitive economy that Heidegger deploys in his thought? Even accepting Heidegger's valuation of "simple rough existence,"[34] his own concern with *dwelling* might suggest radically different forms of primitivism generating radically different base lexicons. Nomadic herdsmen and fishermen might come up with the tent and the boat of Being respectively, and, joking apart, the associative chains attached to such modes of dwelling could be quite different. Heidegger has, I claim, attempted the dehiscence of Being (as identity) through belonging, having, reaching, sending—through primitive modes of human interaction refigured as modes of mediated self-relation, and developed with a certain autonomy. As primitive forms, we might suppose they would be at least universal and hence philosophically illuminating. But they are not presented as a lexicon at all, let alone as a primitive stratum. They are deployed as ways of articulating Being without representation, without, one could say, writing. The hidden law here is that Being shall not be contaminated, corrupted through articulation. Articulation shall not pass through the ontic in any essential way. This lexicon cannot be linked to a particular economy of existence. But what, then, do we do with Heidegger's reference to an inner relationship, the intimate rootedness of his work in peasant life? Can we seriously leave things there?

Heidegger explicitly refuses to be bound by the ontic roots of his terminology. Remarks in that vein about care (*Sorge*) in *Being and Time* spring to mind most readily. But the motif of purification, of decontamination, is not only itself infected with the very same difficulty of shedding the ontic; it relies on the possibility of subjecting the play of language to psychic pacts (agreements between writers and readers to understand a word a certain way). This seems wholly implausible in itself, but even more so on Heidegger's view of language.

These difficulties are serious impediments to our continuing naïvely to deploy the discourse in which the later Heidegger has schooled us. That we continue to do so may best be understood within the wider discourse of investment.[35]

The second dimension of difficulty lies in what I have called the "logic" of Heidegger's thinking. I use this word of course provocatively, to suggest that we might begin to think the unthinkable: that what Heidegger calls thinking might be structured in ways it does not (and in some ways cannot) itself think—ways, indeed, that it explicitly excludes.

In *Mémoires for Paul de Man*,[36] Derrida offers us a very subtle discussion of the massive upsurge in artificial memory, and indeed the technology of memory, in the course of a comparison between Heidegger's claim that science doesn't think and de Man's own account of the relation between thinking and techno-memory. There is one particular sentence I would like to pick up on. Derrida has commented on Heidegger's strategy of separation and subordination of *science* to thinking, and goes on: "The Heideggerian argument which operates everywhere to justify this division and hierarchy, when it is reduced to its essential schema, has the following form and can be transposed everywhere: 'The essence of technology is nothing technological.'" What interests me in this is the idea of a "schema which operates everywhere"[37] in Heidegger's thought.

It might even help us get clear about the "hidden law" that commands his work. But more interestingly, it would surely take us to an outside inside Heidegger's work. Heidegger cannot understand himself as operating a logical machine. He cannot allow that thinking could be reduced to an algorithm, or a cluster of them. But what about us? What if we were to say, "The essence of thinking is nothing thoughtful." I do not mean that Heidegger has not thought about thinking; the play between thinking and thanking[38] is clearly an expansive articulation of thinking, and the various ways in which he distinguishes it from reasoning, calculation, and so forth show the same concern for its differentiation. And of course it is Heidegger who declares that the most thought-provoking thing is that we are still not thinking.[39] But does it have no secret law of its own? Could there not be machinery operating, something without intrinsic value that generates sequences of sentences in ways judged productive? When Heidegger writes that "all metaphysics leaves something essential unthought: its own ground and foundation," can *we* not answer that this very pursuit of ground and foundation is the unthought in thinking? Consider the crucial moves in *On Time and Being* in which the *es gibt* emerges:

> We do not say: Being is, time is, but rather: there is Being and there is time (*es gibt Sein* and *es gibt Zeit*). For the moment we have only changed the idiom with this expression. Instead of saying *it is,* we say *there is, It gives.*
>
> In order to get beyond the idiom and back to the matter, we must show how this *there is* can be experienced and seen.

We could look also at the parallel moves in "The Principle of Identity."[40] After quoting and quickly translating the crucial Parmenidean fragment: "Das Selbe nämlich ist Vernehmen (*Denken*) sowohl als auch Sein" ("For the same perceiving (thinking) as well as being"), he tells us that Parmenides does not help us hear what *to auto* says. And yet "we must acknowledge the fact that in the earliest period of thinking, long before thinking had arrived at a principle of identity, identity itself speaks out in a pronouncement which rules (*Verfugt*) as follows: thinking and Being belong together in the Same and by virtue of this Same."

> Unintentionally [*Unversehens*] we have here already interpreted *to auto, the Same.* We interpret Sameness to mean a belonging together. (*ID,* 29)

This, he goes on to say, has now been fixed, but quite what it means is unclear. We have to take a closer look and "let the matter speak for itself."

If we judge these sequences of sentences in terms of the links from one to the next, we can only suppose that part of the Heideggerian text is missing. Then we realize that what legitimates these sequences are Heidegger's references to *saying* and to the *matter* of thought.

But a less tendentious way of understanding what is going on would be to say that a certain logic is in operation and that the principles of this logic guide the sequencing of sentences: Seek the third that dissolves static representational dualisms. Pursue such discourse as allows the articulation of subject/object relationships in ways that undermine any simple distinction. Transform questions of identity into transactional ones.

These ideas can be characterized by the drive to the primordial. I have already discussed this in the first section with reference to the claim that "temporalization is the free oscillation of the whole of primordial temporality." In *On Time and Being* after Heidegger has reached three dimensions, he asks for the *source* of their unity, which he characterizes as the "interplay (*Zuspiel*) of each toward each." He then asks about the *giving* in the *"es gibt sein"* and discovers "an extending opening up," and then asks *what gives?* to which the answer is *Ereignis*, appropriation (*OTB*, 15–17). Heidegger's genius lies in the modulation of these moves, but the underlying schemata involved are not too difficult to discern.

If, as it has been suggested,[41] Heidegger's work is in the last analysis (which never comes) the most rigorous defense of presence, that is only the name for the clustering (perhaps belonging-together!) of a diversity of operations, procedures, devices, which are not only in principle capable of repetition, but whose often predictable repetition underpins Heidegger's opus. It could be said, then, that Heidegger's texts are textual productions generated by the recursive application of a finite number of procedures.[42] If these play at least a part in what is called thinking, they are not themselves thought through. This is our task and Heidegger's fate.

We might perhaps here return to the question I raised above about Heidegger's discussion of undergoing an experience with language. Heidegger's strategy here is familiar. He opens up a radical opposition to a taken-for-granted attitude and then gives a *particular specification of the alternative*. But it is then only too easy to lose sight of the space opened up. In this case,[43] Heidegger is engaged in inducing in us an inversion of our usual sense of being subjects in control of language, by suggesting that we will arrive at the essence of language by "undergoing an experience with language." By listening we will hear language speaking, we will experience the "granting that abides in Saying." Words will be seen not just to name preexisting items in the world, but to give them being, to arise with them. But what of the listening that listens to words such as *grants, abides, obeys, summons,* and so on, and hears reactionary politics, or hears theology, or hears the worldview of the peasant farmer? Such a listening is no less a radical break from the ordinary use of language; it is no less an experience which one can undergo with language.

Derrida once said that he did not see eye to eye with Heidegger on language; it was perhaps just such a change of ear that he was alluding to.

These two difficulties, forms of constitutive exteriority of Heidegger's texts, are intended to give us pause in considering the fate of time in the later Heidegger, and to give some reason for a reprise of the abandoned program.

Time as Destiny

Heidegger makes great play of the destiny of Being, the *Geschick des Seins.* Being somewhat allergic to the language of both fate and destiny, extending a more positive welcome to chance and the messiness of Being, I want to look at a small selection of his remarks on destiny as a symptom of the dangers of his allowing his thinking about time to be subordinated to ontology.

I want all too briefly to distinguish three approaches to destiny: existential, ontological, and textual. The first two I attribute to Heidegger, and the last I associate with Derrida. In each of the first two approaches, I want to argue for importantly contestable assumptions, which when brought out and taken seriously would transform them into more modest and plausible areas of investigation.

The existential approach to destiny, which already appears in a strong form in Nietzsche, can be found in section 74 of *Being and Time* (on Historicality), and of course Heidegger is riding heavily on etymological echoings here.

I will quote only a short passage:

> Destiny is not something that puts itself together out of individual fates, any more than Being-with-one-another can be conceived as the occurring together of several Subjects. Our fates have already been guided in advance, in our Being with one another in the same world and in our resoluteness for definite possibilities. Only in communicating and in struggling does the power of destiny become free.[44]

What Heidegger is trying to achieve in this section is a synthesis of the idea that the repetition of tradition opens up our destiny, that Dasein's ecstatic temporality is the ground for historizing, that destiny cannot be just a summation of individual fates, and that a community can realize its destiny through communication and struggle.

The distinctive function played by destiny in this passage is to provide a way of transcending the more arithmetic addition of individual fates and to introduce the presumption of a *terminus ad quem* into a community's historical reflection. The strategy of Heidegger's thought here is to provide what looks like *a* solution to what seems to be a pressing problem and to represent it as *the* solution.

My central claim is this: the word *destiny* functions in such a way as to imply that there is a truth, or a space of truth, to be won by such struggle. Even if every word prescribes a law, this one is essentially legitimating in its function, and when Heidegger talks about the power of destiny becoming "free through communication and struggle," he is eliding the importance of coming to some collective vision of the future with success in discovering one's true destiny. This elision eases, though it does not prescribe, the slide into totalitarian thought, because the need to arrive at and enact the truth can easily be made to override questions as to how one arrives at it. Hence the leadership principle. Remember Parmenides' goddess: "Come, I will tell you—and you must accept my word when you have heard it."[45]

Heidegger, it is only fair to say, would repudiate any such direct reading. He writes, for instance,

> Always the destining of revealing holds complete sway over man. But that destining is never a fate that compels. For man becomes truly free only insofar as he belongs to the realm of destining, and so becomes one who listens and hears, and not one who is simply constrained to obey.[46]

This draws on his account of freedom to be found in "On the Essence of Truth."[47] And Heidegger is quite right to insist that we cannot think of truth or freedom except within what we might call an opening. But nothing requires that disparate openings historically coincide or that this or that opening is compelling.

Unless we are to have philosopher-kings, it is important to keep separate the continuing need for revolutionary thought, the need for radical change at certain times in history, the impossibility of giving a wholly rational grounding for any particular projection of the future, and the supposition that there are privileged revelations of destiny. Perhaps we need a god to save us from believing that there is no conflict among poets. But we also need to ask whether poetic eschatology should be privileged over that of economists or ecologists. And then we must ask who privileges, where, and when.

It could be objected that what I mean by patience is merely the avoidance of risk and that there are times, surely, when we have to risk all to win all. Consider Nietzsche on Wagner's Bayreuth: "The event which lies like strange sunlight upon recent and immediately coming years, designed for . . . a future age" and which "must transform every notion of education and culture in the spirit of everyone who experiences it . . . a curtain has been raised on a future in which there are no longer any great and good things except those which all hearts share in common."[48]

Nietzsche bet on Wagner and lost. As he wrote later,

This essay is full of world-historical accents. This is the strongest "objectivity" possible. The absolute certainty about what I am was projected on some accidental reality—the truth about *me* spoke from some gruesome depths.[49]

And Heidegger even wrote, "We must produce the illusion, as it were, that the given task at hand is the one and only necessary task" (*MFL*, 158).

What is beyond dispute is that no model of action is adequate that does not address questions of risk, crisis, investment, commitment, decision, failure, death—but also the most radical opening of one's relation to the future, one for which Reason always comes too late.[50] Time may always be revolutionary, but there are also revolutionary times in which action can legislate and not just follow rules. But genuine absence of rational grounds for projecting the future must not spawn metaphysical simulacra in the form of destiny. Destiny is *at best* the name of a projectable space of possibility within which my (or our) actions would make sense.

This takes me on to consider Heidegger's use of the *Geschick des Seins*, the destiny of Being, Being as destiny. Everything I have already said about the privileging of a primitive economics applies here too.

Reference to the *Geschick des Seins* is meant to translate the *es gibt (Sein)* into historical terms, as the fluctuating of Being as gift, giving, and withdrawal, to complete the process of withdrawal from the stage of existential analytic represented in *Being and Time;* and it is meant to occlude the importance of "history" not only as a sequence of events but even as understood in the accounts of historicity in *Being and Time*.

Heidegger's central and continuing task is to think "Being without [reference to any foundational relation to] beings." The surpassed "metaphysical" account did, however, have one advantage—that of offering a distinctive and constitutive *relation* against which Being could be clarified. The *Geschick des Seins* relocates this relationality in a movement of giving or sending, and holding back or withdrawing. This is not what we ordinarily think of as history, though it may look like it. Heidegger writes:

> Being does not have a history in the way a city or a people have a history. What is history-like in the history of Being is obviously determined by the way in which Being takes place and by this alone . . . this means the way in which *es gibt Sein*. (*OTB*, 8)

Sending is defined as "a giving which gives only its gift, but in the giving holds itself back and withdraws."

> What is historical in the history of Being is determined by what is sent forth in destiny and not by an indeterminately thought-up occurrence. (*OTB*, 8–9)

The theme of the accidental is pursued more explicitly when he writes:

The sequence of epochs in the destiny of Being is not accidental, nor can it be calculated as necessary. . . . What is appropriate shows itself in the destiny. What is appropriate shows itself in the belonging together of the epochs. The epochs overlap each other in their sequence so that the original sensing of Being as presence is more and more obscured in different ways. (*OTB*, 9)

Heidegger is clearly right when he says that these remarks are to be referred back to *Being and Time*, section 6, the discussion of the history of ontology, and not to the later discussion of historicality. The reason is surely this: Heidegger has taken his own expression—"the destruction of the history of ontology"—and thought it through more deeply. The result of that pondering is the attempt, first, to eradicate any sense of linear chronology or teleology in "history," and second, to think through the double genitive of the "of" in the history *of* ontology, through the implications of the *es gibt (Sein)*.

How are we to understand "Being withholding itself" and "turning away"? As a *reaction* to a predominantly subject-centered tradition, it is understandable, but precisely as such is it not problematic? The discourse of destiny importantly attests to both the structural invisibility of the conditions of what appears and the transformation in history of the deepest forms of those conditions. But how convincing is the story of scene-changing in a transcendental theater? In particular, is not Heidegger's supposition that *epochs* would be prior to, and would condition the shape and fate of, representation undermined by the narrative itself?

In his essay "Envoi," Derrida asks whether the repetition of envois (epochs, sendings), including that of representation itself, might not be subject to an unthought law of representation, namely, the constant repetition of the envoi, the great Greek epoch. This question would affect

> not only the whole ordering of epochs or periods in the resumed unity of a history of metaphysics or of the West [but also] the very credit we would wish, as philosophers, to accord to a centered and centralized organization of all the fields or all the sections of representation grouped around a sustaining sense of a fundamental interpretation.[51]

This is not just a problem about Heidegger's formulation of the epochality of Being. It is a problem about *what it is* he is trying to formulate. And yet it is arguably the question of formulation, and then commitment and reception of thought that actually provides a locus for the very saga Heidegger is relating. Does not the discourse of the *Geschick des Seins* capture rather well the risks of reading, writing, and translation?

This very treatment of Heidegger makes perfectly clear the importance to him of this question of the reception of his thinking, and it is not at all difficult to treat giving, withholding, concealing, and so on as a language for articulating the drama and the stakes of writing, reading, being read, translating, interpreting, and so on.

This issue clearly did concern Heidegger. There are numerous remarks offered in guidance to the reader or listener—to ignore the propositional form, to follow the movement of showing (at the beginning of *On Time and Being*), and that "the Saying of Appropriation in the form of a lecture remains . . . an obstacle" (*OTB*, 24). And his readings and translations of Parmenides again make appeals to various powerful ways (e.g., listening to the saying) of recouping the losses embodied in centuries of tradition. I would suggest as a project for some other day a careful study of the point-by-point parallel between what Heidegger says about the destiny of Being and what he says about writing as transmission. The issue is already problematized elsewhere, particularly by Kierkegaard and Nietzsche, and it is of course discussed in Derrida's essay "My Chances."

In "My Chances," Derrida transforms his promised topic—psychoanalysis and literature—into proper names, through whose destiny as signs the problematic of chance and necessity can be thought through more generally in a "*logos* or *topos* of envoi."[52] The link in the *Metaphysical Foundations of Logic* between Heidegger's thrownness (*Geworfenheit*) and its dispersion (*Zerstreuung*) allows him to introduce, at least as a model, the essential iterability of a mark, by which it is continually divided and multiplied, which, as he puts it, "imprints the capacity for diversion within its very movement." If we suppose that this structure of the trace or mark is not only "fundamental" but also pervades every "constituted identity," then the effect would be to introduce intrinsic deviation or dispersion within any such determination as destiny, somewhat like the Epicurean swerve. Writing about Freud, Derrida says,

> In the destination [*Bestimmung*] there is thus a principle of indetermination, chance, luck or of destinerrance. There is no assured destination precisely because of the marks and the proper name.[53]

By the introduction of chance, and in particular, the alignment of the question of destiny with the structure of the trace, Derrida has exploited the connection Heidegger insists on among thinking and Being and language in ways Heidegger would not have anticipated. If Derrida has a hand in shaping Heidegger's destiny, it will not have been entirely by chance, because the centrality of language for Heidegger always made it a hostage to fortune.

At the risk of being labeled one of the last men from whom nothing great or good ever comes, and who, as Nietzsche put it, sacrifice the future to themselves, I would like to suggest the possibility of converting this whole discourse of destiny and chance into a more cautious domain of reflection.

In saying this, I am trying to respond to what Philippe Lacoue-Labarthe described as the suspicion with which one must always now read Heidegger.[54] I am proposing a cool, modest, gently analytical (with a small "a") approach to these questions, because we cannot, as philosophers, divorce the style and shape of our pronouncements from the wider possibilities of their rhetorical transformation. The wider public discourse of destiny is not separable from wars of mass destruction. I do not mean the *word* destiny so much as its confident use. There is an important difference between mentioning it, discussing it, analyzing it, making it the site of questioning, and so on, and its approved use even in the course of what claims and promises to be a program of radical interrogation. I take up again the politics of destiny in "Art as Event," chapter 12, in the context of American landscape painting and the doctrine of manifest destiny.

Let me give an example that will raise more problems than it resolves but that we must address. In *Ecce Homo* ("Why I Am a Destiny" [*Schicksal*]) Nietzsche did not write, "there will be a wailing and gnashing of teeth"—a problem, as he might have put it, for dentists. He wrote, "there will be wars the like of which have never yet been seen on earth."[55] What does this mean? What do we tell our students it means? Or ourselves? He writes of geological upheavals, of the advent of "great politics," and talks of the war of truth against the lies of millennia. I will not here discuss the performative rhetoric of apocalyptic discourse. I will confess that what I and, I suspect, many other teachers of Nietzsche have explained is that the war he is describing is one carried out in books, conferences, debates, arguments, and so on. It is the struggle against lies, against stupidity, against smallness, against morality—the struggle to overcome *man.* And we clearly separate this from the struggles that have littered our century with trenches, camps, and burnt-out cities, struggles that still gnaw at our consciences and plague our screens. We make this distinction, we draw these lines. But what if the fate of the lines we philosophers draw, in our thinking and writing and speaking, is to be immediately overrun on the ground, on the street? What would such a fate mean for responsibility?

In the first paragraph of "Why I Am a Destiny" (*Ecce Homo*), Nietzsche wrote, "I am no man, I am dynamite." (He was repeating a description made of him by a reviewer of *Beyond Good and Evil,* which perhaps holds a lesson for reviewers.) If the word *destiny* is typically linked to a rhetoric of arousal, then *destiny* in this sense has a destiny. Quite apart from our doubts about its metaphysical legacy, the speed with which it can be deployed in the cause of political and military mobilization surely ought to give us pause. Our precautions, our warnings, footnotes, and so on are no safeguard if destination is, precisely, not able to guarantee the preservation of identity, but is intrinsically divided, delayed, diverted.

What then would this discussion about destiny tell us about time? If we read Heidegger literally, not very much. The real continuity of this later work with *Being and Time* is that the question of time is only a means to another end—that of awakening and preserving a certain experience of the truth of Being.

I promised at the outset that I would suggest ways in which we might come to think of Being, the a priori, transcendence, the ontological difference, and so on in a new way. I will now pursue these matters a little further.

The obvious way in which to rethink Being, the ontological difference, and so forth is to follow the path already beaten by Derrida, who offers us powerful strategies for undermining both the character of the primitive and the primordial as well as the textual drive and desire that takes us in these directions. Derrida's classical gestures here centered around a kind of parodic substitution of an impossible origin within a transcendental framework. This is the legacy of *différance,* trace, supplement, and so on. In *"Ousia* and *Gramme,"* Derrida explicitly repudiates the idea of another, primordial time that could underwrite ordinary time. In doing so, he brings ruin to much of the language of the later Heidegger. But of course part of what is being questioned is the very idea of a transcendental (or quasi-transcendental) framework. I want to suggest a way of expanding the erosion of the transcendental other than by this substitutive displacement. This would attempt to reopen the field of *intratemporal constitution* by pursuing forms of inter-referential and articulatory complexity. In a graded series of levels, this would involve attempts to articulate the temporal forms of transition, dehiscence, difference, repetition, interweaving, entanglement, and superimposition. As well as the Derridean displacement of the origin (in favor of repetition, and *différance*), I am suggesting we pursue the possibilities of multiplicity of temporal series, of the complexity of their constitution, and of the capacity for cross-determination of one series by another. Such an account will take considerable analytical work, and I cannot take it further here. What drives this thinking is what I would call my *principle of all principles*—that it is always too soon to abandon the resources of the temporal. And the continued use of terms like horizon, spacing, transcendence, even *ecstasis* requires of us at the very least a textual circling back, to break open and rearticulate their temporality.[56]

Let me give two examples of persistence with or fidelity to the temporal. First, Heidegger often asks us not to read his work as a series of propositions, but rather to "follow the movement of showing." It would not be difficult to present this request as critical for our understanding of Heidegger, what a military commander would think of as a bridge that *had to be kept open.* But what is it to "follow the movement of showing"? What is it to come across this request again and again, at both the beginning and at the end of a paper? Consider:

1. *Showing* is already a repetition that renews or recovers by a return that repeats a more original sense of allowing to be seen. (See Heidegger's account of phenomenology in section 7 of *Being and Time*.)
2. A *movement* of showing is a textual movement both in the sense of the continual vertical upsurging movement[57] (what Heidegger would call presencing) that sustains the text at each instant and in the sense of a movement of succession (and the transcendence of succession) through the course of the text.
3. *Following* such an already double movement will subject it to the most complex processes of ongoing and reflexive temporal synthesis and releasement, which no result will quite capture and yet which cannot be quite distinguished from the series of the results of such readings, and so on.
4. Such a resonant response to this double movement of the text will both bring to bear the most complex coordination of hidden and overt agendas, pasts and futures, and be itself taken up into that tangle of ear and eye and nose by which we will subsequently live and act and . . . read. I am trying to suggest we can translate "following the movement of showing" into a language that gives voice to an open coordination of rhythms within rhythms and repetition of repetition, a co-temporal *fracticity.*[58]

I would now like to offer a second example of the kind of repetition of the temporal I am suggesting—that of the ontological difference. This again is a central notion for Heidegger. My line of thought is this: it may be vital to be able to shift from ontic discourse, discourse about beings and their relation to each other, to discourse about Being, about *Ereignis,* about the *es gibt,* about withholding, and so forth, but that does not preclude what could be called backdoor entanglements between the ontic and the ontological. One way of explaining this would be to insist on exacting the pound of flesh from the debt owed by the ontological to ontic language, to insist that there is no proper way of paying off this debt, that giving, withdrawing, responding, turning away *bind* the ontological to the ontic in ways Heidegger appears to resist. It may be vital because I treat this very attempt at an articulation of temporal fracticity as a radical shift from everyday models of time, a shift famously adumbrated by Augustine. But this discontinuity is not the announcement of another realm at all. The transcendental, if you like, is nowhere else but *in* the empirical (cf. Merleau-Ponty's *in-visible*).[59] The best model for this unity of absolute distinctness *at a time* and wider continuity, is offered, I believe, by the Möbius strip (a flat ribbon, twisted once and joined in a circle) at any point of which there are two quite distinct sides, which are yet, when traced through, seen to be only a single surface. This neither proves nor explains anything, but it illustrates how one might begin to think *transcendence within temporality.*

Addendum

One radical criticism of the position outlined here would be to suggest the need for another reading of Heidegger's itinerary after the 1920s, a reading that shows that he is engaged *in this very project.*[60] On this reading, time does not disappear but continually erupts—as overcoming the spirit of revenge (in *Nietzsche*), as *Ereignis* (in *Contributions to Philosophy*), as reserve and efficiency (in "The Question Concerning Technology"), as thanking and commemoration (in *What Is Called Thinking?*), as restitution (in "The Anaximander Fragment"), as founding and presencing (in *On the Way to Language*), and so on. It is perhaps a sign of some lingering nostalgia on my part to want a more systematic and programmatic treatment of temporality than this, one that would reconstruct the geological formation that gives rise to this archipelago of instances. Temporality will become the infinitely complex site of the *re-* from which the specter of primordiality will have been finally banished, never to return.

5

From Representation
to Engagement

Space and (Its) Representation

Is representation a threat to time? Philosophers of many different stripes, from Kant and Hegel to Heidegger and Bergson, would agree on this. But this formulation of the question is unhelpfully simplistic. It prematurely glosses over the many senses of "representation," *mis*-representing their unity, as one might say. And it does not tell us how it is that "time" suffers from being represented. It would run the risk of too closely tying Heidegger's concerns to those of Bergson to claim that his central concern in *Being and Time* is to ward off the dangers posed by representational or objectified time, even if the way he poses the question of Being does point in this direction. Moreover, it is clear that Heidegger's *acknowledgment* of time beyond representation did not stand still. What Heidegger calls the question of Being (in *Being and Time*) is arguably the attempt to renew thinking about the relations, structures, and conditions that precede representation—substituting, as we might say, existential for transcendental structures. But the aim of his project is not simply to get clearer about the locus of time—for example, to show how fundamental it is. Thinking time in terms of temporality is the first step in posing the question anew—in terms of the shapes and structures of— of our engagement with the world. However, Heidegger's treatment of these matters in *Being and Time* has come in for some harsh criticism and is no longer fashionable. I try here to defend the unfashionable.

If the *acknowledgment* of time, an acknowledgment both philosophical and "practical," is threatened by representational thinking, what precisely does "representation" mean here? We need to distinguish (at least) two figures or shapes:

First, a representation that accepts and reinforces, or delights in and celebrates, a kind of timelessness, and works within that abstraction (think of logic and mathematics, and of structural representations such as diagrams, maps, grids). Here we find either no declared problem over time or an active recognition that it is only in this willful abstraction from time that certain possibilities arise. Arguably, within its own limits, such detemporalization is not a threat to the acknowledgment of time. It only becomes a threat when we lose sight of those limits.

Second, a representation that symbolically includes time (Dali's clocks, narrative painting), or even attempts to acknowledge the impossibility of reducing time to a component of representation. But even here the relation between "space" and "representation" is far from simple. Not all representation is spatial—we need only think of the temporal arts (drama, film, music, and song). Spatial representation is typically spatial in a rather limited sense of space—two-dimensional and flat—as in paintings and maps. And then there is the abstract sense of "spatial" that we might employ in speaking of conceptual geography, structures of op-position, and matrices—where we are not only dealing with a spatial representation but we are deploying *a model or representation of space.* In other words, the "space" deployed in representation is not "real" space, but something closer to an "extensive dimensionality" or even a form of intuition.

On this Kantian formulation we might come to see both the need to supplement space with time as a release from a restrictively spatial sense of representation, and the limitation of such a supplementary strategy. Limited, that is, precisely to the condition of representation. And this would raise the further question—what would it be to think at one and the same time both the need for a temporal supplement to space *and* the need to overcome the representational framework with which the very distinction (and hence the formulation of overcoming) gets formulated?

What would it be to *overcome* our representational understanding of space and time? There is a sense in which if we cannot think "repre-sentation" in terms other than those it provides, we would be stuck with a representation of representation and not have escaped the circle. When Heidegger talks about Being, he is trying precisely to think beyond rep-resentation, and with the word *thinking* he marks the need to change the way we go about this.

What would it be to overcome our representational understanding of space and time? Our discovery of an intimacy between the space of rep-resentation and the representation of space is a clue here. What does such an intimacy reflect? A logical circle? Or something else? Clearly, there is a kind of logical circle. But this is not sui generis. Logical circles do not just appear; the interconnectedness they embody reflects a mode of engagement. This is the justification of what Heidegger calls *equiprimordiality* and for his repeated defense of the circle as a structure of thought. The issue for hermeneutics, as he puts it, is not how to avoid the circle, but how to enter it properly.[1] And this means understanding the kind of interconnectedness exemplified by a circle. I have used the expression "a mode of engagement" to plant a flag somewhere in the right territory, but whether "mode" is not too specific and whether "engagement" is not too general remains to be seen.

To pause for a minute with the circle, note that it figures or prefigures many of the issues we are looking at. Is not a circle both a spatial figure and a figure of space, the archetype of that representational space par excellence that we call geometry, challenged in this status only by such honorable contenders as the line and the point? And yet the circle has to be more than this if we want to speak of "knowing how to enter the circle." For now the circle is not just a shape or a figure but simultaneously a movement. What does it mean "to enter a circle"? Is that already a "circling around," or does it imply being trapped by a rigid and alien form, as one might be caught in the ruts of an old farm track? Or is it an embracing appropriation of the significance of the circle—the kind of repetition that Kierkegaard recommended? If we understand the circle as fundamentally a certain kind of circling, are we temporalizing space—or doing something more, breaking out of those abstractions we call space and time? How can we speak about this? Directly, indirectly? Easily, with difficulty? What could be involved in this breaking out or twisting free? And where are we then? Are we in another place? Or another way of occupying a place? Or perhaps another way of *going on*?

These questions, perhaps from a certain distance, are intended to rehearse at least some small part of the problematic of *Being and Time,* and some of the movement of Heidegger's subsequent thought. To talk of time as the horizon of the question of Being is to enter a path in which the recursive critique of representation embedded and embodied in the word *Being* progressively consumes the very idea of time, first by making it a horizon, then by introducing temporality, and ultimately by trying to think time-space as something like dimensionality "itself." To describe Being as embodying a recursive critique of representation is not just to say that to think Being is to enter a circle in a certain way, but to say that the risks and dangers of relapsing into representational thinking must be repeatedly warded off. Why is this?

Heidegger's thinking is methodologically unified by his acknowledgment of the centrality to philosophy of a certain instability. On the one hand, the attempt to mark, to give voice to what exceeds a certain representational oppositional thinking, runs the risk of offering little more than formal indicators, pointing in the right direction but without content. On the other hand, the attempt to construct an independent domain of intelligibility runs the risk of esotericism, getting lost in another way.

The Young Heidegger

In my view, this danger is unavoidable for an important reason, one that Heidegger struggled to articulate: thinking of Being is modally different from representational thinking. I will try now to enter the circle in a different way, through Heidegger's early concerns with the nonrepresentational resources of religious thought. I begin with a quote from John van Buren's *The Young Heidegger:*

> What Heidegger attempted to do in the early 1930s and in *Being and Time* was to conceptualize ontologically precisely the experience of kairological temporality in primal Christianity, which now became the paradigm of all experience for Heidegger. . . . Here we come across the sources of many basic Heideggerian terms: e.g., the "kairological character" of experience, the moment (*Augenblick*), repetition (*Weiderholung*), "wakefulness," keeping silent (*Schweigen*), the passion (*Leidenschaft*) of temporal enactment and the inauthentic time that involves idle talk and the calculative awaiting of a fixed future. (195)

Heidegger turned away from Catholicism to Protestantism because it supplemented the narrowly theoretical take on intentionality that he had found in Husserl with concepts and categories that involved the whole person and his subjective relation to his life and death and to its significance. Protestantism, like Husserlian phenomenology, involved a restless inner working and reworking of sense, not its passive reception or metaphysical systematization. The categories of Christian thought and the way it replaced a passive inheritance of sense with an active tension of constitution and reconstitution (see, e.g., Kierkegaard's sense of anxiety) provided Heidegger with a critical alternative to the theoretical, representational, epistemological, and metaphysical traditions.

The fascination that Nietzsche exercised on Heidegger was that Nietzsche seemed to have succeeded, where *Being and Time* had held back, not merely in translating Christian categories into a religion-neutral discourse, but in abandoning the lingering temptation of a traditional "ontological" treatise. Moreover, Nietzsche seemed to have found a way of doing justice to a kind of transcendence within immanence without drawing on even the phenomenological roots (or residues) of religious thought. But if the will to power at one level is clearly opposed to and supplements "representation" (which is why "the will to truth" is such a powerful thought), it is not difficult to see its power to do this as derivative from that very same metaphysical distortion that governed representation: the "subject." The will-to-power promised much because in principle it was responsible for any idea we might have of the subject, so it promised to contribute to a deconstructive genealogy of just such central "representational" concepts. It opened up a whole series of what we could call syntheses of engagement and self-engagement, not just theoretical constitution.

Ultimately, Heidegger's real objection to Nietzsche was not his atheism as such but the discovery in Nietzsche of a new kind of closure. This closure takes the form of the failure to recognize that the truth (and "life") lies in one's participation in a certain dimension, and that it is this dimensionality that preserves us against fixity and allows repetition. As far as the movement from Heidegger's thought after the 1930s is concerned, what I take to be central is his recovery of the *religious* dimension in its *phenomenologically undeniable form*—that of givenness, of dependency, or a certain passivity, as constitutive of the dimension of receptivity, of activity/passivity, or time-space, which ultimately inherits (in a transformed way) the problematic of time as the horizon of the question of being.

It is easy to suppose, as Levinas does[2]—and John Caputo seems to follow him here[3]—that the importance of Being for Heidegger lies in its deep impersonal ontological neutrality, that it marks, if it does not exactly mean, the exclusion of the other as other and of the ethico-political questions of mercy and justice. I believe, on the contrary, that Being functions in Heidegger as something like the recursive dynamic ground of what Kant called regulative ideas, of which Justice would be a good example, which can never be given in intuition (and which, as Derrida claims of democracy, is always "to-come").[4] This claim will take a certain amount of unpacking, but its methodological implication is this: that "Being" and "the question of Being" name the elusiveness of any intuitive presentation, the fragility of any and every attempt to specify the dimensionality (presencing, opening) within which such presentation might be pinned down, and the recessive quality of our engagement with that dimensionality.

To understand how and why this is, we could do worse than ask: how enduring is the claim in *Being and Time* that time provides us with the horizon for thinking and questioning Being? I want to try to show that it does endure, although Heidegger's understanding of what it means will change. And I shall argue that with Heidegger, as with Derrida's recent discussion of double duties and aporiae, that what is ultimately at stake—and that allowed Heidegger at one point even to call himself a theologian, and that provided the thrust of the pre–*Being and Time* essay, "The Concept of Time"—is what we might think of as the practical or ethical or existential question of how to take up an adequate relation to time. And if we are our time, how to become what we are. We might *think* of this question as practical, ethical, or existential, but for Heidegger these expressions all get things the wrong way around, supplementing, compensating for inadequate understandings of what they augment. In parentheses, I would add that one of the most repeated and productive insights Heidegger has is what I would call the *artefactuality* of philosophical problems (and I suspect of problems in every "science," including theology).

Why is *taking up an adequate relation to time* so important? And so important to philosophy? There is no doubt that for Heidegger this question not only unified many otherwise separate philosophical questions, but it also served to expose and transpose them into the dimension in which alone they could become significant. If "I am my time" (1924), if the most apparently objective philosophical questions are first relational, then self-relational, and ultimately questions of comportment, then it is not so much the question of time that is important as that of my relation to the various constitutively temporal dimensions of my being. We could then say, as Heidegger said of language,[5] that it is not a question of offering a new theory of time so much as bringing about a new relation to time or a new experience with time.

It is important to stress a number of the ingredients that go into what Heidegger calls thinking:

1. Heidegger has a finely tuned sense of what we could call the withdrawal of time (not unrelated to the withdrawal of Being). That this withdrawal is grasped as such offers at least hope of a reversal of some sort but does not guarantee it. An example of this withdrawal of time that predates Hegel is Marx's account of commodity fetishism, the invisibility of the labor that goes into making what we consume as things without history. The withdrawal of time appears in Husserl's account of the natural attitude, and Heidegger's account of everydayness. We are blind to the presencing within presence, to the appearing within the appearance, that bracketing out, or the step back, can make visible.
2. The withdrawal of what we could call fully engaged time is facilitated by the rise to dominance of an external world time, time mediated by stacked structures of representation.
3. The possibility of the recovery of engaged time (cf. Kierkegaard's account of repetition), which could be understood as a movement of the soul (*metabole*), will then itself wither on the vine.
4. The horizon of my mortality is, as Heidegger says, tranquilized away, facilitating the withdrawal of engagement.
5. The loss of a sense of my (our) historicality deprives me (us) of a context of self-situatedness.

Constitutive temporality is invisible in a constituted world. We may suppose that the idea that things can only be what they are by virtue of some transcendental temporality or synthetic activity is an idealist myth. But my own transparently grounded temporal engagement in the world is not constructive idealism but the genuine condition of a certain fullness of Being. And importantly, it consists, not just of self-defining creative action, but equally of suffering, and perhaps more importantly still, of living temporally within the dimensionality established by possibility and necessity, activity and passivity, the finite and the infinite, and being fluent in the various modes of temporality that these open up both for the self and to the Other.

Heidegger is a philosopher of death, not in the obvious sense of taking being-toward-death seriously in *Being and Time,* but in the sense of identifying value, truth, intelligibility with experiences in which what is in each case at stake must be enacted and reenacted, and can never be stored up as some kind of abstractly recoverable truth. Time, or temporality, is at the heart of the very self-showing of phenomena (and even of their being hidden), of the self-relatedness within history that constitutes my grasp of my mortal existence with others, and of the need for the repetition of the tradition, for reworking, replaying, reenacting what has been passed down.

Heidegger was a revolutionary thinker. But revolution is a turning that must never stop.[6] The extraordinary inventiveness with which he embraced and then rejected position after position is not to be put down to indecisiveness, but to a persistent, recursive, and driven search for dynamic dimensions of presentation and then engagement, jettisoning each time the dispensable conceptual baggage, especially where that threatens to close down the revolution.

For my part, I want to repeat, rework, and reconsider my own doubts[7] about Derrida's claim that the concept of time is itself metaphysical and that there can be no alternative concept that would escape this judgment. There are a number of reasons why this claim is an important clue: first, the very idea of a concept is already a judgment about the temporal stabilization of meaning; and second, the concept of time *as a concept* is explicitly tied to representation.

Derrida opposes the possibility of something like "temporality" or "authentic time"—and hence Heidegger's apparent attempt to discover an *Urzeit,* or original time. But what this does not exclude is something like time (or the temporal) being the site of our most fruitful interrogation—and not merely interrogation as a means to an end, but as a way itself.

Derrida may say that Heidegger's specific quest for an authentic temporality subjects time to a suspect metaphysical determination in the shape of (say) self-presence, but could one not equally say that the recognition of the incompleteness of any presence (for example, that democracy is always to come) is another favored candidate for just such a refurbished temporality? There is a danger here of continuing to misunderstand what "kind of thing" we are dealing with when we speak of "temporality"—the issue is no less vexed than was the problem of "defining" Being. I have already suggested one approach: treating time and temporality as the site of engaged interrogation. The virtue of this formula is that, like the *question* of Being, it builds interrogation, hence trembling and anxiety, into our inhabiting of time. So, for example, my relation to the past is not just fixed as recollective memory—where I am in charge. I am also haunted by it, formed by it, deformed by it: there is no one stable way of determining by "being as having been." And this instability, which cannot just be resolved into modes (for example, authentic/inauthentic), characterizes my relation to the past. It does not so much disrupt as enrich my being toward the past. On this account, we retain a sense of temporality(-ies) as a horizon of engagements in the world, even as this horizon supplies the ground for tensions, contradictions, and so forth. The drawback of this way of thinking and talking is that whatever the advantages of horizonal thinking, it can distract us from some very direct ways of pursuing the intrinsic temporality of our being. And here I want to open another front.

Feasting off Christianity

One straightforward deficiency of representational time is that we cannot, on that basis, make sense of the concepts, categories, narratives, and anxieties that feed our deepest capacities for (self-)understanding. Aristotle, phenomenology, mediaeval philosophy, Christianity, German poetry, and Nietzsche—just to begin the list—were explored and successively scavenged by Heidegger for concepts, schemata, and orientations that would remedy this deficiency. Van Buren has an excellent account of just how Heidegger feasted off Christianity:

> This is the philosophical way that he used Paul's attacks on the vanity of Greek philosophy, the mystic's *via negativa* to the efflux of the Divine Life, Luther's scathing critique of the *theologia gloriae* of Aristotelian scholasticism, Schleiermacher's antimetaphysical regress to the feeling of absolute dependence, and Kierkegaard's paradoxes of modern speculative thought in the name of the earnestness of ethico-religious *Existenz*. Heidegger [he sums up] had become a philosophical rebel, and his first allies in this reawakened battle of Greek giants about being were neither Heraclitus nor Aristotle, but a group of anti-Greek and anti-philosophical Christian thinkers.[8]

Here van Buren is confirming the critical destructive resource that Heidegger found in these Christian thinkers, which supports my sense that at no point was it their doctrinal commitments that interested

Heidegger, but rather, the conceptual and phenomenological resources locked up in them. Interestingly, as Kisiel also points out, even when it is the rich positive content of "primal Christian experience" that draws his attention, what he takes away is transformed into the neutral categories of phenomenological ontology.[9]

It has become fashionable to distance oneself from at least the systematic form of the extraordinary achievement that was *Being and Time*. But part of what is aimed at in that project can be understood more productively and sympathetically. Part of the function of developing something called fundamental ontology is to protect its insights from being treated as mere secular translations of religious phenomena. Indeed, it is to claim quite the opposite: that religious experience may well be "ordinary experience" misunderstood. We might then suppose that what is often said of the very project of fundamental ontology—that it is a misconceived repository for genuine insight (that its systematic form repeats in routine fashion the traditional shape of the metaphysical treatise)—is in this respect equally true of religious discourse itself. Heidegger's hubris, which I continue to find appealing, is to be able to think, to pursue something called thinking that, even as it answers to its time, is not reducible to an ideology, a religion, a "philosophy," or to being an expression of the concerns of the age, a *Weltanschauung*.

The secret of the phenomenology of religion would be that it delivers to us, and legitimates, experiences and concepts that can at least be grasped independently of the doctrinal content on which it might otherwise be thought to lean. But the problem of the phenomenology of religion is that it is blind to what I will call genealogical or artefactual problems.[10] To illustrate what I mean here, let me suggest two different radicalizations of the content of religious thought and experience:

1. Religious thinking preserves more or less intact concepts and experiences that prevailing (scientific, representational, metaphysical) modes of discourse exclude. Its "representational" language (God, angels, heaven, etc.) is a mere convenience (or inconvenience), mimicking the discourses it supplements.
2. Religious thinking is to be understood as a compensatory supplement that corrects what is inadequate about natural or everyday experiences, but only by confirming the fundamental error involved in that understanding. "God" (and all allied concepts) is an artefact, an error that does something to correct an original error but repeats a more fundamental mistake. Suppose, for example, that a man became emperor and took himself to be all-powerful until the day his luck ran out on the battlefield. He might at this point recognize correctly that he was *not* all-powerful, but he might (incorrectly) suppose that some other being was all-powerful, retaining the schema, reassigning

its contents. Or to take another case, Kant supposes that we should not kill or injure ourselves because our bodies belong to God ("God is our owner; we are His property"[11]). Now it may be true that my body does not belong to me, but it does not follow that it does belong to some other being. It might just be that "belonging" is an inappropriate expression in this context. Here again, if God were invented as the owner of bodies that do not (cannot) belong to themselves, he would be an artefact. And if that were true, *thinking* could not rest with an ontological translation of religious phenomena.

Take, for example, Wittgenstein's remark that "we have the feeling that we are dependent on something. Be that as it may, we are in some sense dependent. That on which we are dependent we may call God."[12] This claim pretty much repeats Schleiermacher's claim that religion is a matter of feeling or intuition, and in particular of our consciousness of a "feeling of dependence" on something, a claim that itself influenced Heidegger.[13] These phenomenological treatments of the religious are in themselves deeply unstable. They could be understood reductively ("God is nothing but . . .") or, more ambiguously, as an explication of the significance of religious thought.

When Heidegger says that philosophy is essentially atheistic, it is because a faith that accepts answers to religious issues puts an end to that questioning that keeps religious experience truly alive. For Kierkegaard, for example, anxiety is the space in which faith receives its necessity and perpetual repetition. Heidegger doesn't just repeat the identification of "God" with "the feeling of dependence." But the power of the experience of a succession of Christian thinkers lies in the way they allow us to thematize general conditions of human experience that representational thinking easily occludes. Heidegger borrows not just a feeling of dependency but a structure of receptivity on which what we think of as an activity rests. The relation between thinking and thanking is one example (in *What Is Called Thinking?*), and the *es gibt* and the *Zusage* (pledge, promise) of language are others. In his essay "Die Sprache," Heidegger, drawing on Humboldt, works through almost dialectically from a simple consciousness of our activity ("Man speaks") to its "opposite" ("Language speaks"), and then to a more nuanced, considered position. ("Man speaks insofar as he listens to the speaking of language.") We could treat this as the translation of a Christian claim about the danger of hubris, but if Heidegger is right, it is much more than that; it is a general truth about experience—that our powers depend on what we take for granted, that activity presupposes "passive synthesis," and so on. To call it a general truth seems to reduce it to another neutral discovery.

But of course the significance of the discovery or rediscovery of this active/passive, or middle-voice dimensionality is that it precisely captures, or begins to capture, the authentic shape of our engagement—with others, with ourselves, with and from history, our time. It does not give us solutions; rather, it gives us the beginnings of a dimensionality in which to think. And as a consequence, it provides a nexus in which certain kinds of concepts can adequately operate—concepts such as judgment, care, engagement, honesty, acknowledgment . . . responsibility, which essentially require both a relation to the other and a self-relatedness. These concepts, however, cannot be thought on the basis of representational/metaphysical time—time as already measured and represented as "out there." Nor will it do to retrofit a phenomenology of internal time-consciousness. What is needed is something like Heidegger's sense of ecstatic temporality in which Dasein is the site on which diverse temporalities bear and in which responsibility involves a kind of openness to all that this brings. "Dependency" here is no longer quite the right word, suggesting a compensatory corrective to an original error—autonomy. What Heidegger is opening up to us is the primacy of dimensionality, the truth of which is ultimately veiled by any word or image we might come up with, and is rather to be found in a certain comportment.[14]

At the end of *Of Spirit,* Derrida imagines a conversation between Heidegger and contemporary Christian theologians in which the ambiguities of translation (reduction v. explication) that I mentioned are exposed and not resolved.

> Heidegger: "I follow the path of a repetition which crosses the path of the entirely other. The entirely other announces itself in the most rigorous repetition. And this repetition is also the most vertiginous and the most abyssal."

Christian theologians: "Yes, precisely, that's just what we're saying. . . . That's the truth of what we have always said, heard, tried to make heard. . . . You hear us better than you think."[15]

Representing Death, "My" Abyss

One obvious source of difficulty with this attempt to reaffirm the problematics of the 1920s is captured by Levinas in *Time and the Other,* which at a certain point explicitly targets the ontological neutrality of *Being and Time.* For Levinas, time is understood as the interruption of sameness, and the exemplary instance of this is not "my death," but the fracturing of self that is brought about by the other person, who opens me to a time and a future I could not have anticipated. On his view, the other person's fragility and mortality shatter my attachment to self in a way that exceeds even the disruption brought by an authentic grasp of my own mortality. My response to this move is not dissimilar to the shape of Derrida's "Violence and Metaphysics," in which, inter alia, he shows that "we" cannot treat the other as "wholly other," that Husserl was right to think of there being some sort of projective pairing of an alter ego. To recognize the other as a person is to say, implicitly, "like me." Analogously, while there is great merit in coming to see the other as an actual or potential shattering of my self-centered temporalizing projection, surely the ethical force of this disruption is dependent on my grasp of the significance of the other's fragile mortality. And arguably, Heidegger's account of being-toward-death supplies just what is needed, not just for the significance of *my* mortality, but for anyone's. On this argument, something like Heidegger's account of being-toward-death is needed for the other to successfully interrupt my self-enclosed being.

At this point it might be said that we need to draw in Derrida's own critical treatment of Heidegger's being-toward-death, especially in *Aporias*. The weight of Derrida's worries falls on such expressions as "my death," "death as such," and the "possibility of my impossibility." It is important for Heidegger that these terms can operate definitively. For one key difference between the human and the animal, on which the distinction between dying and (merely) perishing is based, is formulated in terms of our (human) grasp of "death as such," which we may suppose no animal possesses. Derrida not implausibly takes seriously the work of those (like Aries[16]), who show that death has a history, a genealogy, and that its significance is culturally embedded and cannot just be appealed to as something essential we can know "as such." I have a lot of sympathy with what this implies: that the distinction between man and animal is not so straightforward.[17] But Derrida's argument surely only intensifies the original distinction. For if the distinction between man and animal may not be so easily drawn, "we" are pretty sure that only humans can even begin to philosophize about the difficulty of knowing death "as such." Human beings may well not really understand their own deaths as such, but one is tempted to say that they recognize, whether explicitly or not, that their own deaths are not straightforwardly graspable, that "my death" is not for me an event like any other—and that this sophistication is not available to any other creature.

Whatever the problems Derrida raises for Heidegger's manner of distinguishing the human from the animal understanding of death, we might think that Derrida is more on target when he insists that Heidegger is in retreat from the true *exposure* that death brings when he speaks of it as "my ownmost possibility." Derrida is here reworking a version of Sartre's complaint that Heidegger makes death productive, gives it meaning, rather than (as Sartre puts it) recognizing its complete lack of sense. For Derrida, with a somewhat different twist, death does not intensify "myness," but rather puts it in question. But this is another of those places at which Derrida may be bringing out the deep truth of Heidegger's position even as he tries to contest it. For surely the whole point of being-toward-death is not that it confirms some preexisting sense of my identity, but that it releases me from it. Heidegger *is* making the residual claim that it releases "me" from it, but even Derrida cannot avoid some version of this claim. Even Levinas, who says it is the death of the other that takes precedence and is obscured by a focus on "my" death, must be saying that the death of the other affects me, my sense of propriety, even as it precisely evacuates "my" sense of self.

And the argument can be pressed further. My response to the death of the other (or the mortality of the other) is inseparable from my grasp of the significance of the other's death. It is hard to see how this can be dissociated from my various capacities to value my own existence. I do not necessarily do this egocentrically. My own life is quite a lesson in the miracle of existence, human and otherwise, without any strong sense of possessiveness. The death of the other *may* be more important than my own death. A child may matter to her mother more than her own life. It is only the other's death that I can mourn.[18] But when we respond to the actual or possible death of the other, not simply for its impact on me (the terrible loss of a friend or child or parent), but in some sense *on behalf of the other,* then it becomes critical how, in each case, that other understands herself and her mortality. Surely our grasp of such possibilities will be inseparable from the range of such relations we have managed to model in our own self-understanding. This takes us back to the ineliminability of Heidegger's account of being-toward-death *even* for responding to the death of the other. Without that, we could not adequately distinguish the destruction of a sandcastle on the beach from that of the mouse in the larder, the unknown solder, the neighbor's child. We do not have to be able to justify the different kinds of response these will elicit to know that without the possibility of such a range of differentiation, we would not be responding adequately in each case at all.

Another mark of what I would call the convergence of Derrida and Heidegger on death can be found in the way Derrida will treat the to-come (e.g., in democracy-to-come). He insists that he is not speaking of a "future democracy" in the sense of one that could one day be made present. Rather, we could speak of a certain permanent structure of openness to interruption. We could speak of this as openness to a possibility, but this is not a possibility to be realized. Unless the structure of promise is to be betrayed, what is opened up would itself carry forward this structure of openness. In this precise sense, such a "possibility" is, from the point of view of concrete realization, an "impossibility." This is not a defect, but simply a mark of its recursive openness.

Does Heidegger understand this? He will speak instead of my death as the possibility of my impossibility. But how different is this? Central to Heidegger's account of the temporality of being-toward-death is the distinction between expecting (*erwarten*) and anticipating (*vorlaufen*) death.[19] This is nothing but the distinction between looking to death as a future present event, and understanding it as something that "as such" cannot arrive, just as we cannot ever reach the horizon. Surely Heidegger's being-toward-death is precisely an *anticipation* of Derrida's account of the to-come. And if we are right, this same account does not so much reinforce a possessiveness about "my" life as mark the point of a certain affirmation of dis-possession.

Heidegger's Horizon of Engagement

If we take the word "horizon" in its recursively recessive sense, perhaps the lasting achievement of Heidegger's oeuvre is already to be found in the prominence given to that word in *Being and Time*, when he writes of time as the horizon of the question of Being. I understand him to have discovered that to explicate the claim that Dasein is its time, to adequately *acknowledge* time, we need to develop a dimensional understanding (hence spacing, clearing, opening, trembling, swinging) in which the complex modulation of activity and "passivity" gives rise to a new temporality—not a new concept—rather, an orchestration of an engagement, in which it is the interweaving of various layers and levels of temporality, one that opens onto an unrepresentable future, that supplies the possibility of renewal and repetition in the Kierkegaardian sense that Derrida rightly attributes to Heidegger.[20]

This same dimensionality is what is indicated in those lists of "double duties" that Derrida gives us in *The Other Heading* (such as "the duty to respond to the call of European memory," and *also* to "open . . . it to that which is not, never was, and never will be Europe") that make it clear that it is the privilege and power of philosophy not to give answers but to keep open the aporetic spaces of difficulty, possibility, and even impossibility.[21] The problem of representation is ultimately not simply a question of accurately accounting for time. It is the existential and ultimately ethical and political question of the manner of our engagement in the world.

Unlocking the Image in Thought

We know that Heidegger, even in *Being and Time*, introduced the idea of ecstatic temporality *over and against time*, not as phenomenology had done, to capture my subjective *consciousness* of time, as opposed to that of the clock and the calendar, but to capture my existential *engagement* in time—personal, social, and historical. On this account, it is not that time is *in* me or that I am in time, but, as he put it, "Dasein *is* its time!" Another way of putting this is to say that Dasein has a complex *intrinsic* relation to time. We do not merely have memories or a history; we are constituted by our relationship to these, whether we are *stuck* in the past or can *move on* creatively. Heidegger was not content with the formulations he gave us in *Being and Time*, and much of his later work focused on new strategies for circumventing representational thought. When (at the end of *On Time and Being*) he says that "the [very] form of a lecture remains . . . an obstacle. The lecture has spoken merely in propositional statements" (*OTB*, 24), he is saying that the mode of engagement, participation, and repetition demanded by a lecture is (too) tied up with representation.

Kant had visited this problem of our betrayal by representation before. Kant distinguishes between the schema of a *sensible* concept (dog, triangle) by which concepts are connected to images, and the schema of a pure concept of understanding, that is, the categories (of substance, cause, possibility, modality, etc.). These schemata Kant calls "a priori determinations of time in accordance with rules." And yet, Kant admits, "[The application of] this schematism of our understanding . . . is an art concealed in the depths of the human soul, whose real modes of activity nature is hardly likely ever to allow us to discover, and to have open to our gaze."[22] Kant's thinking about time and the schematism grinds to a halt with this "art concealed in the depths of the human soul." But what if we were to understand the soul here as no longer concealed, but as revealingly articulated by something like ecstatic temporality, a temporalizing *way* of Being, of which *representational thinking*, for example, would itself be a specific *mode*?

It was no bad thing for Kant to *mark* the possibility of this *other* thinking (or mode of Being) as he did, but he captured it with the image of *depth*, and darkness or concealment. Kant, in other words, both marks and *conceals* the need for a *modal transformation* of our understanding of our relationship to time within a representational scheme or image. This is the first of a number of examples of what is involved in unlocking the *image* in thought. It involves interpreting, *reading* those images as disguised *gateways* to a transformed thinking, gateways whose strange function is marked by their sacrifice of a certain conceptuality.[23]

Already in his *Critique of Judgement*, Kant had made a statement on this, when he talked of "aesthetic ideas . . . [giving] the imagination a momentum which makes it think more in response to these objects, though in an undeveloped way, than can be comprehended within one concept, and hence in one determinate linguistic expression."[24] For example, "an artistic rendition of Jupiter's eagle with lightning in its claws expresses the sublimity and majesty of creation by directing judgment away from the logical concept of sublimity . . . toward the sublimity of its own inner capacity for synthesis."[25]

This recognition of the non-conceptual within the conceptual (through the image and symbol) still takes the form of reference back to inner powers (including those of "genius"), so that representation is here outflanked transcendentally rather than existentially or ontologically. For Kierkegaard, for example, the passion of thought, my engaged *participation* in thinking, escapes communication unless it is achieved indirectly and, as he puts it, "in an artistic manner."[26]

Kant expunged all the examples from his first *Critique* on the grounds that those who could understand their point would not need them, and those who could not, would not be helped by them. But the very specificity of the example actually has, dare one say it, a conceptual richness missing from the purely abstract claim. This will help us fill out the sense in which what I have called "gateways" function. (And, yes, the word "gateway" is a gateway!) What Kant was blind to, at least here, is that the trials and complexities of the concrete application of a concept exemplified in a particular example are, as such, exemplary of the very issue of application (for example unrolling in time) that every concept always suffers. Not to use examples on the ground of their (misleading) specificity is to forget that specificity is itself universal and presents the same repeated challenge of application. Even if the application of (universal) concepts to specific cases always raised different specific issues, the fact that the question of how concepts are applied is always an issue means that one could lose out on a wide dimension of concern by eschewing examples.

This allows me to return to the connection between overcoming representation and the question of engagement, guided by Wittgenstein's extraordinary remark: "We do run up against the limits of language. . . . This running up against the limits of language is *Ethics*."[27] What can he mean by ethics here? And in what way do we "run up against the limits of language"?

I want to make a rather strong suggestion, which, whether true or false, will have the virtue of a certain clarity: that it is a common, if not universal, feature of at least a certain kind of philosophical thought that it reaches a limit circumscribed by its commitment to representation. What I mean by representation here is a commitment to some sense of adequacy in the conceptual reproduction of the real, to which we might give the name truth. Philosophy reaches a limit, however, before it has been completed. And in recognition of this *gap*, certain images (symbols, allegories, metaphors, etc.) are generated.

Our task as philosophers is to interpret (unlock) these images in such a way as to free philosophy from its arrested development. I further claim that the effect of this hermeneutic of the liminal image is to contribute to a grasp of its true temporality. What I understand Wittgenstein to mean by ethics in the remark I quoted is precisely a recognition of the limits of representational/conceptual thinking and of the continuing need to make judgments (for example, about the application of rules) where there are no rules to guide us. More significantly, however, I understand him to be saying that it is in these kinds of claims that what we call philosophical truth resides—that the modal character of philosophical truth is cautionary, advisory, orienting, regulative, interrogative—not descriptive. Such claims would have the form "Don't look for the meaning, look for the use"; "Act in such a way that the principle of your action could be a universal law"; "Don't be seduced by appearances"; "Distrust all inherited concepts"; "Go back to the things themselves"; "Interrogate the silent and invisible frame which gives to philosophical concepts and problems their (apparent) stability"; and so forth. Philosophy would be in the business of "assembling reminders," "opening up ways of seeing, establishing habits of connectivity," and reinforcing certain critical dispositions. Philosophical truth is a species of *how*, not a kind of *what;* and philosophy, far from being a science, is a practice of emancipation. In consequence, questions of *reading, reception,* and *uptake* loom large. This bears most directly on the question of the image in thought. If the image is indeed both danger and inspiration, it is because we can understand the image as some sort of resting place, rather than recognize it for what it is, a point of transition, a gateway to a different *mode* of truth.

Allow me to indicate through a number of examples what this claim would come to. I will focus on a small handful of image-words that philosophers have come to rely on to do the kind of job I am describing: abyss, bridge, circle, and way. It is no accident that *all* of these words can be found in Heidegger, but they are, by and large, the common property of philosophers from Plato through Hegel, Nietzsche, and Kierkegaard to Derrida. They are perhaps just some of the props in the theater of the limit, where, I claim, the age-old drama of philosophy lies in the struggle to recognize the proper modality (and temporality) of truth. If the truth lies in the *how* of a practice, as I claim, it is also never completed and always having to be repeated, reinvented, reworked, reappropriated.[28] At an early point in *Being and Time*, Heidegger writes that "if the Self is conceived 'only' as a way of Being of this entity, this seems tantamount to volatilizing the real 'core' of Dasein. [But this worry] . . . gets its nourishment from [mistakenly thinking of Dasein as] a being present-at-hand" (*BT,* 110/H117). There is a deep connection between my analysis of the structure of these two remarks: what Kierkegaard names as "God" licenses, albeit at great risk of later confusion, the whole modality of necessary repetition, which would not otherwise make sense. (Herein lies an entire account of religious discourse.) Heidegger, on the other hand, with such words as "only," "volatilize," and "real core," is bearing witness to the pain and resistance of the modal shift from the substantive to the dispositional, from a nominal to an adverbial sense of self.

Let me give some selected adumbrations of what needs to be said about the abyss, the bridge, and the circle. Each is a spatial image or notion that can be taken as an end point, a limit, or as a beginning, an opening. Each can be understood either structurally or in dynamic and engaged terms. In both cases, the former reading produces entrenchment, paralysis, and some sort of closure thesis; while the latter proposes, with all its own risks, a different modality of discourse. *Aporiae* (lit.: no way through) are symptoms of representational/metaphorical thinking. Nietzsche's account of man as a bridge (sometimes a rope) to the overman needs unlocking in such a way that the overman is not to be found at the other end of the bridge, but is a mode of being defined by "going over," "going across"; the circle is not an extended logical tautology, but a practice of repetition and of recognition of interconnectedness.

And what of the abyss, dear to Kierkegaard, Blanchot, Derrida, and many others? Heidegger's word is *Ab-grund*. No doubt this can be experienced as loss of a foundation, as a logical and existential gap over which it is necessary to leap, as a frightening limit to what can even be experienced at all. But in each case, the abyss is being recognized in terms that are to be left behind, overcome. The abyss is a creature of representational thinking. This void, danger, or gap signals the inability to register fully a temporally and modally transformed possibility of being (and thinking) within representation. The danger is that we will come to have such an affection for the abyss, and such pride in the courage it takes to walk along the edge that we will fail to take the leap, fail to unlock this and other images at the edge of representational thought.

Finally, a brief word about the circle. It would not be inappropriate to anticipate our discussion in chapter 11 of Escher and those extraordinary lithographic circles—*Ascending and Descending, Belvedere*, the lizards emerging from the page, the hand writing itself. What is always in play here is a movement from representation to the real, from transformation to time, to a time in which *"plus ça change, plus c'est la même chose."* And all this takes place *within* representation. Escher's circles, cycles of repetition, mark an *exit* from representation even as they close it off, and in this way they are a fitting *image* of the liminal, threshold structures we are pointing to. This same strange, uncanny shift takes place in Heidegger's remark that he is not so much trying to *get somewhere*, as trying for once to get where we are already.

6

Glimpses of Being in Dasein's Development
Reading and Writing after Heidegger

> Distress varies in the essential beginnings and transitions
> of man's history. But this distress should never be taken
> superficially . . . as a lack or misery. . . . This distress exists outside
> any "pessimistic" or "optimistic" valuation. [Our]
> grounding-attunement . . . differs according to the inceptual
> experience of this distress.
> —Heidegger, *Contributions to Philosophy*

If the practice of philosophy is a certain transformative repetition, how do we read or respond to or repeat a philosopher—in particular, Heidegger—who articulates this very principle in an exemplary way? There is a logical paradox here, but also a methodological problem. In the case of Heidegger, I first show just how self-consciously he engages in a repetition of repetition, how he thematizes this whole question as the question of reading and writing philosophy. And I propose a way of reinterpreting the fundamental relation between Time and Being, one that opens Heidegger's thinking onto other traditions and gives it a future that he himself did not anticipate. I argue that it is the complex temporality of human maturation, our always incomplete development, that gives rise to the question of being. And it is this fundamentally temporalized multiplicity within human identity that needs to inform the mock battles about the primacy of ontological, ethical, or sexual difference. For it is here that they are all intertwined.

Heidegger's Remarks about Reading Others

We are not *required* to read Heidegger in the light of how he reads others or his reflections on philosophy as reading. But these issues are so central, and so much happens for Heidegger here, that we would be foolish not to. I present what I am doing in this way to make it more challenging to those who see themselves as defenders of Heidegger's legacy. For that legacy is, or should be, concerned with the transforming of legacy.

I would like first to demonstrate what I have so far just claimed about the intimate connection in Heidegger's work between philosophizing and the transformative reading of the tradition. Of course, in one sense this is obvious. So much of what Heidegger has published were originally lecture courses devoted to central figures of the tradition, especially the ancient Greeks. But we need to remind ourselves what Heidegger thinks is at stake here, to realize that if he is right, these very considerations apply to our reading of Heidegger himself. We all know that Section 6 of *Being and Time* concerns itself with the need to deconstruct, dismantle, "destroy" the tradition, to bring out its positive possibilities. But let us look at his remarks a year or two later in his *Kant and the Problem of Metaphysics:*

> An interpretation limited to a recapitulation of what Kant explicitly said can never be a real explication, if the business of the latter is to bring to light what Kant, over and above his express formulation, uncovered. . . . [W]hat is essential to all philosophical discourse is not found in the specific propositions of which it is composed but in that which, although unstated as such, is made evident through these propositions. (*KPM,* 206)

> In order to wrest from the actual words that which these words "intend to say," every interpretation must necessarily resort to violence. This violence, however, should not be confused with an action that is wholly arbitrary. The interpretation must be animated by the power of an illuminative idea. Only through the power of this idea can an interpretation . . . get through to the unsaid and . . . attempt to find an expression for it. The directive idea itself is confirmed by its own power of illumination. (*KPM,* 207)

Heidegger claims to have been inspired here by Kant's own formulation of the principle of interpretation:

> Our interpretation is inspired by a maxim which Kant himself wished to see applied to the interpretation of philosophical works and which he formulated in the following terms at the end of his reply to the critique of the Leibnizian Eberhard: "They do not understand the intentions of these philosophers when they neglect the key to all explication of the works of pure reason through concepts alone, namely the critique of reason itself (as the common source of all concepts), and are incapable of *looking beyond the language which these philosophers employ to what they intended to say.*" (*KPM,* 206)[1]

Heidegger here distinguishes two kinds of interpretation: recapitulation and real explication, and emphasizes the need for the risk, violence, and daring called for by the latter. Curiously, this "real explication" is no less directed by the "truth" than recapitulation. The claim, however, is that *the truth at this level* can only appear through the illuminative power of a directive idea, which the reader brings to the work.

This idea, developed later by Gadamer,[2] helps resolve what otherwise looks like a difficulty in Heidegger's use of Kant here. For it seems as if

Kant writes everywhere of what the *author* intended to say, while Heidegger, by contrast, speaks of what the words intend, or, in the passive voice, of what "is made evident through these propositions." Is Heidegger here deploying a certain interpretive violence at the very point at which he is crediting Kant with being the source of his inspiration? Turning again to Kant himself, this time to the first *Critique,* we find Kant's deployment of the famous words (italicized below) in the context of a discussion of Plato, and of the importance of Plato's understanding of the Idea, precisely for *not* being a purely subjective property or merely a creature of the understanding. It is here that Kant writes,

> I need only remark that it is by no means unusual . . . *to find that we understand [an author] better than he understands himself* [my emphasis]. As he has not sufficiently determined his concept, he has sometimes spoken, or even thought, in opposition to his own intention.[3]

These remarks in a way reproduce within themselves the difficulty in reconciling Heidegger's version of what is at stake in a real explication with that of Kant. I am tempted to say that what Kant really means here by the sufficient (or full) determination of a concept is close to what Plato really meant by an Idea. And while for Kant an intention, or at least the kind of guiding intention that informs a philosophical work, directs itself, knowingly or not, toward an Idea, Heidegger adds that the reader needs to provide an illuminative idea so that something of at least *the right order* can be crystallized. In other words, two principles are put in play here, potentially pulling in different directions: first, the need to recognize that philosophers are typically on to something whose precise shape they may not grasp; and second, that a "real explication" is required to try to get at *something of the order of* what a philosopher is on to. Heidegger's solution to the possible divergence of these two desiderata is validation through the illuminative power of a directive idea. Here, it has to be said, Heidegger is endorsing in a completely serious and rigorous form, a certain experimental orientation.[4] The seriousness and rigor, however, prescribe a certain quality to a successful reading. Heidegger is not saying that it is better to be wrong but interesting, but he is saying that without a certain level of reanimation, we don't have thinking, but a dangerous and widespread impostor, sometimes called philosophy!

In *What Is Called Thinking?* Heidegger distinguishes between going counter to a thinker and going to his encounter.[5] On the one hand, polemics; on the other, thinking. In the end, we have to conclude that, as Nietzsche said about friendship, we cannot exclude *polemos* from thinking. To think with someone is to struggle with them over what matters. The point is that the struggle is a matter of entering a space in which struggle would be significant, rather than just missing the point. Heidegger makes just this claim at the very end of *Being and Time:*

We must look for a way [footnote: * "Not the 'sole' way"] to illuminate the fundamental ontological question, and *follow* it. Whether that way is at all the *only* one or even the *right* one can be decided only after we have followed it. The strife in relation to the question of being cannot be settled *because it has not even been started.* (*BT,* H437)

To capitalize on my initial selectivity, I would like to make some remarks on the specific responsibility of Heidegger's readings of Kant and Nietzsche, namely his pursuit of the question of time. Each in different ways, these two readings will enable me to open up the possibility of a further reinterpretation of Heidegger himself.

The central thrust of *Kant and the Problem of Metaphysics,* in the terms we have already announced, is that Kant cannot just be read as an epistemological thinker, that the question of knowledge is subordinated to the question of man's relation to the world, a relation that is ontological in character, not just in the traditional metaphysical way, but in the sense of our having constantly to deal with the strangeness of this relation. Kant's failure to grasp the full extent of his own thinking has to do, on Heidegger's view, with his failure to divest himself of the traditional model of time:

Rather . . . the laying of the foundation and even in its conclusion . . . are presented according to the provisional conception of the first point of departure. And because Kant, at the time of his presentation of the transcendental schemata, had not worked out an interpretation of the primordial essence of time, his elucidation of the pure schemata as transcendental determinations of time is both fragmentary and obscure, for time taken as the pure now-sequence offers no possible means of access to the "temporal" interpretation of the notions. (*KPM,* 206)

Now what is interesting from our point of view is the temporal model implicit in Heidegger's own analysis of Kant's failure to determine the concept (of time) with which he was working. I do not mean the full-fledged doctrine of ecstatic temporality and being-toward-death in *Being and Time;* I mean the model actually employed in making sense of Kant's failure. It is Heidegger's claim that Kant's failure was a failure to revisit the temporary provisional model of time with which he started off, in the light of the subsequent vistas of understanding he had opened up. Kant, in other words, has failed to rework, to work through, the model that did indeed allow him to begin and progress. The "fragmentariness and obscurity" of his account of the schematism itself reflects a temporal deficiency, namely, having failed to update his provisional starting point, while precisely acknowledging the necessity of provisional starting points. This, of course, is a quite different account from that in *Being and Time,* where Heidegger insists on the need for a *Wiederholung,* a repetition that would give us access to "those primordial sources from which the categories and concepts handed down to us have been in part quite genuinely drawn" (*BT*, H21).

My second focus will be Heidegger's reading of Nietzsche in *What Is Called Thinking?* I begin by showing how Heidegger's understanding of the forcefulness of reading has changed somewhat from the formulations of the 1920s. It is Heidegger's claim that despite the powerful resources Nietzsche marshals to affirmatively overcome the spirit of revenge that drives metaphysics, this whole venture nonetheless rests on a still unthought representational view of time. What is particularly striking is how this "critique" is framed by a deep recognition of the extraordinary achievement of Nietzsche's thought. He writes of respect and acknowledgment, and of being "shaken to the depths" by what remains unthought, "the greatest gift that thinking can bestow" (*WCT*, 76).

Respect for the other is a receptivity to his thought in which that thought is already construed as a response. It is just such a formulation that undermines any naïve opposition between the ethical and the ontological. Philosophy is a response to the vulnerable space of the other's response.

Pursuing the theme he had already worked on in *Contributions,* that the necessity (*Notwendigkeit*) of philosophy lies in its being a response to *Not*, to distress, to difficulty, Heidegger fastens here on Nietzsche's lament—that the wasteland grows. His response to Nietzsche is driven by a reflection on the very willfulness of the desire to overcome. That is, by the recognition that the required transformation can only be met by transforming the very shape of the desire that projects us forward. I believe we can find in the shape of human development, understood not just psychologically, but "ontologically," the fundamental basis for a critique of the will. And in our capacity for adumbration of pasts that we cannot completely recover lies the shape of our faith in what both Kierkegaard and Derrida would call the impossible.

I have already thematized the idea that this reading of Heidegger would significantly fail, in Heidegger's own terms, if it did not come with a certain transformatory intent and an "illuminative idea." For this guiding idea to stand a chance of taking root, some preparatory remarks are in order. I will be trying here to bear in mind the following: that Heidegger's method concerns itself with problematic, impeded repetition, suggesting that the past is not readily available to us; and that Heidegger is right to think that the model of time as a leveled-off succession of now-points is a hopeless basis on which to open up the question of being. It flattens the dimensionality that opens up the possibility of freedom, authenticity, transcendence. Heidegger is quite right to insist that man's being is essentially temporal, that the ontological grammar of our *ecstasis* is distributed in three dimensions, that the economy through which we acknowledge our being-toward-death is critical to any judgment of au-

thenticity, that being is historical in the sense of suffering epochal transformations, that we misunderstand what it is to think if we believe it is
possible to complete philosophy or to return to the beginning, and that
linear time constantly leads us down the wrong track.

The refusal to think of time either as succession or as the teleological
directedness to an end, a future present, a completion, has consequences
for philosophical practice itself, given that philosophical texts appear at
least to begin and end, to argue for and arrive at conclusions. Add to
this the refusal to think of language as a mere means of expression or
communication or naming, and philosophy is inexorably drawn toward
the question of performativity, in which the very shape of its practice
embodies these claims. These concerns are evidenced by Heidegger's insistence that "our task is to cease all overcoming" (*OTB*, 24), that he does
"not want to get anywhere. We would like, only, for once to get to where
we are already,"[6] and that these have just been "a series of propositions,
[what matters is] rather to follow the movement of showing" (*OTB*, 2).
I will pursue the question as to whether a certain understanding of performativity, which seems required by a certain responsibility, might itself be a dangerous seduction.

What was at stake in Heidegger's raising anew the question of being?
Heidegger was trying to create or re-create an immanent basis for transcendence in the face of the otherworldly mystifications of theology and
the one-dimensional threat of domination by representation posed by
science and technology. Because the very idea of Man opposed both to
God and to Nature is caught up in a hopelessly entangled matrix, it is
better dropped. The recovery of the question of Being is the recovery of
a dimensionality within existence that makes truth, freedom, and responsibility genuinely possible. Such a dimensionality is, as he says in
What Is a Thing?, the strange space of the in-between.[7] Why does time
seem like the key to such a transformation? First, the experience of strife
within our experience of time is common currency—common, for example, to Kant, Nietzsche, Bergson, and Husserl. But equally, time has
already been put at the service of a certain transcendence in its religious
partition into the "temporal" and the "eternal," life on earth and life
after death. Heidegger is essentially reclaiming the power of this distinction from the traditional model of time that it presupposes. Life after
death is not one dimension of time *following* the first. Heidegger's distinction between everyday and authentic temporality, and his later accounts of time-space are attempts to secularize the resources made possible by transformations in our relation to time. And not surprisingly,
this centers around our relation to death. Different modes of being-in-
the-world can coexist, so to speak, as different possibilities of existence,
and do not need to be thought of successively.

There has been a certain interest in recent years in Heidegger's rela-

tion to questions of sexual difference, especially from Derrida and Irigaray. And mostly, it is his neutralization of Dasein's sexuality that has
been discussed. There has been a struggle for a certain primacy between
the ontological difference, sexual difference, and just plain difference.[8]
The key to this intervention is to show how what may just appear as an
empirical difference (sexuality) is (quasi) transcendental in its function;
in other words, that it serves to distribute other values and concepts. But
if this is so, at least as strong a case can be made for the role of childhood,
and indeed, human development in general. It is hard to imagine temporality playing a more constitutive role than in human development
through childhood and beyond. I will try to argue now that what Heidegger calls the question of being is intimately tied to our condition as
beings who are essentially the product of development. My main focus
will be on individual human development, but some of these remarks
apply to history too. I propose to offer a rather schematic account of human development that will free us from specific allegiance to particular theories (though I will give some specific illustrations). I argue further that with this directive idea, we can illuminate many of the claims
Heidegger wants to make, and that this developmental perspective gives
Heidegger's thinking a new future.

Developing the Idea of Development

Dasein, for the most part, seems to mean adult Dasein.[9] There is clearly
a significant difference between a human who has developed through
a series of stages, both physically and psychologically, and the infant
crawling on the ground. The adult has acquired capacities—motor skills,
capacities for empathic relatedness, survival skills, language and communication, knowledge, critical skills, moral judgment, and so on. The
adult has acquired a complex mix of independence and new forms of
dependency. The adult has in some respects "come into her own," become free. In introducing these kinds of concepts, we are making it
harder to confine what is at stake to the realm of the empirical. When
we talk about skills, we are tacitly supposing an unchanged bearer of
such skills. But we know that this is not how it is. We know that these
developments involve wholesale transformations in our way of being-in-
the-world, dramatic changes in the ways we negotiate the in-between.

The kinds of changes I have in mind here are those marked, for example, by Lacan, as the mirror stage, and the entry into the symbolic.
These each involve a transformation in what we could call the economy
of being. In the first, we accept the synthetic power of the image in giving us, albeit at this specular level, a sense of ourselves as a unity. In the

second, we accept a position in language, an identity through naming, in exchange for accessing the powers of language. I am not here arguing for Lacan's particular account.[10] What it offers us, however, is a glimpse of what is at stake from a structural point of view, in development.[11] Irigaray's account of the primary constitution of a subject boundary through touch, through the caress, would in this respect be no different. Heidegger's later discussions of language are precisely of this order—transforming, not our theory of language, but our *relation to* language. It is hard not to see this as a further step, building on the achievements of childhood development. The very difficulty of conveying this change reflects the opacity of changes in which a whole economy is at stake. If for a moment we were to glance at history more broadly, we would find in Heidegger's account of the epochality of being, an account with at least some analogous features. These epochs are not commensurable, and what qualifies as an epoch is something like an economy of being. The way he describes technology as the era dominated by *Gestell* is perhaps not wholly different from the spectrality of the mirror stage.

So far, then, I have tried to show that there are at least candidates for stages of human development that would qualify as different modes of Being-in-the-world.[12] What significance would Heidegger give to such stages? We know that in the case of the evolutionary steps—marked, however complexly, by animal existence—he treated their alterity as a form of impoverishment, or indeed, absence of world. Does this uncharacteristic re-emergence of a kind of teleological ordering principle suggest a kind of urgency to the question of the animal, anxiety in the face of the animal?[13] There is every reason to do the same with the child—or the infant, if we are really concerned to move thinking forward.

One might give two extreme versions of the development of a certain complexity through a series of stages. On the first model, the early stages fall away, having done their work, like booster rockets or a taxi one takes home, simply a means to an end. On the second model, all the early stages remain transparently available at the later stage, which nonetheless grasps its own privilege in relation to them. Neither of these models seems appropriate to human development. So let us suggest a third option—that some kind of memory of earlier stages may be available, but that access to these stages is extremely difficult, not least because even in the absence of conspicuous trauma, the very way in which "experience" was formatted has changed. And we must also ask whether the transitions from one stage to another have been wholly and successfully completed.[14] In the way that Freud understood neurosis to be a universal phenomenon only writ large in neurotics, I will assume that in the normal situation these transitions are never quite completed.

Heideggerian Corroborations

If all this were true, what would adult human experience be like? First, it would be riddled with the being question as well as with normalizing pressures to deny the significance of such questions. For even the marginal availability of other modes of being in the world, activated, reactivated, and transformed within adult experience, makes the question of being visible. Second, our experience would be haunted by the possibility of something like self-fulfillment, even as that very idea is being made problematic. Third, the experience of *Angst*, the uncanny, and the anticipation of death (and even what Freud calls the fear of castration) would all become closely linked to one another. Such interconnectedness, as I see it, argues in favor of our proposal. I propose that the common source for all such experiences of *das Nichts* lies in the incomplete transitions from one economy of being to another. From the vantage point one is leaving, a new economy can easily appear as death. And from that of the new economy, the prospect of slipping back into the previous regime can seem like death too. We may not, as Derrida reminds us, be in any better position than an animal to experience or know death *as such*,[15] but we are only strangers to the experience of the horror or fear of extinction, of our relation to the world breaking down completely, if we have completely sealed ourselves off from childhood.

My basic point here is that when "beings as a whole slip away,"[16] the experience is not that of the loss of the world, but the loss of a certain grasp of the world as whole, which is exactly what is at stake in our developmental transitions. In this way, we find an oddly inverted reprise of Plato's doctrine of anamnesis. On Plato's story, if we are lucky, we recover the soul's transitional preterrestrial glimpse of the forms. On our story, if we are lucky, we are neither wholly shut off from those transitional experiences nor reflectively incapacitated by them; they give us access, not to the Forms, but to Being, precisely at the moment of its being put into question. I would claim too that it is our access to such experiences, and sometimes our ability to escape from them, that allows us to think, or at least grope toward thinking, what Husserl described as "that there might no longer be any world" (that it might cease to have any meaning),[17] or what Blanchot calls disaster.[18]

If this is right, then, the secret connection between time and being is indeed through Dasein's existence, and it does indeed become visible through a transformation of our grasp of Dasein's temporality, and ecstatic being-toward-death points to what is at stake here. But the truth about Dasein's temporality lies in its developmental incompleteness and the way in which a complex of different economies are nested in our being-in-the-world. I would like to have shown how these different economies are themselves different ways of economizing time. It is a cliché, of course, that maturity and education bring about a capacity to cope with delay and frustration of immediate gratification, hence, a different economy of time. To the extent that overcoming metaphysics involves moving away from the privilege of presence, and that ceasing all overcoming involves a recognition that something like presence still survives as the telos underwriting the desire to overcome, then we can see that Heidegger's sense of the subsequent possibilities of thinking continues to involve transformations in the economy of time. I should add here that while for the sake of a transformative inhabiting of Heidegger I have emphasized the connection between economic transition and the sense of death, *Angst,* and so on, there is no reason to assume that our developmentally generated ontological layeredness is not also marked by benign boundary dissolutions—ecstasy, pleasure, *jouissance*—even as one may precisely have a problem owning these experiences.

All this would suggest that Dasein's temporality cannot be thought without this grasp of our having each inherited not just a tradition but also an ontologically ingrained complex of incompatible and unintegrated temporalities. If the word *economy* grates on the ears of those used to Heidegger's horizon, dispensation of being, or time-space, the uneasiness that haunts each of these alternative expressions is about whether what is fundamental is time or *a certain horizonality of time,* that is, a certain dimensionality that might not be quite separable from space.[19] The relation between time and economy repeats that uneasiness.

How specifically does this account graft onto Heidegger? Most obviously, it gives us better access to why Heidegger was so obsessed with Nietzsche. For Nietzsche's whole thought of *ressentiment,* of the spirit of revenge against time, and of the affirmation of the eternal return, is precisely an attempt to overcome both the sense of loss associated with the past and the crippling psychologies we develop to deal with that loss. This account is isomorphic, at least, with much of what Heidegger says about the need to retrieve the past (and the difficulty of doing this), about reanimating the tradition, and about our (and Kant's) getting stuck with provisional versions of things.

This would be the place to bring together all that Heidegger has to say about pain, the threshold, distress, and so forth.[20] For now, let me return instead to our opening quotation from *Contributions.* When Heidegger says that there is distress "[*Not*] in the essential beginnings and transitions of man's history," he means, of course, not an individual biography, but our involvement in the history of being. Heidegger is not speaking about individual development. But he is more than open to the shape of this thought—that philosophy is born from the pain of transition and renewal. My claim, if you like, is a loose version of the claim that ontogeny repeats phylogeny[21]—that individual human development exhibits the same *kind* of traumatic transformations as are to be found in human history, that our own memories give us access to the *difficulty of access* to the past. And in my view, Heidegger (and others like Merleau-Ponty) gives us all the resources we need to resist the idea that we will just drown in psychology if we move in this direction. All this makes it understandable why Heidegger should speak of the need for and the difficulties of a new beginning. The need for what Nietzsche called overcoming is precisely, as Nietzsche and Heidegger agree, the need for a new economy of being, which for Heidegger (contra Nietzsche) is thought in terms of *Gelassenheit*. And the idea that we must cease all overcoming is precisely an attempt to not allow our practice of thinking to bear with it the seeds of transformative failure. Hence performativity.[22]

Finally, I offer a series of remarks that bear on this experimental interpretation of Heidegger, that lend a little credence to our directive idea, and that encourage us to dwell awhile on the strangeness and the unwelcome aspects of this thought.

The temptation of performativity is obvious, natural, and in some ways surely productive. If a philosopher comes to see the possibilities of transformation as tied up with taking up a new relation to language,[23] it is hard to resist the idea that the difficulties of bringing about that change, or even adequately articulating it, might be tied up with the fact that in one's very announcement of these possibilities one may be perpetuating the very relation one is trying to overcome. Performativity would be the attempt to put that right. The idea that pursuing the question of being is most successful if it follows up the connection, first with time, and then with shifting economies of time and being, gives a clear direction to such performativity.

I make the following suggestions:

1. The performative dimension of Heidegger's own trajectory of philosophical experimentation is driven by the need to come to terms with this nestedness of times and economies that we inhabit and that inhabit us.
2. The insistence and persistence of these economies may make opening a new beginning into an infinite task.
3. There will naturally arise a certain temptation, one to which Nietzsche was more sensitive than Heidegger, to strive for a certain coincidence between the *what* and the *how*, or content and style. This may seem obvious. Surely the opposite of coincidence would be a certain dissonance, sowing the seeds for failure by reproducing just what one is trying to move beyond.
4. Nonetheless, it may be wise to raise the performativity to another level, not to try to mirror in one's writing some pure coincidence between the *what* and the *how*, but rather to deploy a whole range of

styles and strategies, accepting, at each point, both opportunities and liabilities. We cannot, for example, think or write without making propositional claims, comparative judgments, critical remarks—in other words, we cannot just allow language to speak itself. Whichever way we turn, we take risks, we enter territory in which we are not entirely in control, and it is through risking failure that we may find success. This is not only unavoidable, but it is something we could celebrate. That would be a second level of performativity— affirming the risks, dangers, and impurities associated with thinking anew, without aiming at a pure coincidence. I have learned from Nietzsche and Derrida to seek more of this in Heidegger, and sometimes to find it.

Does this reading simply open the way to a psychoanalytical absorption of Heidegger? That is not the aim. But we are moving to a point at which what psychoanalysis indicates—that structural transformations are inherent in human development, that humans are essentially developmental creatures, and that these developments are essentially incomplete—are truths that are independent of a specifically psychoanalytical interpretation.

Furthermore, there is something of a parallel between the way in which Husserl's phenomenology grew out of Frege's charge of psychologism, and the way in which Lacan transformed and reworked the biologistic basis of Freud's thinking in the light of a certain structuralist logic. This said, there remains the question of whether Lacan completes this process of transformation or whether he too gets stuck at a certain point. Thus, while in *Of Grammatology* (1967), Derrida specifically mentions psychoanalysis as the place, outside linguistics, in which the "deconstitution of the founding concept-words of ontology" is most likely to see a breakthrough,[24] by the time of "Le Facteur de la Verité" (1975), he is claiming that for all its radicalism, psychoanalysis in Lacan's hands is committed to the mastery of truth: "Abyss effects are severely controlled here."[25] Derrida sees Lacan as finding in castration a new site of truth. The question then for Derrida would perhaps be this—could there be a disseminative psychoanalysis? For us the question is a little different. The picture we are developing is one in which human development is marked by a movement through a series of structures of psychosomatic organization, or economies.[26] These economies would each constitute different regimes of truth, different ways of distributing self and other, man and world. To the extent that *dissemination* captures the dynamic (associative and substitutive) consequences of the differential basis of meaning and identity, the restlessness of any presence, it would operate *within* any economy and as a principle of leakage or permeability between economies. In these ways, dissemination operates as a principle that prevents closure. But it cannot itself account for the differences *between* the economic organization of different stages.

Derrida's remarks about Lacan attempting the mastery of abyssal effects open up a parallel thought about Heidegger and death. I have suggested that developmental identity transitions are, or are potentially, abyssal in quality, that they are reexperienced as *Angst,* and that such experiences provide us with the lived experience of extinction, or death. Surely Heidegger's own thinking of death, and of the possibility of an authentic being-toward-death is caught up in just this struggle for mastery over the abyssal dimension of death, and even a struggle with the desire for and value of mastery.

The short answer to the question about psychoanalysis is that the question of the relation between philosophy and psychoanalysis is a reprise of the situation that brought about the birth of phenomenology. We have to trust that whatever empirical content we pursue philosophically will eventually yield a logic, or an economy; the question of being can be constantly refreshed and reworked only by these forays into the *Sache selbst.*[27]

I conclude in a speculative way with a story that I would graft onto Heidegger's discussion of the danger and the saving grace of technology, a story that supplies the answer to a question. I have offered here a way of thinking about the relation between time and being that makes common cause with all those interested in trauma, in mourning, in nonlinear and problematic understandings of memory, and so on.[28] There is something of an ongoing debate between those who see narrative or narrative imagination as a way of supplying both personal and national identity with sufficient substance to be able to bear ethical responsibility,[29] and the more skeptical apostles of postmodernism. Theoretically, this project seems to be threatened by attacks on the status of narrative from postmodernism, threats of which Kearney is well aware and to which he responds. But suppose we read this debate symptomatically. Suppose we bring together Heidegger's diagnosis of technology (as a kind of enframing that prepackages the real in ways that conform to that frame's principles of relationality) with Deleuze's and Guattari's accounts of deterritorialization, and our commonsense grasp of the way economic relations (of exchange) increasingly dominate, that is, ultimately *define* the real for us. We can *now* understand Nietzsche's account of our cultural and moral wasteland as a diagnosis of our failure to answer a question posed to us by history.

If individual human development is quite standardly a traumatic journey in which different stages are incompletely traversed, one that leaves each of us with a nested bundle of modes of being, times, and economies, then we may ask ourselves how people typically have dealt with this constitutive personal legacy. I suggest that in the past the central coping mechanism has been the work of socially integrative narrative at every level, but that what we are witnessing today is a crisis in narrativity as it becomes displaced by technological, calculative modes of explanation and legitimation. This corrosion of the traditional power of narrative has the effect of exposing the incomplete work of human development, much as a high tide exposes the shipwrecks buried under the sand. What we might call the crisis of narrative is taken up below in chapter 10, "The Dark Side of Narrative," and chapter 12, "Art as Event."

This is at least one lens through we can glimpse the shape of our distress. And this distress supplies the historical pressure under which we are coming to see that time does indeed operate as the horizon of the question of being. This is a secret locked in the heart of the human soul.[30] But if nature hides it from us, it is history that unlocks it.

Heidegger's confrontation with Nietzsche could be said to have culminated in Heidegger's transfiguration of the will-to-power into performativity, most powerfully in his claim in *Contributions to Philosophy* to be *thinking from Ereignis*.[31] The will-to-power is not just a vitalistic critique of truth as representation, because it puts in question the very idea of life, even as it draws on it. Heidegger could be said to have found the truth of the will-to-power in the ineliminable performativity of philosophy, that philosophy cannot ultimately be "about"; it must itself eventuate. And it eventuates as a form of self-transformation, one marked by "life," "affirmation," "creativity," precisely to the extent that it draws us back into the truth of *Ereignis*. This is the shape of Heidegger's reenacting responsibility toward Nietzsche. This responsibility requires that we sacrifice truth as (mere) accuracy, for truth as a kind of living in relation to disclosure. Responsibility requires that one live with risk.

I have myself taken up the challenge here by bringing a particular illuminative idea—that of human development as a fundamentally incomplete ontological journey—to the interpretation of Heidegger's fundamental question. Such a story not only allows a certain naturalization of ontology, but it allows us to stage again the whole question of the relation of the ontic to the ontological. On my view, which Heidegger at times shares,[32] the ontological is already *in* the ontic, rightly construed. But it is hard to hold on to this idea!

Finally, it might be asked, what is the specific responsibility of choosing this illuminative or guiding idea rather than another? The fact that it continues the thematic of time and temporality is not unimportant. Its distinct advantage over the ways in which Heidegger will develop this question (toward time-space, and the truth of *Ereignis*, and a possibility to come) is that the whole issue of human development is like a courtyard opening onto, and opened onto by, the most pressing concerns of our time—historical, political, educational, and environmental. Our continuing responsibility consists in the willingness to keep exploring these passages, opening these doors, and not resting reductively on the attractions of any single account.

PART III. THE EVENT OF TIME

7

The Event of Philosophy
Heidegger, Foucault, Deleuze

> History also teaches us how to laugh at the solemnities
> of the origin.
> —Michel Foucault

> Everything now returns to the surface. This is the Stoic
> operation . . . the unlimited returns.
> —Gilles Deleuze

> Beginning is going on. Everywhere. Amidst all the endings, so
> rarely ripe or ready.
> —Catherine Keller

If the history of philosophy is the record of a certain attempt at recollection, an antidote to the deadening repetitions of everydayness and dispersion, a selective reading of the last century would suggest that another lineage has been launched, one that would free us from the trajectory and investments of this longing for a return. That other lineage would wean us from the compulsive repetition of a certain metaphysical desire, the desire for presence, perhaps even for a certain death. In each case, what is at stake is a certain economy of time. I want to pursue the question of an *other* economy by focusing on a small cluster of contemporary thinkers of the event.[1]

Imagine reading the words: "The philosophy of the event is the event of philosophy." The palindrome form would suggest Blanchot as its author. But in the provocative implication, we could equally imagine it coming from the pens of Heidegger, Foucault, or Derrida—perhaps even Deleuze. In each case, what qualifies these for inclusion—and there are surely others, such as Lyotard—is first a sense of the breakdown of the productive power of the speculative proposition, which in Hegel's hands would generate a progressive movement of thought. Here, instead, there is a circling back, a reversal, a mirror-imaging. We certainly learn something, but it is a disruptive, not a constructive insight, a thought that promises turbulence, not triumph. More specifically, this reversal suggests a connection between a focal concern of philosophy, that of time, and philosophy's own temporality. I want to show how this structure, which is abyssal in only one of its interpretations (that which focuses on the event), generates both the diversity and, in some sense, the unity of our contemporary "critical" enterprise, an enterprise that would resist the very language of *generation, unity,* and *critical.* I will argue for a new sense of philosophical progress linked to the idea of repetition, for which minor scandal, as you will see, I should not too quickly be forgiven.

I begin with a reflection on the repetition involved in reading, making sense of, responding to, another philosopher. And I will take Heidegger as an example. As we saw in the last chapter, the way he recommends we read another thinker not only licenses a certain creativity with regard to reading Heidegger himself but also frees us, in certain ways, for reading others. In *What Is Called Thinking?* Heidegger distinguishes between going counter to another thinker, and going to their encounter. "Going counter to" we could call criticism, and "going to their encounter," thinking—with and through the other thinker. The objection to criticism (especially in the form of negation, polemics) is that it tends to reaffirm the original frame of reference in which the other thinker thinks, notwithstanding that, or precisely insofar as, it engages in a reversal (negation). Heidegger, on the other hand, writes of addressing a thinker's unthought, describing this unthought, not as a failure on the part of the other, but as his greatest legacy or gift.

Let me pause for a moment. Heidegger is offering here a model of philosophizing as repetition, together with an account of how that repetition can escape the trap of empty repetition by a *displacement,* which reworks and replays some more original scene. Heidegger's position here is exemplary for us, because in this displaced repetition that replays an original scene, there is an attempt to think philosophy as event. (I will discuss "original" shortly.) And we know that from the 1920s to the 1960s, Heidegger pursues, sometimes in subterranean ways, the question of the horizonality of time, concluding with an account of time as event—*Ereignis*—an account that turns out to be closely linked to the need to move from philosophy (tied in his mind to framing, *Gestell,* representation, technology) to thinking. The thought of *Ereignis* is an attempt at a kind of condensation of the philosophy of the event and the event of philosophy. Or, we might say, it is the effect of the sacrifice of philosophy in the service of a performative reduction of the tension between these two wings: thinking as event.

For his predilection for a return to an origin, Heidegger has often come under fire, and I will shortly turn to Foucault's contrasting insistence on a genealogical method. But even here we need to pause once more to ensure that we are not, in this often-tempting understanding of Heidegger, engaging precisely in empty repetition, shallow criticism, and so on. Words can easily mislead us, and we need to get into clearer focus how and why this connection between the event of philosophy and the philosophy of the event has become so pressing, and whether Heidegger succumbs to it.

What would empty repetition be? It is not difficult to hear here the phenomenological lament to which Husserl had given voice—that words were losing their meaning both in everyday discourse, in our public culture, and in the sciences, including philosophy. The point of his *Logical Investigations* was to demonstrate the groundedness of what might otherwise look like purely formal, mechanical connections in ideal (mental) acts, where neither the word *act* nor *mental* is quite right, once ideality is brought in. Empty words, *flatus voci*, seem to bypass the meaning-bestowing function of ideal acts, a condition symptomatic of cultural crisis. Overcoming this condition was to be achieved by reactivation. The origin in question (as in Husserl's "Origin of Geometry," or Heidegger's "Origin of the Work of Art") is not a historically locatable event or act, but nonetheless a re-experienceable proof or demonstration. In a teaching situation, for example, one can "begin geometry again" as if one were an Egyptian general, and calculate the width of a river from one bank without getting one's feet wet. If you do this slowly, you will discover yourself reinventing straightness, lines, angles, and even the very idea of ideality, approximation, and so on. It is an experience, and it is exciting, and this reactivation does indeed, in some sense, repeat the moves that made geometry, an ideal science, possible. By analogy, philosophy itself could be thought of along the same lines—as a witnessing to the production of idealities. And this raises the question as to whether there might not merely be varieties of phenomenology, but varieties strung out on a scale of dis-possession, de-stabilization, as the artifice necessary for the production of ideality was increasingly revealed.

It may be, too, that we misunderstand Heidegger completely when we understand him to be pointing to, calling for, insisting on, some point of origin. For Derrida *différance* was not an origin, not least because it had no single, resolvable meaning. If it was original, it was in an ironic mode, not a unity, but a difference, and thus incapable of operating as a legitimating ground, which was the *point* of positing an origin. But in that case, why not say the same of Heidegger's various formulations, in which he traces back thinking to a four-dimensional time-space, to the fourfold (*Geviert*), or to the strife between earth and world?[2] If we suppose that, nonetheless, he privileges gathering, weak closure, over (say) dispersion, we should still be slow to pass judgment. It may be that some such movement as this is unavoidable, even when arguing for dissemination, dispersion, and so on.

I am toying with the proposition that empty repetition might be overcome by a return, not to some point of origin, but to a certain space of distribution or to a conflict of forces. If *this* is metaphysics, then so too would be Nietzsche's account of Apollo and Dionysus in *The Birth of*

Tragedy, and indeed, Deleuze's account of Plato in *The Logic of Sense.* Consider these sentences from the section "What Is an Event?":

> In Plato, an obscure debate was raging in the depth of things, in the depth of the earth, between that which undergoes the action of the Idea, and that which eludes this action (copies and simulacra). An echo of this debate resonates when Socrates asks—is there an idea of everything, even of hair, dirt and mud, or rather is there something which always and abstractly escapes the Idea? In Plato . . . this something is never sufficiently hidden, driven back, pushed deeply into the depth of the body, or drowned in the ocean. Everything now returns to the surface. This is the Stoic operation . . . the unlimited returns. (45)

I am drawn to this passage for the way Deleuze's reading of Plato appeals precisely to an origin of this expanded sort—a primitive strife. How telling is it that Deleuze speaks of a strife within the earth, whereas Heidegger speaks of a strife between earth and world?

This sense that the dangers of a certain phenomenology can be counteracted by a return to an origin primitively divided against itself can be seen again in Foucault's Preface to *Madness and Civilization.* First he speaks of "returning to that zero point in the course of madness at which madness is an undifferentiated experience, a not yet divided experience of division itself." He later distanced himself from this formulation. But even on this first page, he develops his thought: "What is constitutive is the action that divides madness, and not the science elaborated once this division is made, and calm restored. What is originative is the caesura that establishes the difference between reason and unreason."[3]

What each of these remarks shares is the sense that empty repetition can be avoided by a return, not to a ground but to a space of division, dispersion, and scission (though Deleuze will in effect contest this too, in thinking the rhizome), and that it is on the basis of this space or this question that this emptiness is filled out, that false forms of fullness are banished, and that new thoughts are generated. It is perhaps no accident that Foucault, Deleuze, Derrida, and Heidegger have each distanced themselves from what we could call phenomenological repetition. There is a deep reason for this, one that goes to the heart of a certain phenomenology—namely, that however much phenomenology would like to be purely descriptive, its engagement with language, and then its entanglement with the logic of what it merely describes, render it subject to the very dimension it took itself to be sustaining. Phenomenology perhaps never was or could be what it thought it was. Its desire was always doomed. And the emergence of concepts like chiasm in Merleau-Ponty, a kind of immanent aporia in our perceptual experience, makes this clear.[4]

All this suggests that we can steer clear of empty repetition without subscribing to a discredited version of reactivation of origin. I am working on the assumption that the event of philosophy is tied up with repetition, but it is clear that various senses and levels are entangled here. When I speak of the event of philosophy, it is not implied that there is but one event that took place at some particular historical moment. Nor is it implied that there is one distinct type of event marked as philosophical whenever it occurs. Rather, philosophy would have as its *telos* opening our eyes to the everyday eventuation of the real. The repeated event of philosophy would appear in such openings.

In this sense, we could speak of events as transformations, disclosures, reconfigurations of the economy of thinking. If we ask ourselves what is happening each time, and how we are to describe the shifts in the tectonic plates that occur, we would in each case find a rearrangement of a certain space and time of thinking, new orders of representation, new circuits of forces, new maps of the terrain. Even as I attempt to home in on one good way of describing what happens in each case, my efforts are dispersed, as if language allows me only so long the illusion of my control as it secretly toys with me. Each of the events of philosophy is a transformation and a displacement of a field in which words and things, man and world, space and time are configured. These transformations are privileged in that, as Heidegger would put it, they draw forth "preservers"—not just toilers who would protect a valuable insight against its detractors, but circumstances that enable these reshapings to catch fire across the landscape. And we may wonder whether Heidegger, in his "The Origin of the Work of Art," is only talking about art when he speaks of it as opening a world (OWA, 44). For in speaking of the strife between earth and world, in attempting to mark out a certain space of dimensionality and a time of preservation, is he not also exemplifying, and hence also opening the way for, a certain auto-reflection of philosophy itself?

Philosophy does not need to dream of totality to be driven to think itself. Indeed, the sense that the strife that echoes in its depths might be inseparable from the drawing of lines, and from a kind of transcendental aesthetics, teaches it a lesson both troubling and pleasing. The first troubling aspect is that the world of lines, maps, diagrams, and boundaries, of centers and decenterings and displacements is not one in which there are experts, and certainly philosophers have no privilege here. Moreover, it is equally clear that these lines and demarcations, centers and peripheries are no mere diagrams; they are the shapes of our deepest investments, and as such, are both responsive to and formative for our political and practical existence. We speak glibly of the error of Cartesianism, which installs a subject at the center of its field. But we may sometimes suspect that our ability to focus in on this structure is linked to the fact that it reflects an achieved economic and psychic reality, even if that reality is an ideologically sustained formation.

The promising aspect of this recognition of our insertion, as thinkers, as philosophers, into a space determined and overdetermined by forces, interests, and investments is that it may pull the rug out from under a certain project of mastery. While such a project itself reflects just such a space of investment, it equally opens up philosophy to possibilities of a different order—to questions of strategy, to what is possible within the play of limitations once the unlimited has been vanquished.

This move was anticipated, perhaps, by the Stoics. It was shouted by Nietzsche, echoed by Bataille, and celebrated by Foucault in his brilliant "Preface to Transgression."[5] On Foucault's account, the significance of eroticism and sexuality for Bataille is that it is the experience of the transgression of limits, even as the rift is healed again behind us. And all this is in the wake of the death of God and the displacement of all that yearning for the limitless back onto the finite space of "a world exposed by the experience of its limits, made and unmade by the excess which transgresses it" (*LCMP,* 32).

It is a specifically philosophical transgression that Bataille enacts when, against the eye of pure reflection, of the transparent gaze, of the sovereign subject, he sets the "spectacle of erotic death, where upturned eyes display their white limits, and rotate inwards in gigantic and empty orbits," and then gets paired up with "a bull's white testicle that had penetrated Simone's black and pink flesh" (*LCMP,* 52).

Foucault explicitly names the death of God an event—one that "not merely . . . gave shape to contemporary experience as we now know it; it continues tracing indefinitely its great skeletal outline" (*LCMP,* 32). But what does his own subsequent work and that of those he admires tell us about how or whether "we" can respond to such events? And what more might be asked of philosophy?

It would be tempting to make a distinction, a binary distinction, between those philosophical events now part of our history, and those we have still fully to work through and exploit. On this path, we would contrast past errors with current transformations, albeit incomplete: before and after the death of God, for example. This is tempting perhaps, but fatal. Such a construction of the past would perpetuate a simplistically linear understanding of time. It would restrict itself to a superficially homogeneous reading of the events in question. There would be no room for "In Plato, an obscure debate was raging in the depth of things." And it would be blind to the ways in which the past never quite leaves us be.

This barrage of objections to the idea that we might distinguish between philosophical events that are merely part of our heritage, and those that are alive and ongoing, might itself be questioned. Is it not clearly animated by the spirit of responsibility and seriousness, as if we could not move on until we had finished with the past? Wasn't the point of Nietzsche's talking of life affirmation, or active forgetting, precisely to release us from this? Is there not a lingering will-to-truth here? Was it not important that Descartes did not see how much scholasticism he was carrying forward? And important that Husserl had not read Hegel, that Freud had not read Nietzsche, that Levinas had not understood Heidegger? Does not the possibility of philosophy as event, in short, rest on leaving behind the broken-backed camel of fidelity to the past, along with the obsession with origins? Isn't the claim that the past is always with us an intolerable burden? And isn't it precisely a characteristic of that philosophical event Foucault called genealogy to release us from this burden, to set the camel free? Isn't there a *necessary* violence in being a lion? Isn't the very focus on repetition an error? Shouldn't we release ourselves from this fetish so we can do something different and move on?

At one specific point in "Nietzsche, Genealogy, History," Foucault explicitly repudiates the haunting of the "always already" (*LCMP,* 160). And I will use this as a point of engagement with the essay, itself an event or the repetition or preservation of an event, one which will help us understand what is involved in understanding philosophy as an event, and why none of the instances of this event are ever really over.

Foucault does not ultimately oppose history to genealogy; rather, as he puts it, "It is necessary to master history so as to turn it to genealogical uses, that is, strictly anti-Platonic purposes" (*LCMP,* 160). Central to this mastery of history (itself a parodic expression, I suspect) is Nietzsche's challenge to the pursuit of origin. What is wrong with such a pursuit? It seeks "to capture the exact essence of things, their purest possibilities and their carefully protected identities, because this search assumes the existence of immobile forms that precede the external world of accident and succession." Rather, Foucault continues, "what is found at the historical beginning of things is not the inviolable identity of their origin; it is the dissension of other things. It is disparity" (*LCMP,* 142). Or again, "Historical beginnings are lowly. . . . History teaches us how to laugh at the solemnities of the origin" (*LCMP,* 143). Genealogy, on the other hand, "requires patience and a knowledge of details." Its movements "are constructed 'from discrete and apparently insignificant movements and according to a rigorous method'" (Foucault quoting Nietzsche; *LCMP,* 140). Genealogy "records the singularity of events outside of any monotonous finality" (*LCMP,* 139).

One of the key consequences of a genealogical approach is precisely the re-emergence of the event. Genealogy liberates the historical sense from metaphysics, for example, in the effective history (*wirkliche Histo-*

rie) that Nietzsche opposes to traditional history. This is how Foucault describes its significance:

> Effective history transposes the relationship ordinarily established between the eruption of an event and necessary continuity. An entire historical tradition (theological and rationalistic) aims at dividing the singular event into an ideal continuity (teleological moment, natural process). "Effective" history, however, deals with events in terms of their most unique characteristics, their most acute manifestation. An event . . . is not a decision, a treaty, a reign or a battle . . . but the reversal or a relationship of forces, the usurpation of power, the appropriation of a vocabulary . . . a feeble domination that poisons itself as it grows lax, the entry of a masked "other." The word . . . is not an ultimately simple configuration where events are reduced to accentuate their essential traits . . . on the contrary it is a profusion of entangled events. (*LCMP*, 155)

As much as I admire Foucault, there are unresolved, probably unresolvable if wholly forgivable tensions in this account, tensions that collect and swirl around the question of ideality. Metaphysical history reduces singular events to their ideality. Genealogy, in the shape of effective history, understands an event, not in terms of its appearance (treaty, battle), but in terms of "a reversal of a relationship of forces," "the entry of a masked 'other'." Foucault insists—rightly, I think—that the search for a pure origin is a metaphysical illusion and that history is the product of chance and accident. But the examples he gives of a singular event are nothing if not idealities: "reversals," "usurpations," "entry of masked other." They may not exhibit any deep historical necessity, and they may be the products of chance, but the character of these events, what makes them events, is precisely their formal properties. This is not to say *abstract*. Such events are material in content, but it is their formal properties that make them significant as events. It is such properties that make events not merely significant, but consequential.

Foucault is confused, I believe, about the place of chance, detail, accident. After all, his whole essay ("Nietzsche, Genealogy, History") is constructed on a formal opposition between materiality/ideality, difference/identity, seriousness/parody—powerful binary pairs. We can see them at work in the forms of his opposition to the three Platonic modalities of history:

> The first is parodic, directed against reality, and opposes the theme of history as reminiscence or recognition; the second is dissociative, directed against identity, and opposes history given as continuity or as representative of a tradition. And the third is sacrificial, directed against truth, and opposes history as knowledge. They imply a use of history that severs its connection to memory, its metaphysical and anthropological model, and constructs a

counter-memory—a transformation of history into a totally different form of time. (*LCMP,* 160)

What are we to make of these oppositional binarisms? Should not Foucault have learned better from Nietzsche the importance of displacement of the field of opposition? ("My style is a dance, an overleaping mockery of symmetries"). Wasn't this just what Derrida learned early on when he introduced indecidables precisely as terms of opposition *and* displacement?

Are we to conclude that Foucault is just displaying a little active forgetting? Or that this very innocence is a memory of the dangers of camel-like responsibility? Or is he calculating, not on the formal folly of mere opposition, but on unpredictable disruptive consequences? At one level, one can read Foucault as simply laughing in the face of dialectical recuperation. It might, like death, be unavoidable, but only in the last analysis. In the meantime, parody can shatter the seriousness of those who would police the real. In his "Preface to Transgression," he compares transgression to a flash of lightning, a flashing line, and writes of the "instantaneous play of the limit and of transgression" (*LCMP,* 35), drawing on Blanchot's sense of contestation as a nonpositive, intransitive affirmation.

All this would indeed suggest that what Foucault is advocating is a transvaluation of time itself, of the privilege of the last analysis. But this position is fraught with difficulty—indeed, logical difficulties, that bite quite quickly. Foucault has assembled a whole apparatus, the value of which is not to produce or facilitate one spark, but the recurrence of singularity, of the lightning. Foucault is not neutral with regard to the value of pure origin; he is committed, and not just temporarily, sparkily, to its fading away. In other words, Foucault's brilliant analyses have a generality, a projective power, an applicability that would undercut any more adventurist snubbing of recuperation. And we have to question some of his oppositions. For example, the new historical sense, licensed by genealogy, "opposes with parody the theme of history as reminiscence or recognition." Foucault speaks of "the great carnival of time where masks are constantly reappearing" (*LCMP,* 161).

Monumental history, veneration of the past, closes off "the actual intensities and creations of life." But Foucault is harnessing Nietzsche here to a false opposition. Parody is far from the only way of avoiding or countering the veneration of the past; indeed, it can serve as the most frightening mark of precisely the empty repetition we discussed earlier. The return to a pure origin would itself be a parody, not least because if, *per impossibile,* there were a pure origin, it would be utterly different if it were returned to, like the scene of a crime, or Kierkegaard's Berlin.[6]

But it makes no sense to abandon memory ("to sever its connection to memory") or even the ideality associated with it. Even to avoid the seduction of the metaphysical lure is a work (and a play) of memory. Counter-memory is a memory, and I suspect a labor of memory. Even to fantasize a carnivalesque escape is to give expression to this.

I am not here challenging what Foucault suggests, but carnival, dissociation, sacrifice cannot function quite as he supposes. Take the sacrifice he proposes—that of truth. Foucault's relation to truth, just like that of Nietzsche, is far more complex than this allows. Foucault writes near the end of "Nietzsche, Genealogy, History" that the sacrifice of truth is not just a matter of recognizing the finitude of cognition. But in fact, he is deeply committed to truth being found at a level other than the one at which it is usually located. He writes, for example, of genealogy's intention being "to reveal the heterogeneous systems which, masked by the self, inhibit the formation of any form of identity" (*LCMP*, 162). He proposes, in sympathy with Nietzsche, that "history should become a differential knowledge of energies and failings, heights and degenerations, poisons and antidotes." Over and over again, he wants to substitute for an idealizing unification of history an account of its singularity, differential forces, and so on. This is far too interesting a claim about the way things are not to accord it the value of a truth-claim! And in all but name, Foucault does this repeatedly.

For all his hostility to Heidegger, Foucault's affective location of truth can be lined up with that of Heidegger in "On the Essence of Truth." For Foucault, quite as much as Heidegger, truth is tied to disclosure. In neither case is truth essentially propositional. Foucault's account of this space is compelling precisely because it offers a persuasive story of how this disclosure occurs in the midst of things, while Heidegger's own account is precisely designed to refigure what it is to be in the midst of things!

All this helps us question Foucault's supposition that the only proper response to the idea of history as memory is parody. Foucault is simply wrong to suppose that between chance and idealized necessity/purity of origin there is a wide desert. He himself introduces the very language of the economy of forces that would fill this space. The alternative to parody of the real is effective transformation. And transformation, to return to an earlier theme, is repetition that transcends empty repetition, not phenomenologically, but by an engagement with the shapes of forces that do indeed constitute the real. And it is here, not in parody, that true intensity appears. What parody gets right is that the event (usurpation, reversal) has a form, which is how it functions as an event; but parody is only the shell of a form. Chance becomes effective through the emergence of those transformative constellations that have form.

Reading Foucault's "A Preface to Transgression" today is something of a shock. It is not hard to wonder here, as elsewhere: whatever happened to this extraordinary efflorescence of the 1960s and 1970s? Heidegger once wrote that German Idealism had not been refuted, but rather the German people had not lived up to it.[7] Is this not quite as true of the various critical enterprises launched in the 1960s?[8]

In 1970, Foucault published a review of Deleuze's *Difference and Repetition* and *The Logic of Sense,* entitled "Theatrum Philosophicum," an essay that could be said to have canonized the event that we have come to know as Gilles Deleuze.[9] Much of this review is devoted to showing how Deleuze lays out "the essential elements for establishing the thought of the event and the phantasm." I have not here even been able to attempt an empty repetition of these formulations. I began with the thought that something important happens at the hinge between the event of philosophy and the philosophy of the event. I have tried to show how the event of philosophy, an always singular repetition, is a theme that links disparate bedfellows. I would like, finally, to plot at least some of what seems to me to be at stake in the reversal, which focuses on the philosophy of the event. All of this explains why it is, I predict, that this century will witness, not a linguistic turn but a temporal turn (or return). And it explains why time is central to philosophy, and how, like language, it will flip from being a special topic to being a constitutive obsession.

My claim is that it is the thought of the event that has enabled thinkers as diverse as Heidegger, Foucault, and Deleuze to turn our ordinary linear understanding of time inside out. This turning inside out is itself, of course, an event. And the central terms in this transformation are repetition and singularity. In *What Is Called Thinking?* Heidegger attacks as a great illusion the historicism that would reduce a great thought to the period and circumstances that seem to have spawned it. After all, "history" produces even the ideas that shape our various graspings of history. For Heidegger, history produces singular thoughts, which, we might say, transcend their time, or the condition that makes them possible. I said something similar in criticizing Foucault for seeming to forget at times that for accident and chance to be effective, they have to become event, eventuate, in a way that would not just be more accident and chance, but would reverse and transform the field in which they are located. Heidegger's account here, quite as much as his account of time-space in *On Time and Being,* involves a radical break with time understood as a linear continuum. Rather, time is understood as or through the event, or an eventuation that could be said to distribute the shape of possibilities.

In "Theatrum Philosophicum," Foucault focuses Deleuze's account of the recurrence of difference onto an analogous event-uating, delinearizing account of time, in which Nietzsche's eternal recurrence resurfaces, this time, not as an account of the reappearance of great sequences of events, but as the throb of the new, "the repetitive fibrillation of the present." "What repeats itself," says Foucault simply, "is time." And "the present recurs as singular difference" (*LCMP,* 194).

It is hard not to be struck by the boldness of these remarks, as if time could still be defined, for example, as singular difference. Under most other circumstances, we would be wondering how to *bring about* singular difference (via will), or how to allow it to be this (letting be). If time just *is* "singular difference," what, indeed, would happen to memory, to the operation of selection, to that memory that would remember what not to remember, what to forget, what not to desire (e.g., a simple origin)? This makes one wonder whether it is not so much that there is a truth about time as that there are possibilities for our being-in-time, for being-temporal that our thinking about time-as-such enables us to idealize. The experience and practice of time as singular event seems to be just this, and I suggest that it is this thought that most powerfully constitutes the differential field of forces of contemporary critical thought.

One final thought. It might be thought perverse to draw together Heidegger, Foucault, and Deleuze into one happy little event family. Surely what distinguishes them is far more significant. And blurring distinctions should not be our goal. Certainly, I am tempted by the thought that there is a cleavage, a break, between Heidegger's often reverential tone and Deleuze's often promiscuous, transformative irresponsibility. He must think Heidegger a tree, whereas he is a riotous rhizome. For Deleuze, the event is tied up with transformation, transgression, and invention. And Heidegger? At the end of her essay "Heidegger's Concept of World after *Being and Time,*" Françoise Dastur reminds us that in "Building Dwelling Thinking" (1950), Heidegger links together our abdication of our mastery of the world in the face of our mortality with the "event of the world," which, as she puts it, "appears [even] in the insignificant and inconspicuous appearing of things."[10] What this suggests is that the event of the simple appearing of things arises, not from a return to an origin, but rather from the tension, as a bow is tensed, of fully acknowledged mortal existence. In the most uncanny way, Heidegger here seems to reprise Plato's sense that philosophy is a preparation for death, and yet he finds himself, I believe, on the same shore as Foucault and Deleuze, in wresting philosophical desire from its deadly and deadening compulsions.

8

Political Openings
Heidegger 1933–34

In 1945, Heidegger explained why he assumed the rectorate of Freiburg University:

> I saw in the movement that had gained power the possibility of an inner recollection and renewal of the people that would allow it to discover its historical vocation in the Western world. I believed that, renewing itself, the university might also be called to contribute to this inner self-collection of the people, providing it with a measure.[1]

Heidegger's own recollection of 1933–34 is often self-serving. But I would like to proceed here on the assumption that such remarks do represent what he thought he was doing, so that the philosophical issues that they raise can be pursued. I want to pursue the view that there are intimate connections between his philosophy and his political speeches, not simply to condemn his philosophy, but to deepen our understanding of some of the questions it raises, questions that still haunt us. To put my position very quickly: I do not accept a politically reductive dismissal of Heidegger's philosophy (as that of an "unpolitical petit bourgeois" or, as Heidegger himself suggests, as one that reflects the world of the peasant), for reasons that can be put in logical, hermeneutical, or deconstructive terms. Indeed, the philosophical poverty of attacks on Heidegger is one of the strongest arguments for returning to read him again. If there are parallels and correlations between philosophy and ideology, it is the surplus that concerns me.

I would like to pursue three main topics, topics that for all my attempts to distinguish them are interwoven in Heidegger's texts: apocalypse, identity, and "application." I will conclude with some remarks about Derrida's *Of Spirit.*

Apocalypse

Despair was not just sickness of the soul in Germany in the 1930s; it was also social and economic depression. But for Heidegger, the malaise was deeper. The West was in decline—was, indeed, decline, *Abendland,* land of evening, of the setting sun. It was not only in Spengler that such a view could be found but also in Heidegger's teacher Husserl, who had described the "crisis in European science" as a crisis in the very continuation of the Western intellectual tradition. For Husserl, what was required was a new approach—transcendental phenomenology—which would return the sciences (including, of course, the human sciences) to their grounding phenomena. Signs of disconnection, loss of origin, were manifested by crises in mathematics and physics. Husserl's solution was a certain procedural displacement, the transcendental turn. Heidegger's version, however, was a kind of historical *apophansis* and repetition of origin.

His most obvious inspiration for this was in the poetry of Hölderlin, the poet of apocalypse:

> Hölderlin, in the act of establishing the essence of poetry, first determines a new time. It is the time of the gods that have fled and of the god that is coming. It is the time of need because it lies under a double lack and a double Not: the No-more of the gods that have fled and the Not-yet of the god that is coming. [The poet] holds his ground in the Nothing of this night. While the poet remains thus by himself in the supreme isolation of his mission, he fashions truth, vicariously and therefore truly, for his people.[2]

In fuller flower, Heidegger writes that:

> the spiritual decline of the earth is so far advanced that the nations are in danger of losing the last bit of spiritual energy that makes it possible to see the decline . . . and to appraise it as such. [This is not pessimism or optimism] for the darkening of the world, the transformation of men into a mass, the hatred and suspicion of everything free and creative [make] such childish categories . . . absurd.[3]

This sense of disintegration and the birth of something quite new is not, of course, unique to Heidegger (or Hölderlin). Hegel writes that "it is not difficult to see that ours is a birth-time and a period of transition to a new era" and envisages "a sunburst, which in one flash illuminates the features of the new world."[4] And Nietzsche writes of walking among men as among fragments of the future.[5]

Heidegger shares with Hegel and Nietzsche a deep commitment to a nonlinear temporality, to a level of understanding of time in which the circle is central. The implication, already present in *Being and Time*, section 6, and repeated many times, is that at one very important level, the new is always a productive revelation of the old.[6] But he gives different levels of reasons for the current need for renewal, the flight of the gods. Near the end of *An Introduction to Metaphysics*, he offers a logical reason: "Since it is a beginning, the beginning must in a sense leave itself behind" (*IM*, 160). He offers a fuller account when he writes:

> A beginning can never directly preserve its full momentum; the only possible way to preserve its force is to repeat, to draw once again (*Wiederholen*) more deeply than ever from its source. It is only by repetitive thinking that we can deal appropriately with the beginning and the breakdown of the truth. (*IM*, 160)

The implication is that this need does not arise from some avoidable human failure, but from necessity. Heidegger's claim, elaborated many times elsewhere, is that truth, freedom, authenticity, and science come into their own only in the light of an inaugural event, an event we must continually repeat in various ways. This account of *Wiederholung* appeared in *Being and Time*: "In repetition, fateful destiny can be disclosed explicitly as bound up with the heritage which has come down to us" (*BT*, 438), and it appeared directly in the Rectoral Address, where he is talking about the vocation of science:

> The beginning still is. It does not lie behind us, as something that was long ago, but stands before us. The beginning has invaded our future. There it awaits us, a distant command bidding us catch up with its greatness.[7]

These are sentences of extraordinary power. Heidegger is interweaving and condensing a whole series of moves and positions: that history is opened up by inaugural events, that the inauguration of our history can be recovered and repeated, and that there is some weight or force attached to this particular possibility. Heidegger's layering of time, in which the ontological can slide independently over the chronological, requires a full and separate treatment.[8] But there are difficulties with this retrieval model, which for the sake of economy, I shall simply enumerate.

1. The whole organization of receptivity, activity, submission, loyalty, self-examination, and so on, is modeled on an organization in which everyone knows their proper place, and in which there is a proper place for them to know. No account is even contemplated of the possible conflict of destinies. The regimented rhetoric and the programmatic discourse seems wholly self-defeating.

2. There is no awareness that the very idea of restoration by reversion to an origin might belong to a historically finite epoch, such as a tradition-oriented society.
3. Perhaps what needs repeating is inauguration itself—a new beginning —not some particular, lost inaugural event. (This will get addressed in GA 70, *Über den Anfang.*)
4. Heidegger seems determined to resolve the ineliminable force of memory—which cannot be denied—into the quest for an origin that would allow the memory to arrive, to find a resting place, an end.

Yet Heidegger is quite justified in tearing us away from the presupposition of linear progressive-regressive continuity. This has no absolute foundation, but is a constitutive feature of the everydayness of everyday life. By its very nature, everyday life either does not pose, or swiftly contains (and indeed exploits) the radically new, by aestheticization, commodification, and marketing. Moreover, the presumption of poets or philosophers that the imagination or description or opening of alternative futures might in itself be the slightest bit efficacious is increasingly a mark of folly. A version of Heidegger's position that is not wholly implausible is that the power of thinking and poetizing to enable radical transformation (except locally) is dimming in the face of the economic and technical management of the world. The question is whether this is a tragedy for us, for philosophy, and for the West; and if it is a tragedy, how long will tragedy last as a category with the power to move us?

An address not long ago by a president of Yale warned freshmen to be on their guard against the apocalyptic style, as he put it, diagnosing it as a mere symptom of weak hearts, of spiritual weariness. Should we be so wary? Kant warned against it[9]; Hegel warned against it.[10] Heidegger seems to embrace it. What should we do?

The problem with the apocalyptic style is that it claims an urgent priority over all else. Preparing for the end of the world or the beginning of a new one supersedes taking back one's library books. But an openness to the dimension of the apocalyptic is another matter, and it is one of Heidegger's virtues that he encourages this. Apocalypse can be understood in many ways. By "apocalypse," I mean revelation of the possibility of a dramatically transformed future in which what we know and understand will have come to an end. But there are two distinct versions of this, which I will call an apocalypse *in time* and one *of time*, that is, in history and of history. Levinas has claimed that Auschwitz meant the "End of Theodicy."[11] If theodicy is or was a historically constitutive a priori, then Auschwitz was, in some sense, an apocalyptic event announcing the absence, if not the death, of God for all to see. If Heidegger had been right about the linkage between Greek civilization, the West, Europe, Germany, and the possibilities opened up by the Nazi revolution, the failure of the Third Reich could also have been seen as apocalyptic. It would have been the extinction of a certain kind of life (as spirit). Marx's idea of a revolution being the beginning of history (that is, the history that humans make for themselves) would be another example of an apocalyptic transformation of historical time. The meaning of the Revelation of John would come into the same category. Heidegger keeps such possibilities open. The literal content of John's apocalypse—of plagues, foul malignant sores, every living thing in the sea dying, the sun burning people with its flames—are each the substance of urgent contemporary concern, a concern that complacent linear projections of the future would never reveal. It gives us another sense of apocalypse, one within history, or at least within time, to which we ought equally to be attuned![12]

Identity

Under the heading of "identity," I want to gather together the following concepts, which are deployed by Heidegger in a highly troubling way: authenticity, nation, nationality, Germania, community, fate, and destiny.

It is one of the lasting achievements of Heidegger's work to have *articulated* the self, to have taken it outside itself. To the Cartesian conception of the self as substance—something that needs nothing to be itself—he opposed, in *Being and Time,* a being essentially constituted by being-in-the-world, being-with-others, and a projectively temporal relation to its own possibilities—in the last analysis, that of death. Authenticity is initially defined as a modification of everydayness. For the most part, "The Self is lost in *das Man,* the they. It understands itself in terms of those possibilities of existence which 'circulate' in the 'average' public way of interpreting Dasein today" (*BT,* 167). Raised up out of this limitation by the voice of conscience, Dasein confronts its ownmost possibility, as he puts it, in its appropriation of its own death. Prima facie, this sounds like another form of self-containment, but our thrownness, the dimension of our existence into which we are thrown and do not choose, supplies us with a heritage, determinate possibilities, and, eventually, a fate. This grasp of "the finitude of existence snatches one back from the endless multiplicity of possibilities which offer themselves as closest to one—those of comfortableness, shirking, and taking things lightly—and brings Dasein into the simplicity of its fate [*Schicksals*]" (*BT,* 435). The next and final stages draw on my essential being-with-others to argue that my fate is bound up with the destiny of a whole community, a people (*des Volkes*). "Our fates have already been guided in ad-

vance, in our being with one another in the same world and in our resoluteness for definite possibilities" (*BT*, 435).

The language in *Being and Time* is seamlessly continuous with that of
his many speeches in the winter of 1933–34. In *Being and Time,* he had
said that Dasein had the choice whether to authentically choose and win
itself or whether instead to lose itself (*BT,* §9). On November 10, 1933,
he says that (in a plebiscite on withdrawing from the League of Nations)
the Fuhrer "is giving the people the possibility of making . . . the highest
free decision of all: whether it—the entire people—wants its own existence [*Dasein*] or whether it does *not* want it."[13] Heidegger goes on to
argue that this is not turning away from the community of nations;
rather, what is being expressed "is only the clear will to unconditional
self-responsibility in enduring and mastering the fate of our people."
"Such a will," he continues, "allows peoples and states to stand by one
another in an open and manly [*mannhafte*] fashion as self-reliant entities
[*Aufsich-und-Zueinanderstehen*]."

In the Rectoral Address, structured, of course, by the question of identity in the form of self-assertion, self-governance, and self-examination,
Heidegger draws the university into the web of will and fate:

> The will to the essence of the German University is the will to science as will
> to the historical mission of the German people as a people that knows itself
> in its state. (*SA*, 471)

That mission, of course, is to "submit to the distant command of the
beginning of our spiritual-historical being [Dasein]," namely, the space
opened up by Greek philosophy (*SA*, 477).

What is so extraordinary about Heidegger's rhetoric here is its density
of articulation. What he is offering us is a tightly closed network of
interlocking dependencies. It is as if the explosive dehiscence of substantialist identity has to be contained at all costs by a web of necessities that
would equally and effectively eliminate chance, accident, complexity,
multiplicity, and options. Each of these themes would reward further
thought, but I would like to pursue two briefly here: dependence (receptivity, submission), and destiny.

The theme of dependence derives immediately from Heidegger's own
discussion of the mediaeval concept of substance, attributed to Descartes, which distinguishes between independent being (God) and dependent but relatively independent being (man). For it is a structure that
Heidegger has himself taken over. My fully authentic historicality rests
on my submission to the will of a community, embodied in a leader.
My identity is articulated in a fate that comes into its own in a common destiny. This way of understanding the fulfillment of self-identity
through submission to a higher being is found equally in Hegel and
Kierkegaard (not to mention most religions). But is it not too much a

piece of residual metaphysics for Heidegger to lean so heavily on it? Kierkegaard, whom Heidegger had read carefully, had argued that the self was not self-constituted, but rather was constituted by another. (Otherwise, he claimed, despair would always be suicidal.) That other he called a "power."[14] In fact, Kierkegaard's argument shows at best that the belief in such a power is a prerequisite for certain moods common in the West. Heidegger's argument also seems driven by the necessity of arriving at a certain conclusion.

The appearance of fate (*Schicksal*) in *Being and Time* and its articulation with destiny (*Geschick*) entirely assumes the legitimacy of these terms and takes its task to be that of their proper explication. The chain along which we are driven—from resoluteness, to thrownness, to fate, to being-with-others, to community, to destiny, and ultimately (in the case of Schlageter), to a hero's death, and to martyrdom—knows no end but self-surrender: identity through identification. In the absence of a higher being, Heidegger offers us, in different aspects, the West, Germany, or Hitler.[15] There is nothing enormously unusual or original about this. It is the common stock of nationalistic and militaristic rhetoric. The question I would ask is: Is there a point at which the chain could have been stopped? Or is there something wrong with Heidegger's starting point?

Heidegger's radical dehiscence of selfhood is the right move when confronted with self-sufficient substance as the metaphysical standard. I agree that between finite ecstatic temporal projection and historical thrownness a dimension is opened up in which selfhood can be articulated. I also agree that being-with-others is constitutive for the self. But the march of explication disguised as argument that takes us through fate, to community, to destiny, to nation, to Germany, and so on is hard to distinguish from the ideology of social mobilization, governed at every stage by the exclusion of dissent, difference, and doubt: the reduction of the many to the one. The concept of dependence with which I began could be articulated differently, as Levinas, for example, has shown us![16] I have already touched on the question of destiny, and, to be dealt with properly, it would have to be linked with Heidegger's account of the *Seinsgeschick*, the destiny or sending of being. The connection with the question of identity, which is what makes destiny such a crucial concept in all the writings of this period, is through the idea of an inaugural beginning in the fulfillment or repetition of which our destiny, our being, lies.

The reason, perhaps, for the extraordinary absence of hesitation, doubt, or debate here is that for Heidegger, destiny is constitutive of a people, of a nation. To question either the legitimacy of the term itself or what it might deliver to us would be close to sabotage, and indeed, to misunderstand the essence of questioning. It would be a mistake, however, to cease to think about destiny and about the return to origin, even if the legitimating power of this move has diminished, and for a reason parallel to my claim about being-with-others. For the terminus of each drive for closure—such as the nation or people or state (for being-with-others) and the originary event (for destiny)—would, if it did not exist, have had to be invented. Each is essentially imaginary, but not without consequences, often catastrophic. The truth concealed by the quest for a repeatable origin lies in the inescapable centrality of memory, the power of names (such as Germany), and the demands of narrative. The issue of memory became increasingly important for both Derrida and Habermas, and in the particular instance of remembering, not forgetting, the victims of the Holocaust. Habermas's account of the problems of reconstituting a German identity that could "take account of" the death camps would offer a salutary alternative to the language of destiny were it not for the fact that living with Auschwitz seems almost to require that very language.[17]

Application

The third topic I would like to focus on is "application," which I use problematically, and inside scare quotes. The simplest form of the question I want to pursue here is this: What does Heidegger's application of his philosophy in his Rectoral Address and in his speeches in 1933–34 tell us about that philosophy? What lessons, if any, does it hold for philosophy in general?

I want to argue that even if we accept, as I do, what I have called the "seamless continuity" between Heidegger's philosophy both before and after 1933–34, and his often repellent political lectures and speeches, we should not abandon Heidegger's thinking. Tom Sheehan said we should not stop reading him, but start demythologizing.[18] Philippe Lacoue-Labarthe says we can no longer read his philosophy without remembering his political involvements.[19] Neither is suggesting we should read him out of a sense of duty, or simply as a lesson in philosophical error or evil. Why should we keep reading Heidegger?

It could be argued that a philosopher whose work could serve a tyrant or oppressor is a bad philosopher, either in a moral sense for not anticipating that application, or for failing to realize the emancipatory point of philosophy. Before Heidegger, the classic targets for some such claim were Plato, Hegel, and Nietzsche. The difficulty with using this as a standard for condemning philosophers is, first, that there are a great many other philosophies and philosophers that could give succor to totalitarianism, even those most obviously opposed to it (such as Marx);

and second, that this particular trio are far too valuable to lose. But Heidegger's case, it will be said, is different. Hitler's applications of Nietzsche are one thing; Heidegger's politicizing of his own thought is quite another. The moral argument may trail away when he responds that he had not at the time grasped what Hitler was up to. But the argument about the value of his thinking remains.

We are dismayed, I believe, not only by the content of Heidegger's speeches but also by their rhetorical status. He was not making suggestions that could be laughed out of court or discussed rationally. In the Rectoral Address, he was in effect announcing dramatic changes in the way the university would be organized and how, in the future, its values would be set. Even where he is providing ideological justification, the discourse is constructed so as to admit no alternative position. Everything either is, or must be, necessary. The language is one of obedience, loyalty, and strength. I am sure there were no questions after the lecture. This translation of the rhetorical dimension of philosophical discourse from one in which attendance is free and acceptance optional to that of programmatic ideology is a vital part of our judgment. The temptation of playing philosopher-king (or even the king's philosopher) is hard to resist. But the reasons for resisting it can be found in Heidegger's own work in what he says about "action" and "doing." Heidegger writes:

> [T]he constant decision between the will to greatness and a letting things happen that means decline will be the law presiding over the march that our people has begun into its future history. (*SA*, 475)

Heidegger is not only himself *acting*, he is inciting others to act too. But between neutral descriptions of resoluteness within the framework of an existential analytic (in *Being and Time*) and the incitement to others to decide in certain highly specific ways there is a huge gulf. One of the strengths of *Being and Time* was its constant vigilance in discouraging anthropological, metaphysical, and ethical interpretations. *Being and Time* is valuable precisely as a work that preserves itself against reductive readings. The Rectoral Address (and I shall return to the case of "Spirit") seems to throw caution and precaution to the wind. The language may not be new, but the immediacy of its application is. How could this happen?

One possible answer might be this: Heidegger's account of resoluteness and authentic historicality in *Being and Time* is not, as I understand it, explicitly applied to philosophizing. And given that it rests on what is offered as a descriptive existential analytic, grounded independently of such historically specific resoluteness, it is important that it not be so applied to itself. But the danger of such a reflexive application (the resolute assertion of resoluteness) was not immediately apparent. This would offer a way of filling out David Krell's claim that Heidegger's political involvement was, precisely, a failure of thinking—a failure, that is, in his own terms.[20]

When we look at some of his subsequent statements about the scope of philosophy, about the activity of thinking, it looks as though Heidegger came to the same conclusion. Quite apart from their loathsome plans for the Final Solution, the Nazis had the most complex and detailed blueprints for the total restructuring of the German state. Heidegger actively pursued similar ambitions within the university system. But a willful imposition of a blueprint is closer to technology than to any account of the task of the philosopher that Heidegger has offered us. When Heidegger talks about that task—the task of thinking—it is always in terms of preparation without prediction. Thirty years later, in "The End of Philosophy and the Task of Thinking" (written in 1964),[21] having long since worked through the latent metaphysics of Nietzsche's will-to-power, Heidegger explicitly describes his trajectory as that of having "attempted again and again since 1930 to shape the question of *Being and Time* in a more primal way" (*OTB,* 55). Philosophy is at an end in the sense that it is "gathered into its most extreme possibility" (*OTB,* 57). And at the end of philosophy, there remains the possibility of thinking, which is weaker than philosophy, precisely in that "the direct or indirect effect of this thinking on the public in the industrial age, formed by technology and science, is decisively less possible for this thinking than it was for philosophy" (*OTB,* 60). He describes it as preparatory—"content with awakening a readiness in man for a possibility whose contour remains obscure, whose coming remains uncertain . . . a thinking that does not wish and is not able to predict the future" (*OTB,* 60).

Two years later, much the same claim was central to his *Der Spiegel* interview. Any direct efficacy that philosophy had is now exercised through cybernetics. Philosophy has to give way to thinking in order for the essence of technicity to be addressed. Even that essence, he says, is nothing technological, not just to do with causal efficacy, but rather a *Gestell,* a presumptive enframing of the world for man. As was already apparent in *Contributions to Philosophy* (1936–38), the language would all be about preparation, about awakening a readiness, a limitation that affects not only philosophy but also, as he puts it, all human endeavor. It is at this point that he says, "Only a god can save us." Heidegger's *What Is Called Thinking?* from the previous decade elaborates a similar theme. Philosophical action, what I have called "application," is not appropriate to the task at hand—that of maintaining an openness to the possibility of a new beginning. This is an argument against Heidegger's own Nazi entanglements and, indeed, any other attempts at implementing philosophy.

Spirit

Finally, I want to say something about an extraordinary book, Derrida's *Of Spirit*, which has haunted, by its absence, this whole discussion.[22] Derrida attempts to think through four of the most perplexing issues in Heidegger (the privilege of the question, the essence of technology, animality, and the epochality of being) by linking them all to Heidegger's deployment of "Spirit" (*Geist, Geistig, Geistlich*) in the period from *Being and Time* through to his 1953 discussion of Trakl in "Language in the Poem."[23]

Each of these four points of hesitation are sites of difficulty for Heidegger, too—in particular, the difficulty of thinking them through without falling back into metaphysics. Is questioning fundamental, or does it not already respond to something given? How can animality be thought after Dasein has been scoured of any anthropologism? How can we still talk of "essence" in the essence of technology? Is not the epochality of being residually teleological? In each case, Derrida finds Spirit lurking— or I should say *Geist*, for it is its Germanness that Heidegger emphasizes. From *Being and Time*, so the story goes, through to the Trakl essay, Heidegger attempts to retrieve *Geist* from its Christian significance (linked to breath), and finally, he finds in Trakl's association of Spirit with flame a more original sense, one that gives the German language the privilege of being able to name what Greek only embodied.

Hegel understood Spirit to be essentially embodied in the power of negation to supersede everything that had become merely positive. In this sense, Spirit is essentially critical, destructive. For Hegel, Spirit *falls into* world time. Heidegger, however, tries to think Spirit through a more original understanding of time, one that would announce or promise the dawn, or be an originary event (as in *Ereignis*), and as Derrida says, tries to find in Trakl's poetry a way of returning to a point outside, prior to the Christian tradition.[24]

What Derrida's account does is to provide something of a setting within which to read Heidegger's Rectoral Address and *Introduction to Metaphysics*. For a considerable part of the shock we get from reading these texts results from Heidegger's deployment of *Geist* (Spirit), a term that lived in *Being and Time* only in quotation marks or in lists of equally metaphysical terms that Heidegger was systematically avoiding. But in the penultimate section of *Being and Time*, Heidegger undertakes an analysis of Hegel's concept of time, which inevitably raises its relation to Spirit. Heidegger's basic move is not so much to deny that Spirit falls into time as to translate or interpret this claim in his own terms, namely, as a movement from an original primordial temporalization into something like historical time. With only two more pages in the book to go, Heidegger writes: "Spirit exists as the primordial temporalizing of temporality." For some reason, Derrida quotes this and then glosses away the "exists as" as an "is." But in doing so, Derrida misses the force of Heidegger's precise formulation. The claim that Spirit exists as the primordial temporalizing of temporality is a license to deploy the term, not, as Derrida suggests, barely giving it shelter. And there are deeper reasons for this, reasons that would take us back to the question of "application," of the enactment of philosophy. What is at stake here, I believe, is the possibility of the primordial temporalizing of temporality becoming historically actual, or reactivated, in time. Hitler was no messiah, it turns out, but he certainly claimed to lead Germans to the promised land.

I want now to make a suggestion not inconsistent with the drift of Derrida's final (imaginary) conversation between Heidegger and certain Christian theologians. Heidegger discusses Greek, Latin, and German words for Spirit in conjunction with the quest for an originary sense. He does not mention the Hebrew *ruah,* which, as a candidate for a pre-Christian term, would surely rate a mention. We might conclude that Heidegger is simply blind to the Jewish tradition (and again, comparisons with Hegel would be valuable here). I want to quote an extraordinary passage in *Being and Time.* Heidegger is quoting Count Yorck, who is talking about the spirit of history:

> This spirit is one who did not appear to Faust in his study, or to Master Goethe either. But they would have felt no alarm in making way for him, however grave and compelling such an apparition might be. For he is brotherly, akin to us in another and deeper sense than are the denizens of bush and field. These exertions [soliloquizing and communing with the spirit of history] are like Jacob's wrestling—a sure gain for the wrestler himself. (*BT,* 453)

Ghost, spirit, brotherhood, animality, history—it is all there. But there is more. Jacob, we might recall, wrestled with a man until daybreak, at which point the man touched his thigh and asked to be released. Jacob insisted on being blessed first, and the man blessed him by changing Jacob's name to Israel, but would not give his own name and departed a stranger (Genesis 31). Lost in this quotation from Yorck is an attempt to illuminate the spirit of history by reference to what for Jacob offered precisely what Derrida has called the promise of an event: God's blessing to Jacob, the promise of Israel.

Could we ever seriously conclude that Heidegger's obsession with Germany blinded him to the true source of a pre-Christian spirituality, namely, the Judaic tradition? This is neither the point of my elaboration here, nor, as I understand it, Derrida's. Nonetheless, there are serious questions to be asked about any attempt to privilege a particular construction of the tradition, our tradition, as one whose origin we must probe. If, as Heidegger himself claims, every beginning is already, and as such, a decline from the point of view of spiritual renewal, it is the event of inauguration itself that is valuable and not the return to some particular origin. The return to an origin is, after all, a tacit assertion of the unity of tradition, hence the occlusion and suppression of the Babel of voices that actually constitutes any of our pasts. And if that is so, philosophical nationalism should properly elicit our keenest vigilance and suspicion. I would suggest that we favor those traditions that recognize otherness, and that, in our reading of Heidegger, we fasten onto those many instances in which such an opening can be made.

9

Following Derrida

As you will soon gather, the words that follow are not devoted to the communication of information.* Rather, I am offering you something, I am opening myself up, I am risking myself, I am inviting you to follow me. I make no particular promises—to please, inform, stimulate, amuse—though there is always some hope of this. And I do not promise not to lead you astray, not to make feints. But I do not want you to have to listen out of courtesy. I would like to engage you, to have already engaged you.[1]

But perhaps I have already let you anticipate too much. For now you will have already concluded that I am discussing the "ethics of communication." And my sensitivity to my position as speaker will mark me out as one who still harbors illusions of presence, of self-presence, of the presence of the writer to the reader. Have I not learned the fundamental impersonality of speaking, of writing, of the production of signs? Are these very words not just another twitch, a final writhing in the last moments of the dying author?

Consider, I see myself writing, the multiplicity of contexts in which these words are being produced. Allow me this already oversimple schematization: (1) I am, "here and now," my ginger cat purring at my feet, in England, writing these words, reading them as I write them, monitoring them, thinking they *might* receive the right uptake. (2) I am, "here and now" (still in England), imagining an audience listening to

* This chapter was originally a paper delivered to a Derrida conference at Loyola University in Chicago, in the presence of Jacques Derrida (1930–2004). It is here dedicated to his memory.

my uttering these words at a later date—indeed, an audience whose composition, in all sincerity, I could improve on only by acquiring the power of resurrection. (I would begin with philosophers whose names began with H.) (3) I anticipate that these words may be printed, published, distributed, and read, perhaps by people as yet unborn, and after my own death. Indeed, it may be that between the (English) now of writing, and the (American) now of reading/speaking to you, I will have passed away. It may be that one of my friends, or perhaps a stranger will be reading out these words. And then you will be thinking: How uncanny that he should have anticipated his own death! And how much pathos there is in these last words. And how disconcerting that we cannot reply to them, or ask for more, for elucidations. (4) And now that I am actually here, again, in Chicago, I can add a fourth: I am, here and now, reading this paper to you, speaking to you, in Chicago.

But it may be that you are not listening to me in Chicago, but reading me in Tokyo, perhaps even in "translation." This page (or that page) may have fallen from the wrapping round a fragile porcelain figure that has just arrived in the post. Do you not marvel at my prescience, dear reader? And you, my living audience, supposing I have made it to Chicago, do you feel neglected when I address the reader? Or do you believe that subtly I am actually addressing you, that I am reminding you of these possibilities?

Can you be so sure? I have said that at one level I am writing for an imagined (anticipated) audience, one that is (or would be) historically momentous. But the last time I spoke in America at a conference like this, Eugenio Donato was listening. Indeed, I spoke about him, to him. And the time before that, Paul de Man was flourishing. Two great lights have since gone out, and each man's death diminishes me. People I imagine being here may no longer be anywhere. I can only guess the names of the ears my noise will be trickling into.

Clearly, too, whomever this is being written for, and even read or spoken to, it may yet be *addressed* to a quite different ear. To history? To postmodernity? To Rosemary? To the Other? Perhaps to Derrida "himself."

Suppose then, after all this, that the charges are dropped, and I am no longer viewed as a naïve reinscriber of the metaphysical value of "presence"? How then does the fragility of my beginning even begin to make sense? How can I be *offering* you something, *risking myself, opening out, inviting* you to follow me, when "you" are so radically put in question? But the issue is far more serious even than this. Surely, I have begun with what is essentially a kind of plagiarism, a purloined strategy. And whether I admitted this, or invoked in my defense the metaphysical status of the idea of intellectual property that it involved, the consequence would be the same—that the "I" who could *offer, invite, open out, risk* . . . itself becomes a fiction. Sartre, apropos of *Being and Nothingness,* once wrote that *Angst* was not something he had ever felt, but that it was a fashionable topic of conversation in Paris in the early 1940s. Perhaps "risk" and "danger" are similarly just rhetorically intensifying. *Who* is at risk? And what danger can there be in these mere echoes of others' intrepid steps?

Let us say this: what is at stake—perhaps in all words addressed to a living audience—is what I shall call the *residual* question of the presence of the speaker, and of the act of speaking. Words are addressed, a paper is delivered, and everywhere we hear the workings of desire. These words are an invitation to an impossible event.

How friendly, you may say. The ball is in your court. You can say yes, no, maybe. Of course, it is not that simple. I have not explained what the impossible event is. You do not know what you are being invited to. How can you say yes or no? Etymology confirms these suspicions: invite → *invito* (from the Sanskrit *vak-speak; vak'as-word;* compare *vox.* . . .). And the *Oxford English Dictionary* offers us many senses. To treat, feast, entertain. But also to summon, to challenge. And even to incite, attract, allure to transgression.

In issuing such a problematic invitation, I am, as I see it, following Derrida. I will pursue such a suggestion by explaining one or two ways in which invitation moves from openness to seduction and to a crisis of reading.

Let me take first a simple example, drawn from "Le retrait de la metaphore."[2] This essay begins with a discussion of metaphor that becomes aware that it itself takes place in metaphor. The author comes to the conclusion that he cannot talk *about* metaphor without, as he puts it, "negotiating with it the loan I take from it in order to speak of it." On at least three occasions Derrida asks himself, or tells himself, or talks to the reader about the necessary drifting or skidding of his writing about metaphor. Trying to prevent metaphor from creeping into his discussion of metaphor (which plays with transportation, vehicles, pilots in ships, etc.) is futile. Skidding, sliding, drifting are unavoidable.

How should the critical reader respond to this? Derrida is not just indulging himself, but inciting himself to pursue every piece of slippage he comes across. What is meant to be a feature of language in general actually appears here only as a very willful, deliberate act of writing. Derrida doesn't begin to try to control metaphor. He claims he cannot control language, but in fact, he is all the time in control—writing *about* metaphor precisely as he does, writing *about* slippage, and so forth. What is the reader to do? Are we to pretend that Derrida is just unable to control himself? Or what? The beginning, in other words, is a charade, a play, a ploy—one that seeks our generous assent. The reader must accept that the horse *necessarily* runs away with the charioteer.

There are two points I am not disputing: (1) that discussions of metaphor are, indeed, often remarkably unaware of their own metaphors (Searle's paper on metaphor is a case in point),[3] and (2) that the distinction between the literal and the metaphorical may indeed be systematically elusive. But for the reader to follow, that is to accept, to "go along with" these moves, he or she has to accept the pretence, the gambit, that Derrida's horse, and our horse, has always already bolted. This requires an elision of what is true of language itself and the special characteristics of a particular, highly calculating use of language. Derrida is surely *playing victim*, like those bandits who pretend to be involved in a road accident and whose lifeless bodies spring up when the honest citizen stops.

My second case has more important implications. It concerns the broader question of strategy and seduction.[4] We could put it like this: What is involved in acquiescing, going along with Derrida's deconstructive maneuvers? I want to argue that the critical reader reaches a point of crisis in reading Derrida at which a decision both has to be and cannot be made. If for some, the question of *choice* does not arise, for the critical reader, it must. My question will be—what is it for the critical reader *to follow* Derrida?

Without wishing to privilege this early but seminal paper too much, consider some of the claims made for difference in the original "*Différance*" paper.[5] Using the language of transcendental causation (but persistently refusing its metaphysical implications), Derrida substitutes difference in place of any presence or origin of meaning. *Différance*, in which is condensed both deferment and differentiation, is what "produces" the mundane differences we encounter everyday. This term can be said to draw together the various powerful senses of difference generated by a whole range of thinkers—Saussure, Freud, Nietzsche, Heidegger, Levinas. Derrida writes:

> One comes to posit presence . . . no longer as the absolutely central form of Being but as a "determination" and as an "effect" within a system which is no longer that of presence but of "difference," a system that no longer tolerates the opposition between activity and passivity, nor that of cause and effect, or of indetermination and determination, etc., such that in designating consciousness as an effect or a determination, one continues for strategic reasons that can be more or less lucidly deliberated, and systematically calculated—to operate according to the lexicon of that which one is delimiting.[6]

The fundamental reason for this is that metaphysical thinking and ordinary language are inseparable and that it is just not possible to operate on philosophy "from the outside"; there is no such "outside." When Derrida introduces the term *différance* and begins to give it work to do (it "constitutes" or "produces" any code as a system of differences), he is very careful to repeatedly remind us that transcendental language is just provisional and inadequate. Its employment is merely strategic. *Différance* cannot be thought on the basis of old metaphysical oppositions, "which," he writes, "makes the thinking of it uneasy and uncomfortable."

With these words, Derrida simultaneously acknowledges our difficulty and disarms it of any critical force. Let us try to reopen the place of difficulty. First we notice Derrida's deferment to Saussure, to whom so much modern thought is indebted. There is no attempt to evaluate this model of language. Instead, he offers us a kind of deepening of the principle of difference on which it rests. As an antidote to a phenomenological account of language, the force of this is clear. But to those of us who had also struggled with another tradition—with analytical philosophy, with ordinary language philosophy, who had followed Wittgenstein and Austin, this way of setting out seemed (and still seems) in need of justification. Let us put this to one side, however, for the central difficulty lies elsewhere.

I think we are offered two options: (a) We are asked to understand, or at least to acquiesce in, sentences involving the words *produce, constitute, possibility, effect,* without our being allowed to attribute to any of these terms either ordinary or philosophical significance. But if we had this ability to bracket out metaphysical implications, Derrida's position would be both far easier and far more difficult. It would be easier in that he could then exploit this ability of ours without question; it would be more difficult in that it would suggest that his whole program of reading/writing rested on certain powers of abstinence that look remarkably like a transcription of Husserl's *epoché.* (b) We can understand these words in the old metaphysical way, but only for the time being. We are given warning that this grasp will soon be taken away from us. How we follow these instructions is surely doubly problematic. It is bad enough being asked to walk out on a branch that one knows is about to break. But the whole strategy rests on our actually crediting such terms as difference with a power to displace the foundational language of metaphysics, a power that they plainly do not have unless such terms as *produce, constitutes,* and so on, are understood out of erasure.

The key word in the early pages of the *"Différance"* essay is *repartons* ("Let us go on"). Is this an exhortation? A command? A request? An invitation? Who are *we*? Is Derrida addressing all his readers or only those who are still with him?

There are undoubtedly many responses to this. Let me suggest three. (1) It might be said that there is nothing special about this situation. Reading is always, or should always be, an active, participatory affair. It is never possible to eliminate the reader's role. The occasions on which it seems to have happened are simply those in which the moves required conform to the reader's preexisting prejudices. (2) There is a certain special insight and adventurousness required of the reader. The sedentary thinker will indeed be left behind. We have here a *selective* strategy, a book for the few, an esoteric text. If you bet nothing, you win nothing. He who dares wins. (3) Finally, it could be said that our worries would disappear if a certain consequentialism were allowed to displace our foundational prejudices. We have nothing to lose by seeing where it all leads; we can judge the path later.

I will not attempt to judge this matter now. What I will say, briefly, is that not for the first time (for one can make the same remarks about Hegel, about Nietzsche, about Husserl, about Levinas, about Heidegger . . . and it is important that one can) Derrida opens up, within the framework of reading, albeit without thematizing it just here, the whole space of the relation to the Other, of the writer to the reader. And this relation is posed as one of necessary risk.

The status Derrida attributes to the Other seems to us fundamentally problematic. In his essay "Signature Event Context,"[7] it is the absence of the Other, perhaps even the Other's absolute absence, that is the necessary condition for the legibility of writing. What he does not mention here (we would perhaps be repaid by a closer look at his readings of Levinas and Blanchot)[8] is the role the Other might play in the pathos of writing. In this respect, the writing we call philosophical, metaphysical, and even postmetaphysical or deconstructive may have everything to do with the Other.

To help us pursue this possibility, I would first like to draw into our text a poem by Archibald Macleish that, somewhat tentatively, I shall employ as a kind of grid.

VOYAGE WEST

There was a time for discoveries —
For the headlands looming above in the
First light and the surf and the
Crying of gulls: for the curve of the
Coast north into secrecy.

That time is past.
The last lands have been peopled.
The oceans are known now.

Senora: once the maps have all been made
A man were better dead than find new continents.
A man would better never have been born
Than find upon the open ocean flowers
Drifted from islands where there are no islands,

Or midnight, out of sight of any land,
Smell on the altering air the odor of rosemary.

No fortune passes that misfortune —

To lift along the evening of the sky,
Certain as sun and sea, a new-found land

Steep from an ocean where no landfall can be.[9]

Would it be wholly anachronistic to read in these lines an anticipatory commentary on the promise of deconstruction? Deconstruction has presented itself as the only solution to a historically determined situation that can briefly be termed the closure of philosophy. It has heralded the possibility of a new kind of writing, one that neither makes a radical break nor merely works from the inside, but one that weaves together both strategies. And, what is crucial, one that refuses to understand itself as relating to philosophy as a "negation" in a way that would allow it to be merely absorbed in a dialectic of history. Deconstruction claims, in this sense, to mark an absolute difference, not to be recuperable! But suppose this were merely the dream of a new dawn, of a new beginning?

In this poem, Macleish is warning against the tragedy of false hope. Is deconstruction perhaps just a "smell on the altering air," "flowers drifted from islands where there are no islands"? Or is it not precisely an affirmation of ocean without nostalgia for new islands? Does deconstruction offer a way for philosophy to carry on, to survive, or does it simply strew flowers on philosophy's watery grave?

The reading underlying such exorbitant questions is not without its difficulties. I merely note that the reader sensitive to deconstructive maneuvers could easily refocus the question away from the smell (the odor of rosemary) and onto the "altering air," away from the flowers to their drifting. And the question about whether deconstruction offers a way for philosophy to carry on leaves open the issue of whether one actually accepts its diagnosis of philosophy.

Unless we read this whole poem ironically (and I shall leave this problem unexplored), Macleish is operating with a fairly clear distinction between truth and illusion, innocent adventure and tragic mirage. We are warned against the flowers that drift from "islands where there are no islands." This formulation is not the affirmation of a paradoxical supplementation of origin (as in "trace which is not a trace of anything" [Derrida]). The "islands where there are no islands" are illusions we should steer clear of.

When Heidegger reads poetry, he often picks out those poems and poets for which what is in question is *language,* its limits and productive possibilities, poems that are reflexive, and perhaps performative. One thinks of his account (in "The Nature of Language") of Stefan George's "The Word" (1919). Not only does Macleish not do this here, but he seems even to ignore language's own possibilities. For one way in which the distinction between truth and illusion, between real and apparent islands can surely be made problematic, is through language. The term *fiction* is perhaps a perfect condensation of such ambivalence. Fiction is both negative, that is, error, false, and also productive, creative, even suggesting a certain coherence. What Macleish does not ask himself is whether language itself can supply new horizons, new islands. We have, as it happens, already anticipated a negative answer to this. The account Nietzsche gives of the closure of metaphysics (*Beyond Good and Evil*, §20) is cast precisely in terms of a "prison-house of language" thesis. Nonetheless, it has been the belief of a whole string of philosophers (Nietzsche, Heidegger, Levinas, Bataille, etc.)—who have even risked their labels in pursuing it—that by a change of style, by a changed relation to language, or some such move, something new can be allowed to happen.

Allow me, for a few minutes, a diversion. In the early days of April 1978, I learned at the ordinary, empirical level a truth to which Derrida's meditations on the uncertainties of the postal services (on the possibility of messages not getting through, letters not being delivered, communicative intentions not being realized) only later gave theoretical significance.

I tore out of my daily newspaper a three- or four-page Supplement, carefully folded it up, slid it into a brown envelope, addressed it to Jacques Derrida at the Ecole Normale, and popped it into the letter box. Thinking he might be in America, I added *Please Forward* on the outside, even adding a French translation. Well, it never arrived. I conjectured that it had indeed been forwarded to other continents and then sent on again, following Derrida around the globe until it attained sufficient momentum to be able to circulate freely within the international postal system long after its address had been effaced by the wear and tear of its travels. There, perhaps, it continues to this day, without origin or *telos*, a graphic illustration of the errance of writing.

But the answer to its nonarrival may be found in its content. You must all have seen prominently displayed at least in most American airports a large sign proclaiming that "Security is no joking matter." It cautions against answering the questions of security staff in anything other than a totally serious manner. (If when asked whether you have a weapon, you reply that you have a fully armed Sherman tank in your bag, they will search to find it.) This is not the place, perhaps, to amplify on the theoretical connections between the general concept of security and that of seriousness. I merely offer you this sign in a lighthearted way to suggest an explanation for the nonarrival of my little folded bundle. It was intercepted by the seriousness police.

Suppose it had been received, carefully slit open, and unfolded—
what would the addressee have discovered? What was this Supplement
to a newspaper called *The Guardian*? It had caused a considerable stir
in England. Many people had written in requesting travel brochures,
people who thought they had found a new place to go on holiday. In
fact, as they discovered, it was language that had gone on holiday. The
Supplement was devoted to a political/cultural/economic/geographical
profile of the islands of San Seriffe, with its golden sands; happy, fun-
loving people; and benign military dictatorship. A great deal could be
said about San Seriffe. Indeed, one could say almost anything about it.
To forestall those readers who would seek it out on their maps, it was
explained that the island, formed out of light volcanic rock, had somewhat unusually cracked free from the seabed and now drifted over the
oceans of the world, a floating paradise.

But let us stop this drifting and be serious for a minute. San Seriffe is
a fiction, the veritable incarnation of the floating signifier. Its very name
testifies to its status as a (typo)graphical construction. San Seriffe is
surely an "island where there are no islands," and I am certain that boats
visiting its bustling harbor would often cleave waters strewn with flowers. Macleish, on our reading, was offering us a choice between the res-
ignation of closure and false hopes. Does not the magical island of San
Seriffe show that it is precisely through language or through some ref-
ormation or deformation of language that a third way might be charted?
And is it not deconstruction's path to offer us a third way—neither more
of the same, nor simple otherness, but some interweaving of the two?

We shall return to this poem, but first, another diversion. I would like
to offer a brief note to a footnote to *The Postcard*.[10] On August 22, 1979,
Derrida, in the middle of typing a letter that had mentioned the names
Freud and Heidegger (in that order), received a collect call from the
United States. He writes: "The American operator asks me if I will accept
a 'collect call' from Martin (she says Martine or martini) Heidegger."
Derrida refused the call, saying "It's a joke, I do not accept."

It so happens that open on my desk while I was reading this footnote was Derrida's *Margins of Philosophy*, containing a paper to which I
have already referred—"Signature Event Context," a paper I had heard
"live" some ten years earlier in Montreal. And as chance would have it
again, the book was open at the page on which Derrida was diagnosing
Austin's exclusion, at the beginning of *How to Do Things with Words*, of
"along with what he calls the sea-changes,[11] the nonserious, the para-
sitic, the etiolations." Derrida wonders whether the possibility of language falling into nonseriousness is the possibility of its failure, or an
essential possibility. Might not this risk be its "internal and positive condition of possibility," he asks, "[might] this outside [be] its inside"? And
so on.

When I read "It's a joke, I do not accept," my reaction was strange. The words immediately fragmented into a matrix and reformed themselves into different patterns: "It's no joke, I accept"; "It's no joke, I do not accept," "It's a joke, I accept." The law that favored "It's a joke, I do not accept" was the law of exclusion, of refusal. No expenditure without reserve here. In fact, Derrida even profits from it, in the shape of an interesting question ("Who should pay, the caller or the called . . . a very difficult question") even as he pretends that the footnote itself is a note of thanks, a kind of payment. But let's be serious! Suppose that we respond to the call seriously, what then?

Derrida *refused* the call. We have to ask what was actually refused. Was it (1) the possibility that Heidegger might have made a radical break with the way of life of Black Forest peasants, abandoned the provinces for that radically deracinated and deracinating world we call America? (2) the possibility that Heidegger might have survived death, or Derrida's treatment of him? (3) the possibility that Heidegger was a woman? We take especial delight in the way in which Derrida openly suppresses this possibility (*"un 'collect call', de la part de Martin [elle dit Martine ou martini] Heidegger"*).

And what, we might ask, was the nature of the call? We may think that because the call was refused we will never know. But we can ask whether this refusal did not involve a certain recognition. Consider, just for a moment, *what calls?* In connection with Heidegger, we would recall two possibilities: the call of Being, and the call of conscience. Derrida's refusal of either would be understandable. But let us not forget that the call was beyond the grave, for Heidegger had, by this time, passed on. His time had already come. Perhaps, then, the call was the last call of all, the call of death? Why then did Derrida refuse the call? At this point we might remind ourselves that it was a collect call. This makes the *"es gibt Sein"* reading rather less plausible and strengthens the suggestion that it is death that speaks, that wants to collect its dues. Derrida refuses. This, you may say, is understandable. And yet, does not Derrida, in his writing about Bataille, about Blanchot, about Shelley, not to mention Hegel, Husserl, and others, precisely negotiate for himself, and indeed for others, the most intimate relation with death? Does not Derrida, in effect, and in his own way, affirm death? What charges would there be left for death to collect?

There is a final possibility—that we should not have asked *what* calls, but *who*. There are many clues. The name given, like Heidegger's Dasein, is sexually indeterminate (Martin/Martine). It is the name of one whose voice has been extinguished by death, a radical absence. And it is mediated, absolutely, through an operator, who is both an individual (indeed, a woman), and yet not an individual. We now know, surely, who it is that calls. It is the Other. And if Levinas is right about Heidegger, it would not be inappropriate for Heidegger to be the name used on the *Fernsprecher,* for the question of the Other is still critical for those who have divided up his philosophical legacy—not least for Derrida.

You see the outrageous privilege I allow myself—to give new life, new possibilities of death, to Derrida's lines—the absolute privilege of the reader. Let us suppose that our mine shafts have struck two rich veins—that of death and that of the Other. And that "Heidegger," at least for the moment, is a clue—that he might be the name of unfinished business, that his formulations might still give us more to think, that in some way, he lives on.

I will now confirm this by another strangely parallel example, from another entry (June 6, 1977) in *The Postcard.* Derrida had just given a seminar on "La différance," by then already ten years old, at Balliol College, Oxford. He was stretched out on the grass of the quadrangle, where the discussion following his paper was to take place. A very handsome student, and I quote here, "thought to provoke me, and, I think seduce me a little by asking me why I did not commit suicide. It was in his view the only way of following up [*'faire suivre,'* in Derrida's words] my 'theoretical discourse,' the only way of being consistent and bringing about an event" (25).

Not surprisingly, Derrida gives no direct answer.

The question is not entirely perspicuous. Derrida tells us the question only in indirect speech. We do not hear the exact words. As I recall, it was actually posed at greater length than Derrida allows. I remember only trivia—the creeping shadows of the trees over the lawn and the signature scored on the soles of Derrida's upturned shoes that would leave its imprint on the soft verge of the lawn when he walked away. Perhaps Camus, for whom suicide is the only serious philosophical question, is being cited. Or perhaps something was being made of the role of "difference" in the Stoic discussion of death. The Stoic affirms that he is indifferent to death. He is asked why then he does not commit suicide, and answers "because it would make no difference."

Perhaps, finally, we might note Derrida's setting aside, at the end of "La différance," what he calls Heideggerian hope. The questioner would then be asking: What sort of future for philosophy is provided by laughter, dance, and an affirmation foreign to all dialectics?

The phone call from America was, we are told, "a joke." The question on the Balliol lawn was a "provocation, perhaps a seduction." A strange couple. And strange, too, if death should be their shared theme. Derrida refused the phone call. What did he do to the question? "Instead of arguing . . . I responded with a pirouette, by returning his question to him." A strange parallel. The relation to the Other exhibits an extraordinary inversion, however. In each case, there is anonymity, although in different ways. Derrida never discovers the proper name of his trans-atlantic caller. He is offered a pseudonym, and that indeterminate—between sex (Martin/Martine) and between category of sign, that is, between proper name and brand name (Martine/Martini).[12] Derrida calls him Martin in his footnote. The caller is a pseudonymous *absence*—moreover, one mediated by an unnamed operator. On the Balliol lawn, the interlocutor is totally present and yet unnamed. I do not know whether Derrida omits to mention his name or simply does not know it. For the record, I will tell you the name of this Adonis. It, too, was Martin.

So—a call, a question, some conceits. Sheer whimsy, perhaps, and flimsy at that. And yet so much has already come into play. Let me try to be somewhat more explicit in this last section about what the relationship between writing, death, and the Other might come to, aware as I very much am, how much more needs to be said, how I should have schematized Derrida's treatment of Husserl, Freud, Blanchot, Bataille, Shelley, Heidegger. That I have not done so is a sign only of my own scholarly finitude, not of some lofty gesture. I am guided by the thought that the historical fate of Derrida's writing will, of course, depend on his readers, those who come after him.

I could conveniently begin with Derrida's early discussions of writing as a break with the metaphysics of presence and self-presence, especially phenomenological consciousness. Perhaps I could quote from "The End of the Book and the Beginning of Writing": "What writing itself, in its non-phonetic movement, betrays is life. It menaces at once the breath, the spirit, and history as the spirit's relationship with itself. It is their end, their finitude, their paralysis."[13]

Elsewhere he writes that "the metaphysics of the logos, of presence, and consciousness, must reflect upon writing as its death."[14] Writing is the death of presence in that it inscribes any meaning in a play or economy of signification, which essentially disperses any sense—immediate or mediated—of self-presence, of absolute interiority, or self-relatedness. Husserl's founding of meaning in his own "living presence," as Derrida has shown, perfectly exemplifies the threat writing poses to "life." I have two main responses to this.

1. The words "life" and "death" are, in this very movement, transformed, and their opposition subverted. Dispersion, difference, mark the end of a certain illusion of life that we call self-presence. What this opens up is the possibility of a reinscription, a reworking, of these values within the general problematic of writing. If writing is a supplement to my living presence without which I would not be who I am (I am thinking of Rousseau[15]), is not writing essential to "life" in some sense freed from its traditional metaphysical signification? Is not Derrida, via writing, simply giving voice to a sense of

"life" that even in its vulgar forms (as "struggle," as "disappoint-ment," as "vale of tears," as "for the living," as "bed of nails," or as a "bed of roses") is postmetaphysical, shorn of any illusions of "pres-ence"? In the old metaphysical sense, who, apart from Husserl, is still talking about living?

2. In Derrida's formulation (which we could summarize as "Writing is the death of presence"), there is a definite weighting toward the self-dispersal of meaning. In his account of Husserl's inner speech—which, it is worth recalling, Husserl set up to provide an ideal pure ground of meaning free from the dispersive dangers of *outer* communication— what Derrida focuses on is the way both the "imagination" and the temporal present have an essential relation to what is "other." But, we can ask, what of the fate of public speech/writing? How do the concepts of life/death as they function here involve a relation to the Other?

I wanted to say, at this point, that this is an impossibly difficult ques-tion to discuss in such a short time, that I would need a book. Then, protected by its seriousness, its weightiness, its table of contents, its se-curity apparatus, I might be able to offer myself up to you. But only a transcendental book could afford such protection, as everyone who has been reviewed knows well. I wanted to say that I would not attempt to tell the whole story of writing, death, and the Other, that I would be selective. And albeit in a performative way, I have already let slip the focus I have in fact selected. I will call it the *vulnerability* of the writer. If we think of "writing" in its widest sense, this becomes the question of vulnerability "as such." I will try to broach this question economically and without fuss, fully aware that I am taking certain things for granted, and that I am not fully justifying this focus.

What is the *question* of vulnerability? I thought it was just one ques-tion. In fact, it is several. Most obviously, what sense can be given to vulnerability after the death of the subject, the death of the author? Is there anything left to defend, to protect, to be threatened? Would not affirmation, dissemination, self-dispersal make the question of vulnera-bility into a relic of an outdated logocentrism, a fundamentally residual problem? There is no doubt that the question of vulnerability can take a hysterical form. As proof, let me quote from an early draft of this paper.

"For the last decade and a half, I have followed Derrida around this Western world. . . . I speak today, however, not as a camp-follower, but as his Reader, one of the names of Fate, one of the dark birds circling on high. . . . I begin, then, with an act of displacement, of dramatization, in which I don a mask, the better to speak through. Let me call myself death. Here at this point I feel a mild sense of comfort. I have found a way to begin. And yet there is also the greatest trembling and striving.

He who plays with fire. . . . He who lives by the sword. . . . For I, too, am writing, and you will be the death of me, you who rake through the ashes of my words for the fragments that please you, you who disperse, distort, forget, ignore . . . even enjoy; are you not already preparing to kill? The writer, after all, lacks a face. . . ."

It went on like this. Perhaps you can see how I needed the safety of quotation marks before I could let it out. Here the reader, the Other, is the source of all misunderstanding, of all loss of meaning, and of pain. The question is—is this just the price we have to pay for that *necessary* opening to the Other to which we give the name of writing, or are all such negative, protective responses simply, as we called them, residues of those illusions of ego that an affirmative dissemination might dispense with? (Do we learn nothing from the keen control that Derrida so clearly exercises over his writing and his "natural" concern that it not be misunderstood, that his strategies succeed?) The reader, quite as much as being a threat, it might be said, is the condition of my life, my living on. And yet it is just as such that the reader poses his/her threat. For the reader has the power to appropriate my legacy, to turn it to his (or her) advantage. One thinks of Husserl's disappointment with Heidegger. One can only speculate about Derrida's attitude to Derrideans, those admiring offspring, those who already seek to divide the estate.

What is true of translation—that one lives on, survives, continues, at the very moment of one's betrayal—is equally true of reading in general. (Better read than dead?) Interestingly, the reader, and even more a seated audience, is in the same position: open to pleasure, *jouissance,* ecstasy; but equally, lacking earlids, to boredom, frustration, insult, outrage, and so on. Perhaps to listen, to read, is equally to risk a little death. Perhaps, then, both reader and writer are engaged in a life-and-death struggle that never ends and is never resolved.

It may be that the silent and hidden object of this discussion will one day turn out to be desire and the economy of desire. Only then, perhaps, will we be able to make sense of such concepts as risk and danger, and only then will the undecidability of life/death and the whole question of vulnerability get articulated.

I would like now, before concluding, to offer some brief and tentative thoughts about the desire of deconstruction "itself"—tentative because what I shall say is opaque to me both in its force and its motivation.

Deconstruction is intimately concerned with power. The key to what Derrida called "the general strategy of deconstruction"[16] is the discovery of a conceptual opposition working within a text that structures that text by the systematic privilege given to one of the terms in the opposition. By inversion and displacement, that power-play is exposed and, perhaps, unraveled. It must have been asked before, but does not the deployer of such strategies of reading actually acquire, for him- or herself or for their own texts, enormous power? But of course, it may be said, "And what is wrong with that?" Power is the natural corollary of a productive, insightful reading. If the alternative is the "deaf passivity of commentary," who would want anything else? So when someone laments, as I heard recently, that he had been deconstructed, he is suffering from a misapprehension, his suffering *is* a misapprehension. But in what way? Should one affirm and encourage the deconstruction of one's own writing, perhaps even be honored to be so chosen? Or should one simply enjoy the spectacle of something one never really owned (one's writing) being undone? Should one seek deconstruction, acquiesce in it, avoid it, or what? The case for saying that the cry "I have been deconstructed. Alas, I am undone!" is a naïve one is surely that deconstruction is not destructive, not the same thing as criticism. Any philosophical text, and as such, can be deconstructed. (So, too, can any deconstructive text.) We should not worry. The reason the worry remains, of course, is that the successfully deconstructed text, at least in one respect or at one level, loses its power (which is why, for strategic reasons, before *Specters of Marx,* Derrida has privileged Marx's writings). Surely, we need to ask again: What about deconstruction? What of its desire?

A skeptical friend of mine put his difficulty this way: "Everything I read of Derrida's has one consequence—the production of an invulnerable discourse—a kind of postmodern mastery. It is said that deconstruction is not a position. So it cannot be attacked! It is said that deconstruction 'is' not, at all, that it is not an 'is.' All the better, for that makes 'it' completely immune to criticism. Insofar as deconstruction is the absolute anticipation of philosophy, it is the renewal of the fundamental desire of Hegelian thought. And insofar as it is the interweaving of the only two possibilities of thinking beyond the closure of philosophy, it denies the possibility of any serious competition. Deconstruction has sacrificed the name of philosophy the better to realize its fundamental desire—total anticipation. If one were to pursue this skeptical line of thought, one would add that the admission that any deconstructive reading is, in principle, open to deconstruction, is no limitation at all—it simply confirms the practice of deconstruction in its position of invulnerability."

Now, what is being said here is, of course, paradoxical. If deconstruction is immune to criticism, then these remarks must fail (as criticism). If they are successful as criticism, then they must be false, for deconstruction would then be open to criticism. The simplest way around this would be to suggest that while it can always, in a certain way, handle straightforward philosophical objections, the question of its own power, vulnerability, desire, might prove to be its Achilles heel.

Of course, an adequate discussion of these questions could only really follow a careful consideration of Derrida's texts. On other occasions I have done just that. For now, I shall simply accentuate the difficulty of deconstruction in this way by saying that the reason this question of desire, vulnerability, and so forth is not posed more insistently rests on the continuing power of deconstruction to excite, to allure to transgression, to open up texts to previously unheard-of readings, to raise questions where none had appeared before, and to preserve the space of questioning where others (such as Heidegger and Levinas) have opened it up.

We have repeatedly attempted to bring together the questions of writing, death, and the relation to the Other. Indeed, we raised the whole question of deconstruction within the context of "vulnerability." Is it not curious that Derrida seems to suspend the question of the Other at one of the critical points in his writings at which these themes converge? Discussing Levinas, he talks of the questions surrounding the death of philosophy as "the only questions today capable of founding the community, within the world, of those who are still called philosophers . . . a community of the question about the possibility of the question."[17] This is in many ways a satisfying formulation, which describes the horizon of such "events" as this paper, but does it not rest on an unproblematized notion of "community"?

It will not completely resolve the question of the relative claim of the primacy of the desire for the Other or the desire for "presence" (which is one way of formulating our central question), but I would like to end by returning to Macleish and to the poem we discussed earlier. For our reading was, of course, a subterfuge, a deferral, a holding back. Is the poem really about the illusory dreams of a new kind of writing or thinking that would not be reappropriated by history? "There was a time for discoveries . . ."—is that about the closure of metaphysics? Is the "first light" a version of *lichtung*? Is "the crying of gulls" the anonymous call of Being? Perhaps not.

The surf of any such reading breaks on the words that follow "for the curve . . . north into secrecy." And if that is not clue enough, the secret is soon upon us, unveiled:

Senora: once the maps have all been made
A man were better dead than find new continents
A man would better never have been born
Than find upon the open ocean flowers
Drifted from islands where there are no islands,

Or midnight, out of sight of any land,
Smell on the altering air the odor of rosemary.

Rosemary?

Suppose truth were a woman, what then?

PART IV. ART AND TIME

10

The Dark Side
of Narrative

In "Narrative Imagining," the Epilogue to his *Poetics of Imagining*, Richard Kearney revisits the ethical challenge posed by what he calls narrative imagination to the extreme representatives of nonreferential postmodernism—Baudrillard and Faurrison—and also to the fractured discursivism of Lyotard, Foucault, and Vattimo.[1] His strategy is to focus on the ethical baby being thrown out with the post-metaphysical bathwater.[2]

The central argument is that narrative understanding—especially, but not exclusively, in its literary sense—is the handmaiden of a certain phronesis, offering us imaginative variations of the human condition, allowing us a glimpse of what sense might be made of a human life. To the extent that it broadens our sense of the connectedness of our own life, it allows us to construct our own identity through the "synthesis of heterogeneity," and to the extent that it offers us access to the lives of others, it educates our analogical and empathic capacities to relate to others. Kearney gives us a hermeneutic feast, to which Aristotle, Ricoeur, Nussbaum, Kant, Arendt, MacIntyre, Taylor, Benhabib, and even Joyce are all invited as guests. Narrative imagination supplies a sense of the kind of connectedness and interconnectedness of selfhood that would make promising and ethical responsibility to the other possible— the self as a *socius* within and without.

> The narrative model of identity thus revives the age-old virtue of self-knowledge, not as some self-regarding ego but as an examined life freed from narcissism and solipsism through a recognition of our dialogical interdependence vis-à-vis others.[3]

Richard Kearney's own power of "synthesizing the heterogeneous," weaving a common (though uncommonly plausible) story out of these threads of narrativity, is quite exceptional. I would like to focus more critically, however, on the way he deals with what we might call the dark side, or the underside, of narrative. I will first discuss something of his account in these theoretical texts, and then look at the way what I am calling the dark side gets treated in his own narratives, which will, I believe, offer further support for my doubts.

Kearney's acknowledgment of problems and difficulties of narrative is impressive and important. My first major concern is one that Kearney notices at various times, but does not obviously resolve. In this Epilogue, it appears as the problem of flexibility: "A fundamental fluidity and openness pertains to narrative reading once we are prepared to recognize that it is always something made and remade. Societies which admit that they constitute themselves through an ongoing process of narrative are unlikely to degenerate into self-righteousness." (*PI,* 249).

In "Narrative and the Ethics of Remembrance" he makes a similar claim more strongly—that this openness and indeterminacy follows from the recognition that one's identity is fundamentally narrative in form. He concludes with a cautious "in principle": "This is why, at least in principle, the tendency of a nation toward xenophobic . . . nationalism can be resisted by its own narrative resources to imagine itself otherwise."[4]

Kearney will point out how narrative is central to the "conflict of interpretation," and does not necessarily lead to healing. But it is important to stress this rather than underplay it. Those who tell and repeat identity stories, whether they be Zionists or Orangemen, are clearly in some sense aware of the narrative dimension of their sense of identity, but the idea that such narratives might be *revised* or rewritten in such a way as to allow reconciliation with a counter-narrative is not only *not* implied by a narrative-based identity, but it may precisely be excluded. Identification with a particular narrative, even acknowledgment of the fact of others' narratives, may lead to war just as easily as peace—the desire to kill those who tell a different story. This suggests that narrative consciousness and the kind of imagination that Kearney shows narrative can feed are logically and often practically quite distinct. The move that allows him to connect the two is a specific consciousness of narrativity, that is, a grasp of oneself and of others as narratively constructed identities. But this consciousness of narrativity is not a narrative consciousness. Kearney variously describes it as flexibility, as recognition, as a certain transcendence. These imaginative capacities, in other words, are distinguishable from narrative and only come into a temporary alliance with narrative, like two men in a carnival dragon costume. My question, then, is this—is narrative imagination more of a name for the fortuitous overlap of narrative and imagination, masquerading as an elaboration of the ethical responsibility of narrative? Is not narrative more naturally a Janus-creature with two heads, good and evil?

Kearney's way of dealing with this problem is to explicitly subject the narrative self to self-questioning, "never to forget its origins in narrativity," to endorse the twin importance of the hermeneutics of affirmation and suspicion, and finally to wrap up these responses in the narrative paradox—that is, that objections to narrative draw on narrative form to make their point, whether through the stories that Marx, Nietzsche, or Freud use to teach us about the ulterior ends served by the stories we tell ourselves, or the role of Edward Said's counter-narrative, the corrective role of subversive (including minority) narratives, and so on. Kearney even yokes in Beckett's strategies of decomposing narrative —"Even when narrative imagination is narrating the death of narrative imagination, it is still narrating" (*PI*, 251).

I do have some trouble with this position. Does not the way the idea of narrative imagination comes to the rescue here try to build imagination into narrative rather than allowing this relation to be recursively problematic? The production of counter-narratives does not merely confirm narrativity; it reopens the space of narrative contestation, a space not governed by narrative, but rather by *polemos*. As I see it, narrative imagination is an attempt to recover the power of narrativity to stage this conflict.

Kearney interprets the narrative paradox as a confirmation of narrative, but surely this involves a kind of reduction of the performativity of such paradoxes and closes down a serious question about the role of narrative form. On performativity: Beckett tells stories to subvert storytelling. In what sense does this really confirm narrativity? Could it not be an ironic demonstration of our dependency on narrative *form*? Or a dramatization of the pathos of narrativity in a world that ultimately doesn't make sense? Could not narrative function like a taxi one uses to get to a destination (and then pays off), or a ladder one climbs and then pushes away? Or a persistent conventional frame within which forces and concerns that explode or at least destabilize the very idea of the synthesis of the heterogeneous? It is this that I want to explore by briefly perusing Kearney's wonderful pair of novels: *Sam's Fall* and *Walking at Sea Level*. I will try to show that these narratives precisely fail to contain the issues they raise, issues that ultimately contest the status of narrative. And in so doing, I leave aside the dangers of representing the past, that the other's narrative can crystallize the shape and depth of the enemy's hostility, and that counter-narratives function to correct official orthodoxies within a space of imagination and judgment that is not intrinsically tied to narrative.

If Kearney had not complicated the picture by his political writings,

I would be tempted to speak of his double existence, as philosopher and as novelist. It was a pleasure to read both *Sam's Fall* and *Walking at Sea Level*, which form a pair, a double achievement.[5] And now I am tempted to recount their plots, so that those of us for whom the pleasure of reading these books is still to come may know what they are about. Why do I hesitate? Not just for fear of spoiling your reading pleasure. In fact, I hesitate because it would seem to suggest that the plot, the narrative core, is what is essential to these texts, thus (apparently) trapping me again in the narrative paradox.

The traditional alternative would be to discuss the themes with which the narrative is occupied. We can give minimal satisfaction to both these approaches by quoting some of the jacket material.

Sam's Fall: After a happy childhood in Cork in the 60s, twins Jack and Sam Toland become boarders at the Columbanus Abbey school. Jack is favored by its charismatic abbot, yet it is Sam who stays on as a novice, enlisted in the abbot's quest for the lost universal language of God. But as his twin discovers, Sam struggles to resist the allure of Jack's lover, Raphaelle, and his soul becomes a prize to be fought over by equally determined antagonists.

Walking at Sea Level: Twelve years after the death of his twin brother, Jack Toland is still running from the past. Estranged from his Swiss wife Raphaelle, and with a university post in Montreal, his thesis on the 17th-century Irish philosopher John Toland has stalled and he's drinking heavily. Then, out of the blue, Raphaelle summons him to Geneva to look after their young daughter and promptly disappears. Jack's subsequent pursuit of her takes him from Switzerland to Paris, and on a journey through history, legend and myth which forces him to confront his twin's ghost, and delivers the missing piece in the puzzle of John Toland's life.

So—two ingeniously conceived and brilliantly written stories, each driven by a search, a quest for knowledge and for self-knowledge. In each case a complex interweaving of dreams, traumatic memory, and various devices (such as diaries), for rendering the past and the experience of the Other present, makes these writings triumphs of temporal layering and interweaving.

And, it has to be said, the fundamental dimensions of narrative imagination are demonstrated—identity is constructed through narrative, narrative "synthesizes the heterogeneous," the lives of others illuminate our own lives (both close to us, and those more distant—such as Carpocrates, Gallen, Columbanus, and Toland—all real historical figures whose theology is brought to life sparklingly in these pages), and the border crossings between historical, literary, and lived narrativity are brilliantly negotiated. All this is to say that Kearney's novels richly mirror his accounts of narrative imagination in *The Wake of Imagination*, in *Poetics of Imagining*, in *Poetics of Modernity*, and in his paper "Narrative and the Ethics of Remembrance" (1999).

But what is the status of the narrative frame? The force of the narrative paradox is that it suggests quite properly that there is no escape from narrativity, and one suspects that the reason for this has to do with the temporal articulation of a human life. Now we may rightly be relieved from a certain poverty of presence by such accounts, which draw on the synthetic power of both language and imagination to produce unities of sense out of heterogeneous elements. And it will rightly be said that certain sorts of truths only arise through such syntheses of difference. The idea of a good life, a fulfilled life . . . only makes sense after such narrative syntheses. At this point it is tempting to admit that there are certain dangers here that we need to be aware of, such as allowing narrative to be co-opted by intolerance. The suggestion is that it is imagination that will provide the prophylactic antidote, in the hope, that is, that imagination is not equally subject to the same dark forces. Let us then just remind ourselves that we do not need to fall into the narrative paradox in introducing these novels. We could describe them thematically as meditations on duality, history, and religion, or on "the attempt to overcome duality," or "the battle against oblivion"; and we could add to these themes those of jealousy, the passion of asceticism, and so on. Kearney really is masterful in exploring these themes.

At this point we could attempt to resurrect something of the spirit of Roland Barthes[6] and Claude Lévi-Strauss,[7] for whom time and narrativity are each something of an illusion generated by the articulation of powerful binary oppositions—born from man / born from the earth, good and evil, life and death, and so on. The response both Ricoeur and Kearney (and indeed, I myself) have made to such a view is that the *significance* of these binary elements is itself inseparable from what Heidegger called our being-toward-death, so that the true illusion is that of thinking one has banished narrative or reduced it to an illusion. However, there is something about this structuralist approach that still haunts our thinking and allows us to open up a far more disturbing possibility than either Barthes or Lévi-Strauss ever contemplated. (I take up this again in sustained discussion of Robert Smithson's work in "Art as Event," chapter 12 below.) I argue this point here in a perverse reading of Kearney's book *Walking at Sea Level.*

I mentioned earlier the "theme" of duality. But it is not a *theme* in this book, it is an obsession—a contagious obsession. It is my contention that the narrative success of both books may at the same time be their philosophical weakness, that they subordinate the question of *the double* to the narrative logic of the will to truth and that this precisely gives us an illusion of resolution. The real secret of Kearney's (and Toland's) battle against the double is that it is a battle against another kind of time, a time transversal to that of narrative and perhaps also to another kind of imagination.

The double is the engine of development in both novels. Jack and Sam Toland are twins, rival brothers, hence themselves examples ("doubles") of all those other ill-fated twin brothers that stud history. Fate and accident bring about a reversal in their relative fortunes, then Sam drowns and Jack is haunted by Sam's research project, Sam's love for his wife, and his uncertainty over the paternity of his daughter. Raphaelle, his photographer wife, in love with both men, becomes obsessed with the question of twins, anthropologically, historically, and mythically. And all of these characters are obsessed with the way this issue of the twin permeates theology, especially the Irish tradition. Is God just on the side of good, or does he include evil? Is God one, or doubled? Is God's spirit opposed to matter, or, as in Toland's pantheism, is God identical to matter in space? And if evil is part of God, what does that require of us humans?

But it is not just the characters who are obsessed by the double; so too is the author. One can hardly turn a page without the double appearing somewhere—whether it is Jack's shrouded copulation with Charmaine Le Monde in a quiet part of an airport, in which they resemble a "double-backed beast," two fish in the aquarium, two trees, a newspaper report about Siamese twins. And at the same time, temporal duality repeatedly surfaces in the theme of repetition—Toland's revival of the twin-God idea, various real and imaginary repetitions of the theme of drowning, the return to St. Gallen, the return to the library. And, we might add here, the whole question of Jack's addiction (to cocaine, alcohol, and cigarettes) in which a repetition-compulsion is tied directly to the question of oblivion and death, finally breaking up his marriage to Raphaelle. Finally, there is the conceptual thematic pulse of deception, double-cross, duplicity, betrayal, two-timing.

Kearney sets up his novels in such a way that despite the extravagant bursting-forth at every turn of duality, the double, and the structure of repetition, the uncanny unsettling transversal logic that this ushers in is dealt with, settled, resolved. Jack *does* discover the truth—that Emilie really is his daughter, that one has to learn to live with the hole in Being, and that forgiveness involves a mutual understanding of our deep fallibility, which nicely illustrates the central theme of "Narrative and the Ethics of Remembrance," the ethical significance of witnessing, attestation, and discovering the truth about the past. But the narrative resolution of *Walking at Sea Level* falls short, I believe, of the pathos of Beckett's "You must go on, I can't go on, I'll go on"[8] (quoted approvingly by Kearney).

Consider, for example, the resolution of the book's intellectual adventure. It turns out that John Toland, the real seventeenth-century author of *Christianity Not Mysterious,* on whom Jack Toland is writing his Ph.D. dissertation, is a secret reviver of the Carpocratian heresy—that it is necessary to do evil to experience all sides of God's creation, in order to be able to fully live in his image. And Jack ensures that his contemporary followers who run a child porn ring are jailed. Here I think we have a successful narrative resolution, but a philosophically disappointing one. By taking an extreme case, it suggests that we can indeed (and must) draw the line between good and evil. But extreme cases make bad law. And it has to be said that the theological disputes documented in these books—including the Carpocratian heresy itself—are collectively more engaging and challenging than the resolution Kearney produces to the problems they raise.

An important task for another occasion would be to show that the philosophical (and psychoanalytical) significance of the question of the double—I have in mind, of course, Freud's discussion in "The Uncanny,"[9] Otto Rank's book on *The Double*,[10] Hoffman's short stories[11]—is such that it cannot be resolved in narrative form. Kearney's philosophical thrust is (eventually) to subordinate fantasy to reality, undecidability to the witnessing of truth, doubt to trust, and the time of the event, of interruption, to that of continuity and synthesis. But my sense of what he succeeds in doing, *malgré soi*, in his novels, is to show that narrative, if anything, is a frame that can effectively dramatize the illusion of resolution. The struggle persists between a narrative imagination (in which narrative is supplemented by imagination, and imagination is controlled by narrative), and what I call a certain negative capability, which can allow that there may (equally) be an ethical issue in allowing the voices of ghosts to continue to speak, in acknowledging the power of forces that would interrupt the progressive story of a life and that finally may put in question some of the power of synthesis.

It may be (though this suggestion would have the drawback of introducing a disturbing note of reconciliation) that the true conclusion of Richard Kearney's second book—in which Jack and Raphael find a way of going on—is that the force of a certain narrativity has been purged and that "living on" is precisely to have learned to live *with* and not just against a negative capability, one for which narrative would no longer operate as the ground of intelligibility, but as the frame within which that very synthetic unity is constantly challenged by transversal forms, powers, and relations that put in question the very idea of narrative identity. Enter: the time of the uncanny, a disruptive imagination.

11

Thinking Eccentrically
about Time

The Strange Loops of
Escher and Calvino

Of course, other stories are being continued, rewritten, or echoed here. My title alludes not merely to the title of that extraordinary fugue of a book, *Gödel, Escher, Bach: An Eternal Golden Braid* by Douglas Hofstadter,[1] and to the practice of coupling names by which he announces a homology of minds, but also to the sharpest figure he found for that common structure: "strange loops."

Whereas Hofstadter's explicit interest is in what we could call the mechanisms of mind and the paradoxes of theoretical reflection, I shall be trying to use the sparks that fly from the conjunction of Escher and Calvino to reignite a different project: thinking eccentrically about time.

There are perhaps two more or less obvious ways of thinking about time: both as something fairly objective, out there, which it is our task to discover; and as something constituted, or produced, in one way or another. This latter is sometimes called subjective, but this term is not particularly helpful.

I have usually assumed that whatever we think about the status of "objective" time, it is in the second sort that speculative interest lies. That is, even if we were to hold to some story about the objectivity of simple temporal succession, there is more to be said about higher-order temporal organization, and these features are no more to be found in simple succession than can the shapes of triangles, rectangles, and other rectilinear figures be predicted from the properties of the straight line.

If I now identify simple succession with an objective understanding of time, I make a number of assumptions, the fragility of which I am only too aware. I wish, however, to turn to the second line of thinking—about time as constituted, or produced in some sense. I say "in some

170

sense" because there are many ways of putting the idea that time is open to organization in abstractly describable ways, that is, ways not limited to the particular components involved. A very simple example, one that is perhaps fateful in its importance, would be that of repetition, which cuts into and across simple succession with a new secondary series, while of course naming (and indeed *repeating*) the original principle of succession itself. At no level, however, need we say *what* is repeated, for us to grasp its structure. (Repetition may, of course, be more than a second-order abstract principle of organization; it may actually be the principle by which first-order identities are established as such. This would shift us into a Nietzschean and deconstructive gear.)

Time as Constituted

Let us then focus only on *time as constituted or produced*. Within this most fertile field, I distinguish five different ways of construing this productivity:

1. Time as taking place in some sort of purified experience. Here we would situate a phenomenological account of time such as is provided by Husserl's theory of inner time-consciousness.
2. Time as constituted in or through human existence. Heidegger's account of our Being-in-the-world, a central dimension to which is the importance of human finitude, our Being-toward-death, and the structure of resoluteness, would be exemplary.
3. Time as constituted in and through historically specific human practices. We would think here of the highly structured time (at every level from the day to the year) of the farmer (agricultural time), or of the institutional time described by Foucault (disciplinary time)— the time of the timetable.
4. Time as constituted via the bound signification of narrative.
5. Time as constituted via processes of unbound signification.

To abbreviate a lengthier tale, I see these five categories as picking out distinguishable stages of a gradually more complex intertwining of language and time. Having dealt elsewhere with Husserl and Heidegger, I consider here only the last three categories, sliding toward the last, where, in my view, Calvino is to be found.[2]

The interweaving of language and time is not something that befalls an otherwise clear distinction between signification and the temporal. The power of Derrida's *différance* rests on their fusion at the most primitive level. And then neither time-consciousness nor the temporality of human existence would be prelinguistic, but would contain the seeds and sproutings, respectively, of linguistic signification. But let us confine ourselves to the last three categories.

Foucault's discussion of institutional time is of a time that subjects bodies to routines of daily life via grids and timetables.[3] Time is complexly constituted as a set of successive meanings by the imposition of a spatializing grid. By "spatializing" I mean that the order of the day is best understood as following out the consequences of a written timetable in which the future is predicated on the past, in which the structure of the evening is to be found at the bottom of the time sheet.

Signs are in operation here, but in the most rigidly controlled way, ordered according to numerical succession and to conventions of grid representation. An infinite complexity (of division, and subdivision) is possible; and daily, weekly, monthly, yearly cycles introduce a nestedness of succession not found in simple serial time. But the role of signification is (in principle) strictly limited.

In *narrative*, matters are different and essentially problematic, because quite what counts as a narrative is itself a theoretical issue. For current purposes I propose to construe narrative as, minimally, committed to a representation of a productive continuity of action in time. This is not meant to be infinitely elastic. Nor is it meant to resolve the questions that these terms—representation, productive, continuity, action, and time—each pose. Together they spell out what I mean by the "bound" signification of narrative. By *bound signification* I mean an articulation of signs bound to an ulterior organizing pattern of representation. The most obvious example of that would be a plot. Now it may be that many, or most, or all emplotments are themselves vehicles for the enactment of deeper structures. The structural analysis of narrative found in Lévi-Strauss's account of myth, or Barthes's essay of that name, discovers, in effect, the working out of logical formulae; and values like productivity (comes to something, says something) and continuity arguably involve some primitive commitment to the preservation and/or restitution of identity. It might perhaps be useful to characterize the basic commitment of the idea of productivity in these terms.

The intertwining of time with narrative is both rich and subtle. For Ricoeur, the two are in the end difficult to separate, and in this respect, Ricoeur is endorsing the original suggestion that there may be an intimate connection between time and signification. We are now in a position—with the help of Escher and Calvino—to pose a question that I fear can be posed more easily than answered: Is there not, in all we have said so far, a tacit limitation to the processes of signification that are *allowed to structure* time? For all the ways in which narrative gives depth and intelligibility to our understanding of time, is it not still restricted to understanding signification in an essentially *representational* way? And what alternative possibilities might there be for thinking *ec-*

centrically about time? With this question we arrive at our final category: time as constituted via processes of *unbound signification*. Before reading Escher and Calvino, this category might be thought to be guarded by a question mark. Now, I think, an exclamation mark must be added!

So much by way of introduction. I notice that Escher and Calvino are sitting patiently in the waiting room for their names to be called. It is Escher, currently absorbed in the wallpaper, who is summoned first.

Escher's Line of Thought

Describing his development as an artist, Escher confesses his early obsession with the perfection of his graphic techniques. This involved control over one's tools, "above all," he declares, "one's own two hands."[4] He later describes this as a state of self-delusion, shattered by "a moment when it seemed as though scales fell from my eyes." So the movement is not merely from hands to eyes, but from scaled to unscaled eyes. Escher reworks the visual equivalent to Nietzsche's "ears behind ears." "Ideas," as he put it, "came into my mind, quite unrelated to graphic art." And yet the accompanying "desire . . . to communicate [these ideas] to other people . . . could not be achieved through words, for these thoughts were not literary ones but mental images of a kind that can only be made comprehensible to others by presenting them as visual images."[5]

This is surely unpromising. As we approach Escher, he seems to be walking past us rather than toward us. We have suggested possibilities of signification beyond representation, pointing perhaps to a "poetics of time," and yet Escher goes out of his way to say how words cannot capture his deepest insights.

Indeed, this inadequacy of language renders precarious the very "Introduction" in which these words appear. Most curiously, given their success in aiding our understanding, his images would constitute a paradox of self-reference not entirely alien to the structure of his graphic pieces, and we might come to doubt at a deeper level whether words were so poor.

Perhaps predictably, Escher notices this and, in this very same introduction, resting on a narrow ledge even further down, confesses:

> Reading over [my remarks] about the particular representational quality of my prints, I feel it may be rather illogical to devote so many words to it . . . however . . . most people find it easier to arrive at any understanding of an image by the roundabout method of letter symbols than by the direct route.

Linguistic mediation, he is claiming, is merely a pedagogical necessity. What about visual images? Are they any different? Escher says he is trying to communicate what he revealingly calls "a specific *line* of thought." He writes:

> The ideas basic to [these reproductions] bear witness to my amazement and wonder at the laws of nature [*elsewhere:* "the enigmas that surround us"] which operate in the world around us. He who wonders discovers that this is itself a wonder.

But if language is inadequate, why does he think visual representation can capture these "ideas"? Again, he confesses that strictly, they cannot:

> A mental image is something completely different from a visual image and however much one exerts oneself, one can never manage to capture the fullness of that perfection which hovers in the mind, and which one thinks of, quite falsely, as something that is "seen."

Eventually, he says, "I manage to cast my lovely dream in the defective visual mould of a detailed conceptual sketch."

Escher's difficulty is not new. Philosophers have usually expressed the problem the other way around. Confronted with how we can have an idea of a triangle that was not itself isosceles, or right-angled, or scalene, Kant invented the idea of a transcendental *schema,* which would mediate between sensory specificity and the ideal. Escher is, as it were, describing his grasp of a schema, and his puzzlement over how to represent it. Kant explains this by saying that such schemata *exist only in thought.*

With a certain foreshortening of the argument, I would like to suggest an analogy at least between the *ideas* that Escher is talking about and what, after Kant, we could call transcendental schemata. (And see our earlier discussion in chapter 5, "From Representation to Engagement.")

Kant distinguishes between the schema of *sensible* concepts (dogs and triangles), by which concepts are connected to images, and the schema of a pure concept of understanding, that is, the categories (of magnitude, reality, negation, substance, cause, community, possibility, actuality, necessity, quality, relation, and modality). These schemata Kant calls "a priori determinations of time in accordance with rules."[6] Kant admits that

> [The application of] this schematism of our understanding . . . is an art concealed in the depths of the human soul, whose real modes of activity nature is hardly likely ever to allow us to discover, and to have open to our gaze.

We may wonder whether this opening to the gaze is not what Escher is describing when, he says, the scales fell from his eyes, or whether Kant's remarks are not a salutary warning against trying to use the idea of a schema to illuminate anything.

There is the further difficulty that Kant's account would seem to take us back to the first prelinguistic level of the constitution of time, which we associated with Husserl and phenomenology. Is Escher not a false trail?

The series of Escher's lithographs that includes *Waterfall, Ascending and Descending, Three Spheres, House of Stairs,* and perhaps *Belvedere,* each has to be understood both in relation to time, and as interfering in productive ways with the rules of representation. It is helpful, rather than an artificial introduction, to think of our interpretation of complex wholes as a *synthesis.* In the case of these drawings, in which we are presented with lines, steps, routes for the eye to follow, such synthesis not only takes time but involves an imaginative traversal of a path. It involves a synthesis close to that suggested in a narrative. We imagine the prisoners carrying on, walking up and up and up, and yet going round and round, not getting any higher. Our experience will not gel. There is a break between local success (taking each step) and global failure. It doesn't add up. It is as if we are applying an a priori rule of synthesis and finding it unraveling behind us.

If we recall Escher's remarks about visual images being inadequate to his ideas, it may not be for the obvious Kantian reasons that his ideas are too pure for any particular image to capture, but that they are not ideas such as could provide a rule for a representation or even a properly ordered unfolding of a representation. Here representation functions brilliantly as a way of showing something about the relation between representation and what transcends it. Escher is using representation to point beyond itself. In this he prefigures not just the wider possibilities of the language that he claimed inadequate, but a mode of signification not immediately attached to the real, not reducible to representation. Escher does for drawing what Calvino does for language.

Let me make this claim about Escher just a little clearer. What is the relation between one step and the next in *Ascending and Descending*? It is surely not one of mere proximity, but of signification. The surrounding lines mean "This step is going up." And the succession of steps means "These steps are going up." And yet reflection soon tells us, "These steps *cannot* be going up." A formal principle intervenes: we cannot keep going up and returning to the very same place. Our belief in simple succession is shattered. It is not merely that a series of steps can constitute an entirely different level of Being from that of its elements—compare a tune to a note (which we know), but that what is generated in this case is a whole (a circle) that belies the very principle (going up) being used to generate the series. Escher does not, to answer the obvious question, offer us new constructive ways of thinking about time, but he could be said to warm the seat for our next patient, who, if we may glance into the waiting room, seems to have read something from most of the magazines on the table and is in fact coming to the bottom of the pile.

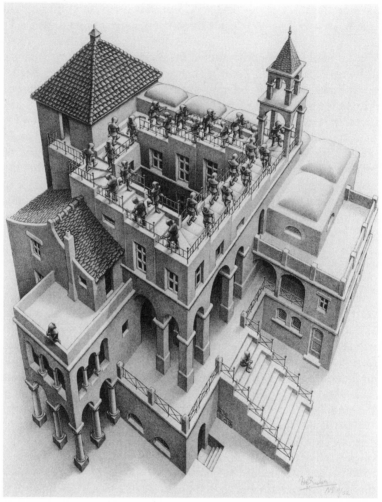

M. C. Escher's "Ascending and Descending."

Calvino and Unbound Signification

In discussing Escher, I was very selective. In the case of Calvino, I shall discuss only *If on a Winter's Night a Traveller*, a book that I admit I have not even finished. I have read it three times from cover to cover, I have read the blurb on the back, but I am not done with it. In this interim report, perhaps I could begin with an observation from the book cover, that "in its course a whole shelf of novels are begun and—for reasons at the time entirely reasonable—never finished." For here we have the ink-ling of a connection with Escher, all of whose connections are, at the time, *reasonable*, but . . .

I shall try to draw out the implications of the basic moves by which the book is constructed for thinking eccentrically about time, and will argue that it is Calvino's relatively unbound use of signification that plays the major role. I shall, further, argue that these moves have impli-cations beyond the book.

It will have escaped no one, however, that Calvino is not content to organize the book in an odd way, from which certain possibilities of thinking about time can then be drawn out. There are also numerous theoretical claims about time scattered throughout the book. We have not long started the book when we read that

> Long novels written today are perhaps a contradiction: the dimension of time has been shattered, we cannot love or think except in fragments of time each of which goes off along its own trajectory and immediately disappears. We can rediscover the continuity of time only in the novels of that period when time no longer seemed stopped and did not yet seem to have exploded, a period that lasted no more than a hundred years.[7]

Yet even in this remark, we meet the difficulty that will confront every attempt to distill a thesis about time from the utterances made within the book—there is no privileged voice that we can rely on. And even if there were, these remarks, as so many, cannot be unambiguously attributed to the author, for they are bound up with the author's report-ing of the thoughts of his reader. Perhaps the necessary confusion of voices is one of the themes of the book.

There are, however, ways in which it makes sense to attribute posi-tions to Calvino, namely, by interpreting the way he organizes the re-marks his characters make. And it is in this way that we can develop a discussion of the themes of the book as well as of its organizational struc-ture. For it is in both respects that it opens up a signifying time. The impact of the book may result from the paralleling of these two.

At the thematic level the most persistent and general theme is that of desire, indeed, metaphysical desire. As we saw in chapter 6, "Glimpses of Being in Dasein's Development," one can find in Lacan a thesis about the relation between language (the symbolic) and desire: compared to a presymbolic relation to the world, language constitutes a radical *break*. And through all its capacities for reference, for description, language cannot restore that original unbroken relation. We can give the name *desire* to that impossible quest to reestablish, through language, a pre-linguistic unity with the world. A satisfactory story (a pleasing narra-tive) would be one that produced and sustained the illusion that, at the level of the meaningful organization of time, the word and the world were one. Calvino makes the desire that underlies this into a theme and ruthlessly exposes it in a number of ways. That such desire is constitutive of reading is made abundantly clear by the long contradictory series of ideal books described by Ludmilla:

> The book I would like to read now is a novel . . . that gives the sense of living through an upheaval that still has no name. (61)

> The novel I would most like to read at this moment . . . should have as its driving force only the desire to narrate, to pile stories upon stories without trying to impose a philosophy of life on you, simply allowing you to observe its own growth. (76)

Each novel, each desire, offers another version of some reestablished contact with the world, a contact that would dispense with signs. The first is precise, concrete, specific; the second a living through; the third, a natural narrative development.

And yet this book is not only made of unfinished books, but makes incompleteness thematic. In the diary of Silas Flannery, we read:

> On the wall facing my desk hangs a poster someone gave me. The dog Snoopy is sitting at a typewriter, and in the cartoon, you read the sentence, "It was a dark and stormy night . . ." and the impersonality of that *incipit* seems to open the passage from one world to the other, from the time and space of here and now to the time and space of the written word; I feel the thrill of a beginning that can be followed by multiple developments, inexhaustibly. (140)

But the spell is always broken:

> The facility of the entrance into another world is an illusion: you start writing in a rush, anticipating the happiness of a future reading, and the void yawns on the white page. (140)

And if this is the writer's experience, it only mirrors the experience of the reader, who either finds unprinted blank pages signaling a discontinuity in the story he is reading, or is interrupted in his reading early on and so on:

> The Reader is beset by mysterious coincidences. He told me that for some time, and for the most disparate reasons, he has had to interrupt his reading of novels after a few pages. (155)

Is he bored? No.

> I am forced to stop reading just when they become most gripping [. . . and] when I think I am reopening the book I began, I find a completely different book before me. (155)

We are being offered a symmetrical necessity of incompleteness on the part of both reader and writer. Language makes promises, opens up desires that it cannot fulfill. To begin reading or writing another book is for hope, or desire, to spring eternal. If this is right, then the status of Cimmerian books is unclear. Professor Uzzi-Tuzzi explains that

> Cimmerian books are all unfinished . . . because they continue beyond—in the other language, in the silent language to which all the words we believe we read refer. (60)

There are at least three different forms by which desire determines our reading (or writing). We aim for completeness (and books respond by breaking off), we want coherence (but are met by fragmentation), and we want reliable beginnings (yet the first page already refers to a preexisting world).

If I may generate a *thesis* from this, it would be that desire structures time through language in the form of unending and unavoidable repetitions of impossible projects, or projects possible only by the silencing of doubts about the aesthetic illusion, doubts about which we now know too much to be able to silence.

This suggests, a propos of Kant's account of the a priori rules of temporalization, that these rules are not neutral with regard to the constitution of the real, but insofar as they embody such ideals as unity, identity, permanence, and so on, they reflect the equally necessary workings of desire.

If we have been ruthlessly reductive about the thematic content of the book, we must be equally bold in considering the lessons its structure teaches us about the possibilities of time. I will not dwell on the multiplicity of levels and the reflexive references between them from author to reader, from reader one to reader two, from author to character, and so on. Nor shall I comment on the structural organization of a sequence of secondary stories around a base story. I want simply to pick out the most important and obvious device being exploited and comment on its implications for the structuring of time.

Novels can be inserted into other novels by the stratagem proposed by Marana to the Sultan, "a character in the first novel opens a book and starts reading" (100). This, of course, is the iterative mechanism underlying the whole book. How should we describe what occurs here? From one moment to the next we can be moved perfectly reasonably out of one story into another. The coherence of this book is the most powerful testimony to the power of such a device to generate a kind of continuity out of a radical discontinuity. Through language we seem to be able to transcend any important connection between meaningful continuity and natural causality. Or rather, the causal links are reduced to an absolute minimum. The relative autonomy of signs from any natural reference allows there to be signs of signs, and hence stories about stories; and it is this that generates unbound signification. No more is the sequence tied to some underlying order or grid. The opening language affords to different orders, levels of language, gives to these simple linguistic devices the power to determine what does and does not count as "continuity." Setting can be radically shifted, characters entirely changed, "worlds" annihilated and created. Still, the book continues.

After reading Calvino, it is a question one can no longer ask, but it is perhaps equally a question we cannot avoid asking—whether what we learn applies only to the extremes of postmodern novels, or whether it has a wider significance. My claim is that Calvino has shown us, writ large, the extraordinary scope that the self-referential powers of language give to our everyday construction of significant continuity in time. When I first read the remark of the seventh reader (near the end of the book) that "the ultimate meaning to which all stories refer has two faces: the continuity of life, the inevitability of death" (204), I took it to be just another comforting reduction. Now I wonder whether the continuity of life is not precisely what, surprisingly enough, gets reaffirmed here.

The man with the suitcase, lost on the railway system, is the man with a past he imagines he can break free from. He can make these radical breaks, but it doesn't work:

> All I did was to accumulate past after past behind me, multiplying the pasts. . . . The past is like a tapeworm, constantly growing, which I carry curled up inside me. (87; translation modified)

Here the continuity that the structure of nested quotation can bring appears as a *necessity* rather than a possibility of freedom. If I make a break with my past, I become the person who has, as it were, put that past in brackets. Every discontinuity can be recuperated. But what if the continuity that we call the self were to rest on nothing more than the mechanisms of quotation that sustain this book?

Heidegger talks of a work of art as opening a world.[8] This book too can be treated as opening a world—not just a literary one, but one in which language and existence are intertwined. Our author, of course, is preparing us all the way through for just such a parallel. And in comparing making love to reading, he seems to confirm Heideggerian usage: "Within both [reading and love-making] times and spaces open, different from measurable time and space" (125).

Beyond Representation, through Language

What is this openness? I would call it the effect of allowing unbound signification to contribute to the intelligibility of our lives. If this, interestingly, names at least something of the structuring of the text, how does it relate to the theme of desire? I understand desire to have as its proper object what we could call the transcendental signified—the "beyond language." I am supposing that the referential and descriptive functions of language suggest a possibility—of direct contact with the real—that language can never achieve, and that every more subtle or persistent use of language necessarily frustrates. What philosophers have thought of as identity through time was described by Nietzsche as a grammatical fiction. At one level Calvino seems to be confirming this. Perhaps it is not just the word "I" that does the work, but the capacity of such linguistic operations as quotation, self-reference, story embeddings, to forge unbound continuities.

In discussing Escher, I concluded that he was using representation to point beyond representation. Perhaps Calvino is finally using the very subtleties and powers of language to point beyond it. The secret is that it is a beyond that could only ever arise through language.

12

Art as Event

There are countless painters and sculptors for whom time, or the temporal dimension of the practice of painting, is thematic.[1] The mutual imbrication of art and time could spawn a whole book series or a very long, highly selective volume. If we reflect that all painting and sculpture (with the exception of kinetic art) has to engage with a four-dimensional world with at least one of these dimensions (time) tied behind its back,[2] and if we take into account the suspension of worldly time often associated with the experience of art, the scope of art's connection with time broadens considerably. Finally, if "time" includes "history"—the depiction of significant historical events (both celebration and denunciation)—or the *making* of history that any artist who contributes to a scene or is taken up by an appreciative audience is involved in, there is increasingly little art that does not bear, and bear witness to, an intimacy with time.

Painting is not the only artistic activity that needs a frame, and it may be that it is only with or against such limits that anything at all creative happens. This exploration of art and time is no exception, operating within very definite, but, I hope, productive limits. The starting point is provided by Hegel's claim that "Art considered in its highest vocation . . . is a thing of the past," and Heidegger's reaffirmation of a certain world-opening role for art.[3] I move from an attempt at a reconsideration of the value of nostalgia in connection to early-nineteenth-century American landscape painting, to critical assessment of the peculiar emphasis on ruin and entropic degradation as the frame of our historical engagement in the work of Robert Smithson. I also draw on Lyotard's post/anti-Hegelian analysis of the significance of the event in the work of Marcel Duchamp and Barnett Newman as a way of assessing the limits of Smithson's engagement with time, proposing a solution to the puzzling absence of time as event in his work.[4]

I

> Amid [these scenes of solitude] the constant associations are of
> God the creator—they are his undefiled works, and the mind is
> cast into the contemplation of eternal things.
> —Thomas Cole

> The work [of art] opens up a *world* and keeps it abidingly in force.
> —Heidegger

There is a renewed interest in early-nineteenth-century American landscape painting, especially the Hudson River school, not least among Europeans. And indeed, it is a good place to look to understand the origins of the idea of manifest destiny and American exceptionalism, or at least the vital embedding of these symbolic resources, tragic liabilities as they have turned out to be, within the American psyche. The valleys of Yosemite, of Connecticut and the Hudson River, the peaks of the Rockies, all bathed in divine sunlight opened and blessed and promised a world, a future, especially for those with the spirit to grasp it. Those who look back may be forgiven for wondering how such promise could have been so blind to its premises and subsequently so often betrayed by the way things have developed. What shape might that path now take if we cannot move without moving forward, without imagining and projecting a better world?

It would be a mistake to suggest that the Hudson River painters simply gave inspiration to those who saw America as a frontier to be conquered. Cole's paintings were indeed heroic in style and scale, portraying landscape in an idyllic and mythic manner (see *The Course of Empire* series [1828–1836]; *The Garden of Eden* [1828]).[5] America was a new Eden, though not unproblematically so. But the emphasis on the sublimity of nature, "untouched forests, soaring mountain peaks, misty beaches and mighty waterfalls," did not prevent a Durand (*View Toward the Hudson Valley* [1851]) from conveying a sense of optimism about progress and man's domination over the natural landscape that he was increasingly cultivating. It is as if the aesthetics of the sublime enables a certain *spiritual* domination, which can then be adapted to practical ends and fall away when it is no longer needed or when it becomes detached from a nation-building agenda. Cole's pupil Frederic Church moved somewhat in that direction, toward luminism, with his paintings of *Niagara* (1857), or *Icebergs* (1861), and he pursued a sparkling realism of nature in far-flung as well as domestic settings—Peru, Ecuador, and Jamaica, as well as the Catskills—celebrating nature in an American way, rather than simply celebrating America.

The movement from a more mythic heroism licensing territorial conquest toward a celebration of light and the beauty of natural settings took place both within Cole's own life and in the succession from Cole to Church and others. There were contradictions within the American dream. The Civil War dates from 1861, the same year that Church exhibited *Icebergs*. Agricultural development, as well as tourism, brought out further tensions in the sublime appreciation of nature. This perhaps encouraged a certain retreat from the early-nineteenth-century confidence in America's destiny and the innocence with which it could stage that coincidence of God, Man, and Nature yoked into the service of Progress.

We might ask ourselves here whether art had betrayed us, or whether we had betrayed art. In the first case, we might conclude that we were seduced by a fantasy, projecting onto a "screen" (landscape painting) a certain idealized natural/social/theological relationship—the gift of property, or promised land—that would open a world only to license genocide, toxic industrialization, the devastation of an earth. Or have we, perhaps, betrayed art? If art has an intrinsic utopian function, is that not betrayed when we shape it into an instrument for our selfish or short-sighted goals? Perhaps there is a third option provided by Hegel's announcement of the end of art. This is not to say that its charms will not continue to work their magic on us. But rather, that art can no longer deliver grand cultural glue and sustenance. We should not be surprised that Nietzsche will both come to idolize Wagner and his *Gesamtkunstwerke* and then repudiate his own hyperbolic projection of what such art might be capable of.[6]

The renewal of interest in early-nineteenth-century landscape painting allows us to articulate something of a general temporal matrix within which to understand the engagement of art with time.[7] There are moments in history at which the way forward seems obscure. And there are times at which great opportunity seems to beckon if we could but consolidate the vision. Sometimes these moments are intertwined. In either case, it is enormously tempting to return to and reanimate a past promise, a golden era, not so much to enable an actual return to that time as to facilitate a return to the promise that it held, or its holding a promise. We do not need to suppose that "life was like that." It is enough that such dreams were once possible.

On the general temporal matrix deployed here, all action—whether individual or collective—projects a future. This space of projection only becomes explicit when our unconscious tacit projections (those reflected in our habits) start to break down.[8] There are many resources on which we can draw in constructing such future projects. But given that there is a premium on their being plausible, it is hard to compete with a picture that purports, at least, to capture a world, and nothing *seems* at least to work as well as returning to a paradise lost. The great deficiency of (say) terra-forming speculations ([re]constructing habitable human space on another planet) is that for anyone with a trace of practical experience, they seem like idealizing fantasies reflecting a kind of humanistic hubris—that such a "whole" could actually be complete and workable, both technologically and spiritually.[9]

A world that has already been tested in reality (or that we believe has been so tested) is more credible. And yet we are increasingly aware that what we return to is typically "a past that was never present"—a creature of nostalgia. Neoclassical revivals are a case in point. But what complicates the picture, and makes the fantasy diagnosis more complicated, is that while there are often deep and genuine illusions built into our nostalgic memories (e.g., airbrushing out the role of slaves in maintaining the lifestyle of the Greeks or the antebellum South), there are other aspects less easily dismissed. If what we return to is not simply a state of affairs but a promise or hope—that is, a state of affairs itself aspiring to certain possibilities—then part, at least, of what we call its illusory or fantasy aspect will be what was unrealized even for itself, but was hoped for and believed to be possible. And of course it is not only not difficult, but often quite cogent, to suppose that there were reasons why these possibilities were not realized at that time that may no longer be operative. Or at least that we can learn from the failures of past dreams.[10]

This matrix suggests that what we may look for in the past is not so much a realized state of affairs as the plausible hope for, or prospect of, such a state of affairs. So we may look back for lessons in how (not) to go forward, in what would be needed to move forward, not necessarily for fully realized worlds. The error or illusion of nostalgia is not merely that of projecting ideal worlds into the past, but of stripping those worlds of their own temporal horizon.[11]

If we modify the role of retrospection in this way, we may come to see the significance of art (and the past) in a new light. Instead of treating the past as a museum of realized states of affairs that might be replayed, we can treat it as a series of open possibilities, oriented sometimes explicitly, sometimes tacitly, toward the future, as well as a series of lessons in the follies of certain kinds of instrumental implementation.[12]

This suggests that the "problem" with nostalgia is not that it looks to the past for solace or inspiration, but that it fails to engage with the temporal complexity of the past. When Heidegger says "The only question is whether an age is ready and strong enough for [essential things]," the big question will be how helpful, in this respect, is his analysis in terms

Thomas Cole, *The Voyage of Life: Youth*, 1840, oil on canvas, 52½ × 78½ in.
Munson-Williams-Proctor Arts Institute, Museum of Art,
Utica, New York. 55.106.

of Spirit.[13] Here, perhaps, art can be quite as much part of the problem
as part of the solution. Taking up again the work of romantic landscape
painters from Turner, Constable, and Friedrich in Europe to the Americans Cole, Bierstadt, and Church, we may interpret it statically as representing the way the world was experienced at the time. Or we may
realize that in its very status as art it transcends representation and articulates possibility, virtuality, a projected future. Space and light are
deployed to articulate time on a flat two-dimensional plane.

This means treating painting as itself essentially taking part in a certain existential or historical virtuality. Everything depends, both for the
artist and for the interpreter, on the dimensionality within which the
painting is conceived to operate. Obviously, this raises complex questions. If we see landscape painting as serving an ideological function[14]—
naturalizing exploitative social relations (unjust property arrangements)
—then painting is an illusion, whether deliberate or unselfconscious, a
cave into whose workshop we are not being encouraged to peer.[15] This
was the complaint made by Roquentin in Sartre's *Nausea*—about the
portraits of dignitaries in the Bouville town hall—that art served to gen-

erate the illusion of (their) "necessity" out of the reality of human contingency.

But equally, to the extent that we are not just passive consumers of art, its very engagement in virtuality makes it the most fertile resource for exploration and analysis. By *virtuality,* I mean the imaginative world projected or suggested or opened up by a work of art. By a *world,* I include the multiple temporal horizons through which that world is experienced: hope and nostalgia, expectation and forgetting, and so on. Such a world is not necessarily represented directly. And it includes what we might call our way(s) of being in a world, modes of human comportment, from the personal to the political and the military. In addition to its virtuality (by which its complex temporal projectivity is exposed), we must also mention the space of contestation in which art essentially operates. To be thoroughly tendentious, we could say that art's virtuality is not normally homogeneous—that we should expect to find in the art of any period a range of virtualities struggling with one another, or active virtualities (anticipating sometimes dramatic new possibilities) warring with more underdeveloped or unarticulated ones. And it might be worth pursuing the idea that one way, at least, in which art can be great is by finding ways of maintaining within itself a range of virtualities in a certain tension.[16]

So far I have explored something of the temporal complexity with which art can "open a world," oriented by the softly social/historical frame presupposed by the Hegel/Heidegger tradition within which these discussions often arise.[17] We have acknowledged a couple of ways in which the failure to grasp art's virtual horizonality can indeed turn it into an instrument of illusion (as Plato first argued). There is a third aspect that now needs to be brought out. If art is not an instrumental blueprint, and if it nonetheless opens up a world and its virtualities, then it essentially leaves open the practical details of how an artist's vision allows us to move forward. Picasso's *Guernica* does not tell us what to do about war, or indeed whether there is anything to be done. And yet we are enjoined by this fact to a rarely acknowledged responsibility in the face of both great and less-great art.[18] If great art dramatizes without resolving the tensions and contradictions of the space it opens up, the challenge to us is to be worthy of that complexity. If lesser art is more univocal or naïve or one-sided, we may yet be able to feed it productively into our own understanding of the space of virtual complexity, to supply from ourselves something of the productive tension that great art would offer us ready-made.[19]

If we follow through the various doubts about understanding the future that art projects in a representational way, an obvious corollary is a certain implausibility in the idea of an end understood as an achieved state of affairs. Such an achieved end, typically understood, does not it-self make room for its own virtuality *within* a transformed grasp of such an end. Such an end would not be so much an end-state as a way of proceeding, of responding. The question I would like to pose is whether we cannot come to a slightly different understanding of art's temporality by pursuing such a reformulated end more directly. Here I turn to a dis-cussion of Jean-François Lyotard and the event.

II

> The modern project . . . does not ground its legitimacy in the past, but in the future.
> —Lyotard

> Art . . . accomplishes an ontological task, that is, "chronological" task. It must constantly begin to testify anew to the occurrence by letting the occurrence be.
> —Lyotard

In various essays from the 1980s, Lyotard laid out both a general phi-losophy of the event and specific reflections on the significance of art in this respect.[20] It would not be an exaggeration to say that he introduces the significance of the event as a response to Hegel's edict *"Wesen ist was gewesen ist"* ("Being is what has been").[21] Hegel and Lyotard agree that there is a radical difference between *what has been* and what is currently happening. And it is only what is past, what has passed, that has the objective character (having been "synthesized") that enables it to be added together, saved, economized. Temporal synthesis, we might say, cannot take place *in* time, but is rather the event of time, occurring, presenting time. "Because it is absolute, the presenting present cannot be grasped; it is *not yet* or *no longer* present."[22] This has implications for what we might call the subject, or self. "That something happens, the occurrence, means that the mind is disappropriated. . . . The event makes the self incapable of taking possession and control of what is."[23]

Lyotard's early phenomenological background rises to the surface here.[24] Later in this essay, he draws broader consequences for this radical break in temporality:

> If thinking indeed consists in receiving the event . . . no-one can claim to think without being ipso facto in a position of resistance to the procedures for controlling time. . . . To think is to question everything including thought, and questioning, and the process. . . . One cannot write without bearing wit-ness to the abyss of time in its coming.[25]

It is such seminal remarks that justify Derrida's saying that we have barely begun to "read" the work of his generation. Lyotard locates the ongoing process of temporal synthesis at the heart of objectification and then offers this site to thinking as its workplace and playground. To the extent that we may treat thinking as inheriting the task of philosophy, time as event, as eventuation is being made the key to philosophy as a practice of resistance to objectification.

This shift, from philosophy to "thinking," echoes Heidegger's similar path, and Derrida's subsequent displacement of thinking in favor of writing. Thinking, we might say, tries to perform and acknowledge, within an essentially representational activity, the ontological limits of representation. If representation occludes eventuation, the inaugural happening of things, thinking at least gestures in the direction of helping us glimpse this. It is true that without conceptual reflection we pay a terrible price. We cannot do without it, but such reflection is not enough, and it generates its own difficulties and stumblings.

The way Lyotard discusses art, especially painting, suggests that he attributes to it a symmetrically inverted power and deficiency, and I will now discuss how he approaches this complementarity between art and thinking in two essays from *The Inhuman*, "Time Today" and "Newman: The Instant," with additional reference to "The Sublime and the Avant-Garde."

It is not that (philosophical) thinking cannot show, or that art cannot think. It may, in fact, be essential that (philosophical) thinking *is* a showing, and that the best art is always thinking. Nonetheless, we do seem to be confronted by two complementary modes of human activity, each of which both requires, and reciprocally illuminates, the other. We will follow Lyotard in highlighting here the significance of time.

If we ask ourselves about "the time of a painting," numerous sites of time immediately spring up (the time of production, of consumption, of circulation, etc.). It is handy that we can tease apart these strands in the temporal skein. Lyotard contends, however, that we can further ask about the time that a painting *is*.

He illustrates this idea via a comparison between Marcel Duchamp and Barnett Newman. On his view, their respective art occupies the site of time in contrasting ways, and in doing so, allows us to see what is at stake. As Lyotard reads Duchamp's *The Large Glass* and *Etant donnés*, they are two "ways of representing the anachronism of the gaze with regard to the event of stripping bare"[26]—where the "event" in question is that of femininity, the scandal of there being an opposite sex. The painting concerns the instant of that event—"the flash of light which dazzles the eye." But the whole gaze finds no place for this. So Duchamp sets up these two works as allusions to a moment they cannot capture, "an attempt to give an analogical representation of how time outwits consciousness."[27] Duchamp is working within a communicative space, trying indirectly to help us see.

Newman, on the other hand, is the artist of the sublime. Instead of "representing an unrepresentable annunciation" à la Duchamp, he allows the painting to present itself. And while the painting is given the force of an obligation ("Here I am. Listen to me"), both author and receiver are evacuated from this purified event. And subject matter? There is a subject matter, but this is the temporality of the painting itself: "If there is any 'subject matter' it is immediacy. It happens here and now. What (*quod*) happens comes later. The beginning is that there is . . . (*quid*)."[28]

Fundamentally, for Lyotard, Duchamp takes "the imperceptibility of the instant" as his subject matter, while Newman's paintings perform it. Newman describes a visit to the mounds of the Ohio-based Miami Indians and his sense of the sacredness of the site: "Looking at the site you feel, Here I am, *here* . . . and out beyond there . . . there is chaos. . . . I became involved with the idea of making the viewer present; the idea that 'Man is present.'"[29] Comparing this account and Newman's subsequent account of his experience of the space of a synagogue he had designed, Lyotard sums up: "This condensation of Indian space and Jewish space has its source and its end in an attempt to capture presence."[30] Presence is the instant that interrupts the chaos of history and that recalls, or simply calls out, that "There is . . ." Being as advent, we might say.

Lyotard understands Newman's art to accomplish "an ontological task, that is a 'chronological' task."[31] It accomplishes it without completing it. It must constantly begin anew to testify to the occurrence by letting the occurrence be.[32]

He subsequently finds in Newman (in "The Sublime and the Avant-Garde") a sense of *now* that is radically different from that phase of consciousness between future and past that we can find in Augustine and Husserl (and Duchamp). Newman's is the sublime sense of "that it happens," cousin of Heidegger's *Ereignis,* which is not only a "stranger to consciousness . . . it is what dismantles consciousness."[33]

Many questions need to be asked about Lyotard's analysis here. Given the contrast between Duchamp and Newman, his specific claims about Newman cannot be taken to be universal claims about art (and painting) as such. Indeed, this contrast is meant to supply us with a certain stretch of possibility within the painting as a "site of time," rather than (just) caught up in a multistranded collection of temporal threads. If Newman's art "accomplishes an ontological task," it does so by performatively addressing time, not just as constituted or as belonging to consciousness, but as something like the creative movement of being itself.

Not just "becoming" in the sense of process, but of origination, eventuation. We might conclude from Lyotard's account that Newman in some sense supersedes Duchamp. After all, he understands both thinking and art as question, or questioning, or what marks the point of the question.[34] And what "dismantles consciousness" would seem to be deeper that what merely points beyond it.

But it would be a thin and rarified account of art that led up to Newman and then stopped, and Lyotard clearly does not mean to suggest this. At the end of "The Sublime and the Avant-Garde," he sounds a warning note, criticizing the commercialization of the avant-garde for confusing the obsession with the new with witnessing the event. But these questions raised by Newman's work are ones that motivate, if not require, a circulation back into the broader expanse of painting (and art) as the site of time, rather than congregating exclusively at Newman's sharp end.

There is, for example, an obvious question about the need (or otherwise) for repetition in art. If the time of the painting itself still has to be experienced each time for the event it witnesses to be taken up, whence the need for a multiplicity of paintings? Is (not) eventuality, happening, the event of life, in some sense always the same just because it has no external object? Well, yes and no. The Miami Indian mound comments ("Here I am, *here* . . .") suggest that the idiosyncrasy of this here, this now, this event is precisely that to which we need to bear witness in its inaugural happening (always assuming that this is today remotely possible).[35] It may not have a constituted content (in the sense of something determined, past). But it may well always have a distinctive character that needs to be addressed, worked with. And we may also need to wean ourselves away from the idea that the event is instantaneous. Speaking of the "instant" is a way of marking a time that is "out of time," a "time after time," not part of the series of constituted nows. But the process of temporal constitution, which is by definition at one level pre-objective, can certainly take time! Think of music, opera, art-events generally.

The implications of what Lyotard says about Newman are broader than the way they play out in Newman's specific embodiment of time in his painting. Lyotard is claiming that the temporality of Newman's painting feeds on the (phenomenological) primacy of the event or the occurrence over its subsequent objectification. But if this is the well from which Newman's sublimity draws, it is, as Lyotard says, an ontological/chronological truth that does not just disappear when one closes ones eyes, even as an artist. So what happens when an artist seems to refuse the time of the event?

I will pursue this question by special reference to the work of Robert Smithson (1938–1973).

III

Robert Smithson emerged from the 1960s as one of the foremost earth artists in the United States and was responsible for the most photographed piece of earth art ever, *Spiral Jetty,* curling 1,500 feet out into the Great Salt Lake, Utah. Just as noteworthy, however, were his innovative artistic practices, involving attempts (not always successful) at engaging mining companies in ways of artistically reclaiming the land they had despoiled. He was a consultant on the design of a new airport at Dallas, Texas, which resulted in some extraordinary flights of speculative and design fancy. He surveyed his own birthplace, Passaic, New Jersey, a site of industrial dereliction and urban decay, as if it contained monuments that needed preserving. And he documented a trip to the Yucatán that echoed the 1839/1842 expeditions of archaeologist John Lloyd Stephens to uncover Mayan ruins, while refusing any repetition of Stephens's colonial gaze by affecting indifference to the very ruins that studded his path. Smithson was at the center of many critical debates (e.g., with Michael Fried) in the 1960s, with seminal essays published in the pages of *Artforum,* and in conversation with the leading artists on the New York art scene. He was a voracious reader and synthesizer of ideas, especially from science and natural history. And he had an overarching sense of cosmic ruin and decay. After his death in 1973 there were countless exhibitions devoted to his work, and critical attention has only increased with time.[36] In the last two years, four excellent books have appeared on Smithson and another with a substantial discussion of his work.[37]

But for all the energy of his artistic production in the 1960s, it can sometimes seem that Smithson has an idée fixe about time and history and that his work is merely a vehicle for its promotion. Is this didactic assessment fair? Or does his predilection for sites of entropic decay and ruin merely supply the necessary limit or frame for his own artistic opening?

It is hard not to think of the minimalism practiced by many of his contemporary artists, with whom he was in constant conversation, such as Carl Andre, Donald Judd, Sol LeWitt, Robert Morris, Ad Reinhardt, Richard Serra, and Frank Stella,[38] as didactic—with its insistence on seriality, structured composites, and spatial clarity and reduction, to the exclusion of any temporal sources of significance, such as narrative.[39] Could one seriously object to such a clear commitment to a fundamental organizing vision?

It is important to remind ourselves that in Lyotard's hands at least,[40] this drifting away from the modernist narrative in the arts did not require an attack on narrative as such. Indeed, the repudiation of the *grand récit* (especially of Enlightenment progress) was meant to allow a thousand *petits récits* to bloom. Anyone residually interested in the political (not a preoccupation of minimalists) saw local narrative intelligibility as a powerful source of resistance to grand overarching explanatory schemes. But minimalism would throw the baby out with the bathwater. Narrativity interfered with the suspension of time that seemed to be required for the visual immediacy of minimally differentiated objects—objects composed of series, repeated units, structured wholes.

Philosophically, the general repudiation of narrativity will seem like a hysterical reaction to the dangers of narrative totalization. The casual drinker will be puzzled by his friend the teetotaler until he discovers that he is a latent alcoholic who cannot have just one or two drinks. By narrative I understand here linguistically mediated intelligible connection in time, where the intelligibility is supplied by a plot or story by which the shape of a temporal sequence is culturally recognized. Structuralist arguments against the primacy of narrative appeared in the 1960s in work by Roland Barthes and Claude Lévi-Strauss. And before that, from the other direction, as it were, doubts were well captured by Sartre's novel *Nausea*,[41] arguing that what we call an adventure is only a retrospective construction, an organized sequence of actions and events in which all the risks and uncertainties have been satisfactorily resolved.[42] But strangely, Sartre's argument is meant to clear the way for our grasp of our absolute freedom, while the minimalist has no time for a subject at all.

The question of narrative bears most sharply on Smithson's description of his 1969 trip to the Yucatán, documented in "Incidents of Mirror Travel in the Yucatan," which appeared as an article in the September 1969 issue of *Artforum* as an "anti-expedition."[43]

What is an expedition? An expedition typically involves exploring what is (to the explorer at least) unknown territory, with a view to bringing back knowledge, stories, booty, maps, and the promise of gold and or property to the sponsoring state or other entity (often a scientific society). Expeditions move from the unknown to the known, the unclaimed to the claimed. They are the advance columns of imperial prospecting—cognitive, mineral, territorial. The grid that the expedition carries with it is one that will aim to open up the possibility of new property rights, in the many senses of property.

Smithson's specific reference here is to the American John Lloyd Stephens's two expeditions to the Yucatán in the 1830s, on which he discovered, cleared, and catalogued a whole archipelago of Mayan ruins, demonstrating the existence of a lost civilization, while positioning the United States and American archaeology as its heir, protector, and rightful spokesman. Stephens was an enlightened man in many ways, but nonetheless his was an imperial vision. The contrast could not be stronger than with the local Indians, descendants of the Maya, who had little interest in or knowledge of their own past. Stephens was the man who could see what was before him, representing a U.S. museum culture to which he was to ship so many artifacts for their better preservation and presentation. It is an exquisite irony that in a matter of months they would all be destroyed in a warehouse fire in New York.

But if Smithson was not following the ideological trail blazed by Stephens, what was he doing? Would it be sufficient to break up every potential site of appropriation, or imperial possession, into one that could not be subjected to such a process?

On one reading, this is what his mirror-displacements are all about.[44] At nine different sites along his road trip from Mérida to Palenque and back, Smithson, in the company of Nancy Holt and his sponsor Virginia Dwan, made temporary installations, using a dozen or so 12″ square mirrors, wedged in trees, leveled with earth, placed on the ground, and so on. These were then photographed. The planes of these mirrors are roughly parallel to each other and angled so as to reflect nothing but the sky—and certainly not the Mayan sites that were the actual way stations of the journey.

Instead of requiring that the site mirror our projective demands or fantasies (ancient civilization abandoned and neglected by current illiterate, ahistorical, and lazy local inhabitants), Smithson introduces literal mirrors that will disperse any attempt to focus objectively on the site in question.[45] No objective synthesis of all the dispersed reflections is possible.

But surely there is something of a dialectical shortfall here. Smithson seems to be saying that art can only redeem us, or protect us from projective seduction, if it refuses any engagement with the ruins of the past whose concrete presence must have been so palpable to him on that journey. Smithson's word for this refusal two years earlier was "indifference."[46]

What are we to make of this? The idea that negation, refusal, reversal, mere opposition is of limited efficacy as a response to what we might want to resist surely does not need arguing. It was a central plank of the thinking of Hegel, Nietzsche, Heidegger, and Derrida, albeit in different ways. If the real issue, the one we ought to be addressing, lies in the frame of reference just below the surface, *opposing* a position may just repeat and even reinforce that frame of reference.[47]

The fact that the recognition of the limits of a reactive negativity is now old hat does not mean that philosophical practice always honors this insight. If the "frame of reference" is (to take an extreme example, but one at issue for philosophers as different as Heidegger, Habermas, and Derrida) the presumed availability of a space of rational discourse, there

Robert Smithson, "Seventh Mirror Displacement," 1969.
Art © Estate of Robert Smithson/Licensed by VAGA, New York, N.Y.

is a certain risk in trying to put that into question, at least for philosophy, namely, that one would cease to do philosophy.

And there is perhaps even less assurance that movements of art will rush to acknowledge this. It may be that taking for granted a particular frame, in extreme reaction to a position internal to that frame, may be a highly productive platform for artistic innovation. Where truth is not the issue, this internal negation may well offer a productive way forward, channeling the energies of those for whom the reigning paradigm of institutionalized art has exhausted itself and is seen to be in need of definitive rejection. As Smithson himself wrote: "The jungle grows only by means of its own negation—art does the same."[48]

It could be argued further that as an aesthetic principle of orientation, nothing works better than a position that is extreme or one-sided—even improbable, ill-advised, or "false"—if it nonetheless licenses or inspires the production of strange new art objects and the ensuing flurry of de-

bate and criticism. For all the formal problems associated with such negation, such objects (and non-objects) may still renew the space of art
and hence its questioning, disrupting power. Smithson fairly baldly opposes objects/appearances, reality/memory, words/things, time/space,
and endorses many other classical oppositions in a way that would give
a philosopher pause.

Many philosophers have disparaged as relativism (which is then said
to lead to nihilism) the thought that thinking and reasoning could be
reduced to expressing a point of view.[49] Yet surely nothing could be more
normal for art? No one would criticize a landscape painting for offering
a point of view, though they might have doubts about the particular
point of view being promoted or the ideological mystification that disguised this fact. But how is this role compatible with what is said to be
characteristic of modern art, that it concerns itself with its very status *as*
art, its own conditions of possibility? To the extent that space, time, and
representation (for example) are just such conditions, this characteriza-
tion might suggest that art should not merely embody a certain stance
(for example, on "time") but that it *take up* the question of art's relation
to time in a reflective and open-ended way.

If this is so, and if Smithson ends up falling short of this standard, a
number of explanations offer themselves. Either (1) Smithson is not a
modernist; he is, as some have suggested, a postmodernist, or a transitional figure between modernism and postmodernism. Or (2) the model
we have offered of the modernist project is itself incomplete or oversimple. Art cannot be a completely open-ended interrogation of its own
status or conditions of possibility. Or at any rate, there can be no questioning or exploring that does not take some things for granted. Conceptual art, for example, while it sets aside the primacy of the object, leans
on the positivity of language (and on the instrumentalization of philosophy) in a way that will subsequently be strenuously critiqued.[50]

There is something to be said for the explanation that Smithson is
distancing himself from the self-absorption of modernism. This is clear
enough in his response to Michael Fried's essay "Art and Objecthood"
in *Artforum*.[51] Fried was defending the need to maintain the art object
as a detached object of aesthetic scrutiny, while Smithson champions a
more dialectical relation, in which the history and materiality of the
scene and situation set up a challenge both to artist and to audience.
Instead of an abstraction, freed from its object, Smithson proposes we
think of art as *obstruction*. The recognition that representation is a form
of idealization, that its difficulties and perhaps inherent incompleteness
are often swept under the carpet, is something that the modernist and
his critic could perhaps agree on. The truly progressive modernist, however, would agree with the postmodernist that what threatens to undo
idealization is vital for understanding the limits and significance of ide-

alization, and hence perhaps of art itself. Here we are close to Lyotard's analysis of postmodernism as the cutting edge of modernism rather than a new stage.[52] Indeed, the new stage account runs the risk of deploying precisely the idea of a progressive series of stages characteristic of modernism.

But the second defense of Smithson, and of any other artist whose artistic exploration is predicated on a platform of assumptions that are not at that moment being questioned, is more intriguing. It is this that we now explore.

To the extent that we can find in painters such as Barnett Newman the awareness of art as event, as an unthematizable opening, Smithson's focus on ruin, on entropy, on the weight of history—all of which resonates with his disdain for the futility of political activism—might seem more like a withdrawal from artistic exploration rather than an example of it. Moreover, if we follow Jennifer Roberts's account of the development of Smithson's work through his often-overlooked religious paintings of the early 1960s, it is not difficult to conclude, as she does, that he was pursuing in that early work a certain transcendence. What she claims, however, is that he did not drop this quest, but that what changed, with his growing interest in crystals and other structures, was the character of the transcendence he sought. Instead of imagining it to be otherworldly, Smithson came to see it as an immanent possibility of this world. He will talk about seeking moments at which time stands still, and he will champion the idea of dedifferentiation, a kind of primal presence, he found in *Ehrenzweig*. What this suggests is an artistic trajectory exploring human temporality across a broad front.[53]

Smithson acknowledges at one point having been influenced by Heidegger's "philosophy of the void." This is a little strange—Heidegger does not speak of the void in quite this way—and it bypasses the whole thematics of being-toward-death that is so central to *Being and Time* as well as the question of time more generally. The issue is to the point because Smithson's attitude toward time and history seems like a very particular mode of being-toward-death, one perhaps echoed in Freud's account of the death-drive, or Thanatos, the drive to quiescence, absence of stimulation, entropic stasis. Smithson's genius consists in his appetite for allegorical linkage and superimposition, his ability to reconstitute the stage of art in a wide array of historical and industrial settings, in his pressing the possibility of "art" and the value of the artist's time and labor, even in the face of a metaphysics of entropy. His refusal of the time of the event, of art as eventuation, had a creative aspect—the recognition of the way history, not least through its material deposits, is never wholly lost and is open to a certain grafting continuance. We may be tempted to charge Smithson with privileging the *end* of time, the state of repose to which every closed system ultimately tends. But does the fact that "in the long run we are all dead," as the saying goes, really offer a privileged point of judgment by which today's ecstasy or discovery or act of generosity must be discounted? Not at all. Human beings—and history itself—are not closed systems, and the law of entropy has only a buffered application to us. And it is just as plausible to suppose that it is the distinctive power of art to counteract our natural tendencies to habituation; to blind repetition; to working, thinking, seeing within rule-based constraints, in order to enact events that open up to us "other worlds," other ways of seeing, other dispensations.

The question we are left with is whether an art-practice—modernist, postmodernist, or ultramoderne[54]—that concerns itself with its conditions of possibility can allow itself to engage with material history, within the broad horizon of pervasive and inevitable decay, and reserve silently and invisibly for its own practice the privilege of creative event, while understanding that practice not as an "event" but as a transformatory graft.

What Derrida says about a writer is true of any creative activity: "The writer writes in a language and in a logic whose proper system, laws and life his discourse by definition cannot dominate absolutely."[55] More broadly construed, "We can always make something of what has been made of us," as Sartre put it. The point is that creative activity presupposes constraints, limits, the given. Such a formula does not prescribe the weighting to be given to this or that pole, to structure, or to creative opening. It insists that there is no escape from this dialectic.

But applying this model to Smithson in particular, and to art in general, raises the question of whether it really leaves room for the distinction we supposed we could make—between philosophical reflection (which knows no limits) and artistic activity (which needs a certain platform of positivity from which to launch its creative exploration of its own condition as art). If we take Derrida seriously, it is not possible to draw this distinction. Philosophy is no less caught up in such a structure, of having to respond to a given, having to take something for granted, having to work with its inheritance, not being able to be completely self-conscious, transparent to itself. We suggested that for Smithson we might conclude that although he does not thematize the temporality of art as event, his own practice bears witness to just such a persistent creative experience. Instead of seeing this as a limitation, we might come to see it as the solution to what we could call the problem of completeness. Recall that Kierkegaard poked fun at Hegel for having devised a complete system that was rendered incomplete precisely by its inability to register Hegel's own singular philosophical passion. Kierkegaard's response was to devise a philosophical practice that exemplified his own position. The same can be said for Heidegger.[56] In these two cases we can at least say that performativity does not sow the seeds of a contradiction. In Smithson's case, we may see his artistic practice as answering what would otherwise be an unanswered question: What is the temporality of the art event itself? And he is making a certain claim—that even the event that opens, that broaches new ground, does so most effectively by an engagement that repeats and reworks a history that was itself always already such a reworking. We take the step *beyond* most effectively by taking a few steps back.

Smithson died before his time.[57] His enduring input is inseparable from his charismatic mega-sculpture *Spiral Jetty*, the most convention-ally beautiful (or sublime) work he made, and from his articulate and wide-ranging interventions in art criticism in the late 1960s and 70s.

There are, of course, those who have independently followed up many of his artistic practices. On the industrial reclamation front, for example, the names of Hans Haacke and Mel Chin come to mind.[58] But it is hard to resist wondering how the trajectory of his thinking and art practice might have developed had he lived. Some of his contemporaries settled for carrying on in the same vein, committing themselves to and getting funding for lifetime projects.[59] It is possible that Smithson would have gone down that path. But the dialectical restlessness demonstrated both by his having transitioned through a religious phase in the early 1960s and by the very different directions of engagement he was pursuing when he died (especially with respect to mining reclamation) suggest someone whose ideas had more miles left in them.

I began by chasing and haranguing the question of how far art can be satisfactorily didactic, can exist to deliver a message, or simply cap-ture or express a position. I have suggested, in a way that broadens Heidegger's thinking about the strife between earth and world, that we might consider art "great" only when it goes beyond delivering a mes-sage to dramatize the tensions and contradictions of which "positions" are only the simplified polar precipitates. I have also suggested that the function of art need not be located in a single work and may also be served by a series of works (often made visible by a retrospective), or by different artists contributing to an ongoing debate or art scene, respond-ing to each other. Clearly, Smithson did this in spades.

What kind of demand is it that art deal with its own status as event? Is it a demand that can be made of any and all art? Is this self-consciousness intrinsic to art as such? Or is it an aspect or dimension of a modernist reflexivity that has itself now been set aside or at least put into question? We have already affirmed, if not demonstrated beyond doubt, our sym-pathy with the view that postmodernism is not so much a break with modernism as its continuing cutting edge. Rationally defended doubt about the inevitability of progress is surely . . . progress. Our earlier dis-cussion of the event of philosophy in chapter 5 had an ontological flavor, situated in the problematic space of repetition marked out by Heidegger,

Foucault, and Deleuze. It is assumed there that even though we are talking about historical contingency, about chance, about the emergence of new discourses and worlds, there are *general* things to be said. And in this chapter we took our lead early on from Hegel's sense that it is precisely the passage of time, in which becoming is converted into being (*"Wesen ist was gewesen ist"*), that provides the inescapable locus of our concern. It may seem, then, that art is just one more thing sheltering under this broader metaphysical umbrella. And in some sense that is so. But what is distinctive about art is that it has come to be seen as one of the most powerful vehicles for witnessing and exploring this fragile and recessive truth about the real, to the point of our wondering whether an artistic project that did not in some way take this up could be taken wholly seriously. I say this even before acknowledging the specific hope of some philosophers that art might offer either a distinct resource (a different access to truth? another mode of expression?) or a salutary lesson, at the point at which philosophy confronts its own limits.

But even if we grant all this, and even if a certain philosophical demand is setting the agenda here, the character of an artist's acknowledgment of art as event cannot be determined in advance. Even our event-champions Heidegger and Lyotard do not agree what is at stake. For Heidegger, the event aspect of a work of art is its opening up a world, setting into play a certain regime of truth, changing the way we live and move and have our being. For Lyotard (certainly in his analysis of Newman), what is at stake seems to be a certain bearing witness to the creative becoming of time as such, the presenc*ing* of what appears. For each thinker, there is something essentially unpresentable, and their views are not necessarily incompatible. But if they are pointing to the same elephant, they seem at least to be pointing to different parts of the elephant. Heidegger, for example, by tweaking our understanding of truth seems closer to offering a cautiously revisionary response to Hegel's sense that art's capacity to answer to and shape our spiritual needs had ended, while Newman's sublime does not seem to have as its goal the sustaining or renewal of community.[60]

The case of Smithson in this respect is, as we have seen, somewhat problematic. In so many ways, both his work and his theoretical contributions—often intermingled as, for example, in "Incidents of Travel in the Yucatan (1969)"—explicitly target assumptions about temporal continuity and intelligibility in favor of all those aspects of experience in which time circles back on itself, stands still, and lets us see all the ways in which our experience is structured by atemporal structures and patterns:

> The current of the river carried one swiftly along. Perception was stunned by small whirlpools suddenly bubbling up till they exhausted themselves into

minor rapids. No isolated moment on the river, no fixed point, just flickering moments of tumid duration.[61]

Yet the envelope within which all this is contained is a metaphysics of ruination. Strangely, this renders him vulnerable to the charge of repeating Stephens's imperial vision, as when (in the Seventh Mirror Displacement in "Incidents of Travel in the Yucatan") Smithson writes that "the world of the Maya and its cosmography has been deformed and beaten down by the pressure of years. The natives . . . are weary because of that long yesterday . . . the grand nullity of their own past attainments.[62]

The role of the mirror(s) in his "Incidents of Travel" is to disrupt any ontological appropriation of a situation by which it would be rendered intelligible and then frog-marched into some linear order. The deep irony, of course, is that for a Hegel, it is precisely reflection that is in the service of such a project. Smithson's mirror reflections are by contrast anarchic and on the side of dispersion, not unity. What are we to make of the philosophy of ruin? The claim that nothing is permanent, that ruin and decay are the norm, can be understood in different ways. It sometimes seems that Smithson has bought into a pop version of the second law of thermodynamics—that the law of entropy governs everything there is, increasing disorder as time goes on. But there is only one thing of which this is certainly true, and that is the cosmos itself, which is the only truly closed system. Perhaps too our solar system, at least as a locus of life, scheduled for final heat death. All other systems can keep entropy at bay, maintaining themselves by drawing more free energy from the outside. We *can* become the accountants of ontological failure, the moments at which, in fact, most systems do decline and fail. But this is a very particular standpoint and has no greater claim to our allegiance than that which celebrates each little ant mound or green shoot that appears miraculously after a searing forest fire. We can check off endings, crumblings, and erosion with our clipboard, but equally the new, the adventurous, the innocent and foolish is always happening and is just as worthy of witness.

Smithson did not, as far as I can tell, understand *time as event* in so many words. But it is my contention that what I am calling his metaphysics of ruination really operates as a foil against which his own unstoppable artistic practice must be set. Compare the case of a doctor who has seen everything and has a somewhat tragic view of human existence. And yet with each patient he may find a renewed reason to hope and care. Smithson is constantly finding creative responses to the situations he engages with. Mining is an interesting case. The extraction of precious products from the earth produces a great amount of value (metal, coal, diamonds) but also a great deal of waste. It can no more be "put back" than Humpty Dumpty can be reassembled after his sorry downfall. But the artist can respond to this entropic slope in a creative way, with an intervention of a different order. That response is each time an event—an event that does indeed embody an attitude and a way of being in the world—and it is in this way that Smithson finds his own way to art as event. It is precisely not a momentary flash, but typically a process or a new monument that makes a statement and marks a new path.

Could this not be said of any art, even that which is most blind to time? It is true that it could be *formally* applied in this way. What is interesting and special about Smithson, as we have seen, is that his own artistic practice—a multivalent grafting onto the material residues of the past—actually reflects a profound meditation on time, followed by a certain ascesis. But his response is one that re-engages and performs time as event in a distinctive way.

I am suggesting that if there is a blind spot in Smithson's engagement with time as event, it is in his very artistic practice, for it is in the particular way he insists on grafting himself onto history that he evinces his own understanding of "art as event." Where Lyotard understands Newman to embody a certain temporal presencing that sublimely escapes objectification, Smithson's version would not be sublime but rather an affirmation of the time of art as a material grafting onto the past.[63] One could interpret Lyotard's insistence on the time of the paint*ing* itself in Barnett Newman, as repeated resistance to the ontological decay of the very transition into the past that turns becoming into being and that generates what Nietzsche called *ressentiment* at time and its "it was." While Smithson's metaphysical frame is and remains for him that of ruin and entropic decay, it may precisely be in his artistic practice (including, for example, his concern with the fate of the submerged *Spiral Jetty*) that the cosmos is rebalanced, as it were.

Notes

Introduction

1. Miles Davis has a CD titled *Time After Time*. And then there's Cyndi Lauper, Eva Cassidy, even Frank Sinatra.

2. Jacques Derrida, *Of Grammatology* (Baltimore: Johns Hopkins University Press, 1976), 41.

3. Jorge Luis Borges, *Labyrinths* (Harmondsworth: Penguin, 1970), 69.

4. See Søren Kierkegaard, *Repetition* [1843] (New York: Harper and Row, 1964).

5. Friedrich Nietzsche, *The Gay Science*, trans. Walter Kaufmann (New York: Vintage, 1974), sec. 341.

1. Interruptions, Regressions, Discontinuities

1. On another occasion, I would follow up the question of the politics of memory raised so poignantly by Marcuse. Memory offers a form of resistance to functional, operationalized language. "Remembrance of the past may give rise to dangerous insights, and the established society seems to be apprehensive of the subversive contents of memory [which] breaks, for short moments, the omnipresent power of the given facts. . . . The specter of man without memory . . . is more than an aspect of decline—it is necessarily linked with the principle of progress in bourgeois society [which] liquidates Memory, Time, Recollection, as irrational leftovers of the past" (Herbert Marcuse, *One Dimensional Man* [New York: Beacon Press, 1964], 98–99). I

am grateful to Pamela Lee's *Chronophobia* (Cambridge: MIT, 2004) for drawing this to my attention.

2. The theme of time being "out of joint" is taken both from *Hamlet* and, more recently, from Derrida's *Specters of Marx*. The question raised implicitly by this allusion is whether this condition is historically specific, something that could be sorted out, or an ineliminable fact. Hamlet confronts the fact of his murdered father and laments that he was "born to set it right." For Derrida, the impetus to grasping how spectrality disjoints the present is the supposed death of Marxism. But this hauntology cannot obviously be exorcised or confined to a particular time.

3. Howard Caygill, *Kant Dictionary* (Oxford: Blackwell, 1995), 129.

4. In this respect it is intriguing to note the pathos of the expression "9/11" to capture the events that took place on September 11, 2001. The baseline poverty of these bare numbers marks the inadequacy of words to capture what happened.

5. The allusion is to Dylan Thomas's poem "Do not go gentle into that good night" (1952), in *In Country Sleep*, written for his dying father.

6. Compare here Schleiermacher's sense of Christian faith being based on a feeling of unconditional dependency, taken up by Wittgenstein, "We are in a certain sense dependent, and what we are dependent on we can call God" (*Notebooks*, ed. G. E. M. Anscombe and G. H. von Wright [Chicago: University of Chicago Press, 1984], 72–75). Freud's critique of religion rests on understanding this as a regressive infantile experience.

7. Francis Fukuyama, *The End of History and the Last Man* (Harmondsworth: Penguin, 1992), 339.

8. Jacques Derrida, *Specters of Marx: The State of the Debt, the Work of Mourning, and the New International* (London: Routledge, 1994).

9. This is reminiscent of Bertrand Russell's example of the problem of induction. The farmyard chickens conclude from experience that the day begins with the farmer broadcasting corn. One day he cuts their heads off instead. So much for induction.

10. This remark has to be qualified in the light of the agenda of neoconservative American Republicans with their *Project for the New American Century,* who keep alight the flame of freedom and its accompanying narrative: "It is dedicated to a few fundamental propositions: that American leadership is good both for America and for the world; that such leadership requires military strength, diplomatic energy and commitment to moral principle."

11. This comes both from the Left and the Right. The Left thinks the agency needed for revolution or resistance requires a strong subject, and the Right grounds its individualism and moralism in such a subject.

12. Derrida's claim that true responsibility requires that we go through undecidability is making a similar point. See *The Gift of Death, Aporias,* etc.

13. Gilbert Ryle, *Concept of Mind* [1949] (Chicago: University of Chicago Press, 2002).

14. See Herbert Marcuse, *Eros and Civilization* (London: Alan Lane: Penguin Press, 1969).

15. See below, chapter 6, "Glimpses of Being in Dasein's Development," which takes this idea further.

16. Martin Heidegger, *Being and Time*, trans. Joan Stambaugh (Albany: SUNY Press, 1996). We should add his remark: "We do not want to get anywhere. We would like only, for once, to get to just where we are already" ("Language" [1950], in *Poetry, Language, Thought*, trans. Albert Hofstadter [New York: Harper and Row, 1971]). On our reading, Heidegger is giving expression to an impossible desire.

17. For example, in Sigmund Freud, *The Interpretation of Dreams* [1900] (New York: Oxford University Press, 1999).

18. See "The Great Earthquake," in Walter Lowrie, *A Short Life of Kierkegaard* (Princeton, N.J.: Princeton University Press, 1970), 67 ff.

19. See my detailed discussion of Nietzsche's eternal return in *The Deconstruction of Time* (Evanston, Ill.: Northwestern University Press, 2001).

20. See Jean-François Lyotard, *The Postmodern Condition* (Minneapolis: University of Minnesota Press, 1979).

21. See Paul Ricoeur, *Time and Narrative*, Vols. 1–3 (Chicago: University of Chicago Press, 1990), and Kevin J. Vanhoozer, "Philosophical Antecedents to Ricoeur's *Time and Narrative*," in *On Paul Ricoeur: Narrative and Interpretation*, ed. David Wood (London: Routledge, 1991).

22. This reference to the "thought-provoking" is to Heidegger's *What Is Called Thinking?* (New York: Harper and Row, 1968). It is worth noting Derrida's "confession" that he has never known how to tell a story in *Mémoires for Paul de Man* (New York: Columbia University Press, 1989). Indeed, one could describe deconstruction as the persistent interruption of the necessary convergences of narrative.

23. See the last chapter, "The Performative Imperative," in my *Thinking After Heidegger* (Cambridge: Polity, 2002).

24. See Walter Benjamin's famous "Theses on the Philosophy of History," in *Illuminations* (London: Fontana, 1977), 255–66.

25. The question of the Event is taken up again more thematically in chapter 7, "The Event of Philosophy."

26. The theme of negative capability (derived from John Keats) is developed in my book *The Step Back: Ethics and Politics after Deconstruction* (Albany: SUNY Press, 2005).

2. Time-Shelters

1. According to Theophrastus, preserved by Simplicius. See G. S. Kirk and J. E. Raven, *The Presocratic Philosophers* (Cambridge: Cambridge University Press, 1971), 117.

2. Most obviously, for Plato, truth. I have a Nietzschean perspective in mind here.

3. Here, and at other places in this essay, there are obvious Heideggerian filiations and resonances. If I do not here discuss his essay "The Anaximander Fragment" (1946), it is not for want of interest. I am trying here to develop a more analytical conceptual matrix with which to articulate some of the same issues, rather than succumb to the pleasures and pains (and inevitable seduction) of reading Heidegger.

4. Gaston Bachelard, *The Poetics of Space* [1958] (Boston: Beacon Press, 1969).

5. See, for example, Ed Casey's *The Fate of Place: A Philosophical History* (Berkeley: University of California Press, 1999); Andrew Benjamin, ed., *Complexity: Architecture/Art/Philosophy*, Journal of Philosophy and the Visual Arts #6 (London, 1995); David Farrell Krell, *Architecture: Ecstasies of Space, Time and the Human Body* (Albany: SUNY, 1997).

6. For the following kinds of consideration: (a) There may be no recognized calibration of the internal event. (When exactly does the bud open? We may be able to say after t1, before t2.) (b) The event itself may depend for its distinct identification on its internal relations to other events within the same shelter. Trans-boundary temporal location may generate incoherence, or at least oddity (e.g., Christopher Columbus discovered America at 3:32 in the afternoon). (c) The value and significance of external and temporal measurement may be extremely limited as compared to the internal temporal order (e.g., a mother's argument against chemically induced labor to suit the hospital timetable).

7. Freud's discussion of the reality principle, the pleasure principle, and the drive toward oblivion, Thanatos, would be an obvious case. And of course, Freud is one of the thinkers who have explicitly used the language of economy.

8. Why, it might be asked, do we persist in talking about time, rather than time and space, or time-space? First, it is harder to introduce time into spatial thinking than vice versa. Indeed, the very linguistic articulation of time begins this latter process. It may well be that all thinking about time ends up (as Heidegger does) with something like time-space, or some other primordial matrix that sustains both space and time. But I am convinced that the long detour of discovering that this is so is preferable to the short-circuit that knows it in advance. This account of time-shelters can indeed be read as a partial explication of why this path to time-space may be unavoidable. Why use the word *economy*? Time is usually understood formally or abstractly in terms of seriality, or "falling-off" (*Ablaufsphänomene*). But if we put aside this abstract description, what opens up are not just the more archaic concerns of the pre-Socratics, but also further formal properties of time, as it functions in identity, for example. The language of economy serves to bring about such a displacement and allows us to *harness* time. NOTE: With Heidegger's discussion of time as "the *horizon* of being" in *Being and Time*, there begins a long meditation on the intimate mutual imbrication of time and space, culminating, perhaps, in *On Time and Being* (1962), and punctuated by sustained discussions on Time-Space in the *Beitrage zur Philosophie* (writ-

ten 1936–38), sections 238–42. See *Contributions to Philosophy (From Enowning)*, trans. Parvis Emad and Kenneth Maly (Bloomington: Indiana University Press, 1999); [hereafter *Contributions*]. See also Heidegger's discussion of Truth and Sheltering (sections 243–47), in which Heidegger makes a non-related use of the idea of sheltering, but one tied into the problematic of truth as concealment.

9. For an extended treatment of such questions, see my *The Deconstruction of Time.*

10. See Gilles Deleuze and Felix Guattari, *Anti-Oedipus: Capitalism and Schizophrenia* [1972] (New York: Viking Press, 1977). They claim that capitalism deterritorializes and re-territorializes every domain or place or unity enclosed by a threshold or boundary. What I claim for time-shelters is that they are sites of resistance to such transformation. And while every time-shelter is *vulnerable* to such invasion, nothing requires that an incursion will *always* take place.

11. I recall, for example, a news report of a man who was allowed to finish his breakfast before being formally arrested and driven off to jail.

12. Paul Ricoeur, *Time and Narrative* (1988).

13. Ibid., 3:241.

14. Immanuel Kant, *Critique of Pure Reason,* trans. Norman Kemp Smith (London: Macmillan, 1964), A141/B180–81.

15. For an extended treatment of this Kantian connection, see Vanhoozer, "Philosophical Antecedents to Ricoeur's *Time and Narrative.*"

16. See Jürgen Habermas, "Concerning the Public Use of History" in *New German Critique* 44 (Spr/Sum 1988): 40–50.

17. Paul Ricoeur, *Freud and Philosophy: An Essay on Interpretation* (New Haven, Conn.: Yale University Press, 1970).

18. Ibid., 261.

19. Ibid.

20. See an attempt at a synthesis of these resources in Herman Rapaport's *Heidegger and Derrida: Reflections on Time and Language* (Lincoln: University of Nebraska Press, 1989). He shows that the trails of linguistic *association* set up in texts (and in life) by such tropes as paranomasia and metalepsis provide a kind of involuntary counterpoint to the harmonies and melodies of narrative organization.

21. See my *The Deconstruction of Time.*

22. Aristotle, *Poetics,* trans. S. H. Butcher (New York: Hill and Wang, 1961).

23. Paul Ricoeur, *Oneself as Another* (Chicago: University of Chicago Press, 1992). His central claim is that selfhood or personal identity does not require the kind of identity we associate with an unchanging self-sameness. Moreover, such a self is tied to a productive dialectical engagement with otherness and the other. Ricoeur's account gives a stunning display of how what I have called the "management of boundaries" might be thought to operate through language, action, and reflection, and the implications for ethics and ontology.

24. I allude here to Husserl's discussion of the possibility of the end of the world, the destruction of all sense (*Ideas* [1913], section 49) taken up so interestingly by Levinas in his "Simulacra: The End of the World," in *Writing the Future*, ed. David Wood (London: Routledge, 1990).

3. Economies of Time

1. I am thinking especially of *Ideas* and *The Phenomenology of Internal Time-Consciousness*.

2. See Husserl, *Formal and Transcendental Logic*, trans. Dorian Cairns (The Hague: Martinus Nijhoff, 1969), and *Analyses of Passive Synthesis* [1918–1926], ed. Margot Fleischer, trans. Anthony Steinbock, Husserliana, Vol. 11 (The Hague: Nijhoff, 1966).

3. Lukács will describe this in *History and Class Consciousness* as the revolutionary movement from the class-in-itself to the class-for-itself.

4. See Hegel, "*Nothing great in the World* has been accomplished without *passion*" (*Reason in History* [New York: Bobbs-Merrill, 1953], 29).

5. Heidegger, *Being and Time*, 232, H250; [hereafter *BT*].

6. See Bret Davis's brilliant treatment of this and related questions in his *Heidegger and the Will: On the Way to Gelassenheit* (Evanston, Ill.: Northwestern University Press, 2006).

7. The path beyond activity and passivity has been productively explored by Charles Scott, "The Middle Voice of Metaphysics," *Research in Phenomenology* 42 (June 1989): 743–64, and John Llewelyn, *The Middle Voice of Ecological Conscience* (London: Macmillan, 1991).

8. *On Time and Being*, trans. Joan Stambaugh (New York: Harper & Row, 1997), 3; [hereafter *OTB*].

9. Pointed out by the translator of *On Time and Being*, 5.

10. *BT*, H36.

11. *BT*, H28.

12. *OTB*, 5.

13. *OTB*, 5.

14. *OTB*, 6.

15. *Given Time*, trans. Peggy Kamuf (Chicago: Chicago University Press, 1992), 9.

16. Ibid., 10–11.

17. Heidegger, *What Is Called Thinking?* See especially Part 2, Lecture II. Parenthetical page numbers in the text are from this work.

18. Note that in *The Gift of Death*, Derrida interprets Matthew's discussion of the heart ("where your treasure is, there will your heart be also") in terms of the sacrifice of the worldly economy for a heavenly one, which requires the operation of a secret (see Matthew 6:3: "When thou doest alms, let not thy left hand know what thy right hand doeth").

19. Heidegger, *What Is Called Thinking?* 142–43.

20. *OTB*, 21–22.

21. *BT*, Div II, ch. 6 note xxx, quoted by Derrida, *Given Time*, 9.

22. See Derrida, "Choreographies" (an interview with Christie McDonald) in *Feminist Interpretations of Jacques Derrida*, by Nancy J. Holland (State College: Penn State University Press, 1997).

23. My response would rescue Ricoeur from the negative implications of his conclusions in *Time and Narrative*.

24. "The Deconstruction of Actuality" [Interview], *Radical Philosophy* 68 (Autumn 1994): 32; [hereafter DA].

25. *For A Justice To Come: An Interview with Jacques Derrida* for the BRussels Tribunal [*sic*] (2004). These themes are developed further in *Specters of Marx* (London: Routledge, 1994).

26. DA, 33.

27. My favorite model for this is the Möbius strip, which shows that it is possible to think together both radical opposition (ontological and ontic) and deep continuity. At every point, two sides with but one surface.

28. Matters as usual are more complicated than they may seem. The quality of an act of generosity might indeed be seen to be compromised by its having a symbolic value if the consequence of that status is revealed in the absence of any follow-up. What is it to save a child's life without addressing the causes of its original starvation? Here we glimpse the horizonal depth of the significance of an act. It would be harder to call merely symbolic a giving that followed through in such a way.

29. Derrida explicitly describes the problem of deciding without rule as "resembling a structure of temporality," *Aporias*, trans. Thomas Dutoit (Stanford, Calif.: Stanford University Press, 1993), 17.

30. Jacques Derrida, *Points*, trans. Peggy Kamuf (Stanford, Calif.: Stanford University Press, 1995), 207.

31. Heidegger quotes this phrase from Nietzsche in a rare reference in *Being and Time*.

32. See especially Lecture II, p. 140.

33. The discussion here makes allusion to a paper by Dominique Janicaud on the myth of Chronos, presented at the Collegium Phenomenologicum (Italy), 1995. See also his *Chronos: Pour l'intelligence du partage temporal* (Paris: Grasset, 1997).

34. And also "Marx and Sons," in *Ghostly Demarcations: A Symposium on Jacques Derrida's Specters of Marx*, ed. Michael Sprinker (London and New York: Verso, 1999).

35. Note that Abraham had already had a son—Ishmael—but he was not legitimate, and he was eventually banished into the wilderness.

4. Reiterating the Temporal

1. Along with chapter 9, "Following Derrida," this chapter is a revised version of a paper published some time ago. It finds a place here because of the vigor with which it offers a defense of the concerns of the early Heidegger in the

face of his own subsequent trajectory and because of my continuing commitment to that project, even as I have subsequently come to appreciate more fully the risks he took in his later writing and what was at stake for him.

2. I have pursued these themes more fully in *The Deconstruction of Time*, 2nd ed. (Evanston, Ill.: Northwestern University Press, 2001); [hereafter *DOT*].

3. G. W. F. Hegel, *Werke* (Frankfurt: Suhrkamp), 2:558.

4. Martin Heidegger, *Sein und Zeit* [1927] (Tübingen: Niemeyer, 1986); [hereafter *SZ*]; *Being and Time*, trans. Macquarrie and Robinson (Oxford: Blackwell, 1962); [*BT*].

5. *SZ*, ix; *BT*, 7.

6. Martin Heidegger, *Kant und das Problem der Metaphysik* (Frankfurt: Klostermann, 1951) [*KDPM*]; *Kant and The Problem of Metaphysics*, trans. James Churchill (Bloomington: Indiana University Press, 1962) [*KPM*].

7. This oversimplifies the situation considerably. William McNeill, for example, reminds me of a lingering reference to authentic and inauthentic temporality in Heidegger's 1934–35 lecture course on Hölderlin's "Germania" and "Rhine" poems. There is much discussion of historical time in *Contributions to Philosophy*, again from the mid-1930s. His discussion here (§242) of "time-space" anticipates the later discussion in *On Time and Being*. (See Miguel de Beistegui's treatment in *Truth and Genesis* [Bloomington: Indiana University Press, 2004]). My own discussion of performativity in *Contributions* also bears indirectly on the question of time. See "The Performative Imperative," in my *Thinking After Heidegger* (2002). And Tina Chanter, in various places, not least her *Time, Death and the Feminine* (Stanford, Calif.: Stanford University Press, 2001), shows how Heidegger's interest in time continues, sometimes in disguise, throughout his writing. Perhaps this issue of the "in disguise"—that the question of time continues in a displaced lexicon—may turn out to be critical. As we see in chapter 7 below, the language of event (*Ereignis*) is a key instance of this.

8. Martin Heidegger, *Metaphysische Anfangsgründe der Logik im Ausgang von Leibniz* (Frankfurt: Klostermann, 1978); [hereafter *MAL*]; *The Metaphysical Foundations of Logic*, trans. Michael Heim (Bloomington: Indiana University Press, 1984); [hereafter *MFL*]; section 12, *MAL*, 198; *MFL*, 255.

9. In addition to the short lecture published as *The Concept of Time*, trans. William McNeill (Oxford: Blackwell, 1992), there is now available a long manuscript by that name: GA 64.

10. Martin Heidegger, *The History of the Concept of Time* [1925], trans. Theodore Kisiel (Bloomington: Indiana University Press, 1985).

11. See Thomas Sheehan's invaluable study, "Heidegger's Early Years: Fragments for a Philosophical Biography," in *Heidegger: The Man and the Thinker* (Chicago: Precedent, 1981). See also Theodore Kisiel's "On the Way to *Being and Time* . . . ," *Research in Phenomenology* 15 (1985). Heidegger scholarship owes an immense debt both to Kisiel for his *The Genesis of Heidegger's Being and Time* (Berkeley: University of California Press, 1993), and to John van Buren's *The Young Heidegger: Rumor of the Hidden King* (Bloomington: In-

diana University Press, 1994). Their jointly edited volume *Reading Heidegger from the Start* (Albany: SUNY Press, 1994) assembles a valuable collection of wider scholarship on this period.

12. See *DOT*, part III.

13. Martin Heidegger, *Die Grundprobleme der Phänomenologie* (Frankfurt: Klosterman, 1975) [*GP*]; *The Basic Problems of Phenomenology*, trans. Albert Hofstadter (Bloomington: Indiana University Press, 1982) [*BPP*]; *GP*, 324; *BPP*, 228.

14. In his *Contributions to Philosophy*.

15. Heidegger, *The Basic Problem of Phenomenology*, 323–24.

16. Heidegger, *An Introduction to Metaphysics*, 1.

17. Though Heidegger insists on the necessary tie between metontology and fundamental ontology (*MAL*, 199; *MFL*, 157).

18. This is more obvious in the case of opening, lighting, clearing, etc. References to event are more ambiguous. We are not speaking of events *in* time, but of time rethought *as* event. See chapter 7 below.

19. See the discussion of "Phenomenology and/or Tautology" by J-F. Courtine in *Reading Heidegger: Commemorations*, ed. John Sallis (Bloomington: Indiana University Press, 1993).

20. *MAL*, 270; *MFL*, 208–209.

21. See "Letter on Humanism" in David Farrell Krell's *Martin Heidegger: Basic Writings* (London: Routledge, 1977).

22. Recalling Heidegger's account of his "attempt to interpret Augustinian (i.e., Helleno-Christian) anthropology in the light of . . . the ontology of Aristotle," it is perhaps not surprising that Heidegger (see esp. *SZ*, 178; *BT*, 223) has the same worries about *entanglement* as did Augustine (see, e.g., "Thou wilt increase, Lord, Thy gifts more and more in me, that my soul may follow me to Thee, disentangled from the birdlime of concupiscence; that it rebel not against itself, and even in dreams not . . . through images of sense, commit those debasing corruptions, even to pollution of the flesh," *Confessions of St. Augustine*, trans. Edward Pusey [New York: Collier, 1961], Book X, 173). Heidegger's attempts to purify *Verfallen* (esp. *SZ*, sec. 38) of its *negative* connotations have to be judged in the light of his retention of so much of Augustine's topology. And if theology were *essentially* a certain topology? Perhaps we have not got rid of God if we still . . .

23. See Cassirer's review in *Kant-Studien*, 36, no. 1/2 (1931): 17, quoted by James S. Churchill in his translator's introduction.

24. "*Ousia* and *Gramme*" in Jacques Derrida, *Marges de la philosophie*, Paris: Minuit, 1972; *Margins of Philosophy*, trans. Alan Bass (Chicago: Chicago University Press, 1982).

25. For a fuller account of this project, see *DOT* (see n. 2, above). The question of *complexity* is obviously central here. Coming after Heidegger's praise of the simple and the stable, it is obviously a crucial question. The issue is whether greater complexity can make for the kinds of difference that make a difference. And that question, too, requires thought. If what is required is a difference of *level*, we have to ask whether the differentiation of levels is as

sharp as one supposes, and whether that sharpness is not itself the product of detemporalization. This suggestion has, of course, extraordinary consequences, for it would affect the ontological difference itself, on which Heidegger pins so much. The claim would be this: that differences of *level* are only ever local, and that there is no guarantee that they can be sustained over time or in the dispersive recontextualization that is the lot of language. For a model that proves nothing but shows everything, consider the Möbius strip, which has at any point two clearly distinct sides, but until it is cut, these sides are in fact one continuous side. I owe this example, of course, to Lacan.

26. In recent work, see e.g., Miguel de Beistegui, *Thinking With Heidegger: Displacements* (Bloomington: Indiana University Press, 2003); Karin de Boer, *Thinking in the Light of Time: Heidegger's Encounter with Hegel* (Albany: SUNY, 2000); Françoise Dastur, *Heidegger and the Question of Time* (Atlantic Highlands, N.J.: Humanities Press, 1998); William McNeill, *The Glance of the Eye: Heidegger, Aristotle and the Ends of Theory* (Albany: SUNY, 1999); Charles E. Scott, *The Time of Memory* (Albany: SUNY, 1999); John Sallis, "Another Time," in *Appropriating Heidegger,* ed. James Falconer and Mark Wrathall (Cambridge: Cambridge University Press, 2000). And as mentioned before, Tina Chanter, *Time, Death and the Feminine.*

27. In David Farrell Krell's *Martin Heidegger: Basic Writings.*

28. See Parmenides: "It is all the same to me from what point I begin, for I shall return again to this same point," in Kathleen Freeman, *Ancilla to The Pre-Socratic Philosophers* (Oxford: Blackwell, 1966), 42.

29. "Why I Stay in the Provinces" (*WSP*) in Thomas Sheehan, ed., *Heidegger: The Man and the Thinker* (Chicago: Precedent, 1981), 28.

30. A very different diagnosis could be drawn from Levinas, for whom the locus of all that I have called a primitive economy would be the face-to-face relation, in which I am always already called (on) by the Other. But would it really *save* the Heideggerian text to relocate it on Levinasian terrain?

31. "The Nature of Language" in *On the Way to Language* [1959], trans. Peter Hertz (San Francisco: Harper and Row, 1971), 57.

32. *WSP,* 28–29.

33. Consider Derrida's "The writer writes *in* a language and *in* a logic whose proper system, laws, and life his discourses cannot dominate absolutely" (*Of Grammatology,* 158). This claim, which itself *repeats* (rewrites) something of the turning inside out of the sock of language that Heidegger attempts in *On the Way to Language,* can be allowed to turn back onto Heidegger's own discourse.

34. We must never forget that unlike his peasants, Heidegger keeps leaving the mountains and *returning.* The *valuation* of simple rough existence is never itself simple. Heidegger is entangled in sentimentality, despite his disclaimers.

35. The question of investment in Heidegger (both our investment in his work and the way certain kinds of economic prejudices work their way through his work) must await another occasion. As far as the latter is concerned, we need to think about (1) the dangers he sees in the *Bestand,* the standing-

reserve that characterizes the *Gestell*, enframing, and (2) the rejection of any neutral currency (such as meaning) in language. Could Heidegger's work be a refusal of money? Marc Shell's *Money, Language and Thought* (Berkeley: University of California Press, 1982) deserves wider philosophical attention.

36. Derrida, *Mémoires for Paul de Man*, 108–109.

37. Cf. Derrida's reference to "the germinal structure of the whole of Husserl's thought," in *Speech and Phenomena*, trans. D. Allison (Evanston, Ill.: Northwestern University Press, 1973).

38. See Heidegger, *What Is Called Thinking?*

39. Ibid., 6.

40. In Martin Heidegger, *Identität und Differenz* (Pfullingen: Neske, 1957); *Identity and Difference*, trans. Joan Stambaugh (New York: Harper and Row, 1969) [*ID*].

41. By Jacques Derrida in *Positions*. I have the same fondness for the early Derrida as I have for the early Heidegger, and as Heidegger had for the early Husserl. A study is needed of "The Early and the Late: the Finitude of Thought," dealing also with the early and the late Hegel, Schelling, and Marx, arguing for some general truths of thanatography: opening and closing?

42. The specification of these rules is here very gestural and incomplete. My confidence in recommending the elaboration of these rules to others is based not just on what could be called rogue "experience with language," in which one becomes aware of the machinery of Heidegger's staging and the sense of the organizing economy of his language, but also the premise that there *must* be such rules (by which I mean, minimally, insistent patterns of repetition), if the language is to make sense. In consequence, what I am saying cannot be a criticism of Heidegger as such. What it does take issue with is his own understanding of what he is doing, of what thinking *could* be.

43. See "The Nature of Language," 57 ff.

44. *SZ*, 384; *BT*, 436.

45. Freeman, *Ancilla*, 42.

46. Martin Heidegger, *The Question Concerning Technology*, trans. William Lovitt (New York: Harper and Row, 1977), 25.

47. In Heidegger's *Pathmarks*, trans. William McNeill (Cambridge: Cambridge University Press, 1998).

48. Friedrich Nietzsche, "Richard Wagner in Bayreuth," in *Untimely Meditations*, trans. R. J. Hollingdale (Cambridge: Cambridge University Press, 1983), 249.

49. Friedrich Nietzsche, *Ecce Homo*, trans. Walter Kaufmann (New York: Random House, 1967), 275.

50. Crucial texts here would be "The Origin of the Work of Art" in Heidegger's *Poetry, Language, Thought*, trans. Albert Hofstadter (New York: Harper and Row, 1971), and the title essay in Derrida's *Psyché: Inventions de l'autre* (Paris: Galilée, 1987).

51. Derrida, "Envoi" in *Psyché*. This quotation is taken from the translation, "Sending: On Representation," 323.

52. Jacques Derrida, "My Chances," in *Taking Chances: Derrida, Psychoanalysis and Literature*, ed. Joseph Smith and William Kerrigan (Baltimore: Johns Hopkins University Press, 1984).

53. Ibid., 16.

54. Philippe Lacoue-Labarthe, *La Fiction du Politique* (Paris: Christian Bourgeois, 1987).

55. Nietzsche, *Ecce Homo*, 127.

56. This movement of circling back is of course itself *temporal*, and it raises the question of whether we should not be able to rethink the movement back to the ontic outlined in Heidegger's discussion of metontology (in the Appendix to *MFL*, section 10) in essentially temporal terms.

57. A way of thinking through such a vertical *movement* that relied less on the idea of presencing could perhaps be found through the doctrine of a double axis of language, of which the paradigmatic, or substitutive, would generate the *verticality* here described.

58. A note on *fracticity*. This neologism deserves a future. It attempts to condense the idea of facticity—which we might gloss as the force of circumstance, our ineluctable engagement with the ways things are in the world—with the fractal, the idea that every arrangement of things, when investigated, discloses further levels of complexity. All the way down. This applies to structures as well as to temporalities.

59. Maurice Merleau-Ponty, *Le Visible et l'invisible* (Paris: Gallimard, 1964); *The Visible and the Invisible*, trans. Alphonso Lingis (Evanston, Ill.: Northwestern University Press, 1968).

60. Allergy to the language of fate and destiny, and doubts about the language with which the *Geschick des Seins* is elaborated should not be misunderstood as a general hostility to the risks Heidegger increasingly takes in his own use of language. If, as I claim, existential temporality is essentially plural, polyphonic, then the language of *stimmung*, atunement, tone, awaits us. And if time is the persistent brinking of otherness (perhaps, specifically, the Other), then the language of opening, lighting, and clearing would become increasingly seductive. Thinking knows no mantric words, nor does it proscribe. What justifies and sustains it is its persistence in returning to the source of its sustenance: time.

5. From Representation to Engagement

1. Heidegger, *Being and Time*, 143/H153.

2. Emmanuel Levinas, *Otherwise than Being or Beyond Essence* (Dortrecht: Kluwer, 1974).

3. John Caputo, *Demythologizing Heidegger* (Bloomington: Indiana University Press, 1993).

4. It is true that in Giovanna Borradori's *Philosophy in a Time of Terror* (Chicago: University of Chicago Press, 2003), 133–35, Derrida distances himself from this Kantian connection, for reasons that are not wholly convincing. Kant does not, as Derrida suggests, think that such ideas are actualizable. And if that is the main problem Derrida has with Kant's regulative ideas (he has others, like Kant's whole architectonic), then he is much closer than he thinks to endorsing them. Derrida admits, with ironic twinkle, "I cannot swear that I will not one day give in to it [the regulative idea]."

5. See Heidegger, "Language," in *Poetry, Language, Thought.*

6. Compare here Luther: "[The believer is a constant beginner] who is always beginning, seeking and renewing his questioning. . . . And he who does not renew his quest loses what he has found, since one cannot stand still on the way to God," with Heidegger: "If God's eternity could be 'construed' philosophically then it may be understood only as a more original and 'infinite' temporality" (*BT,* 564/479) (both quoted in van Buren, *Young Heidegger*) with another remark of Heidegger's: "Dasein . . . guards itself against 'becoming too old for its victories' (Nietzsche)" (*BT,* 308/264). Husserl, too, famously described himself as a "perpetual beginner."

7. See my *The Deconstruction of Time* (2001).

8. Van Buren, *Young Heidegger,* 151.

9. See Kisiel, *Genesis of Heidegger's Being and Time,* 108 ff.

10. See my "The Artefactuality of God: Reply to Caputo," in *Styles of Piety: Practicing Philosophy After the Death of God,* ed. Clark Buckner and Matthew Statler (New York: Fordham University Press, 2006).

11. Immanuel Kant, *Lectures on Ethics* (New York: Harper and Row, 1963), 154.

12. Quoted in Cyril Barrett's excellent *Wittgenstein on Ethics and Religious Belief* (Oxford: Blackwell, 1991), 100.

13. For an elaboration of these comments, see my "Thinking God in the Wake of Kierkegaard," in *Kierkegaard: A Critical Reader,* ed. Jonathan Rée and Jane Chamberlain (Oxford: Blackwell, 1998).

14. This suggests an important way of understanding Husserl's claim, when confronted with the thought of a primal flux, that "words fail us." We echo Wittgenstein's sense that the silence that appears at the limits of language marks the place of the ethical, the turn from words to comportment.

15. Jacques Derrida, *Of Spirit: Heidegger and the Question,* trans. Geoffrey Bennington and Rachel Bowlby (Chicago: University of Chicago Press, 1989), 113.

16. See Philippe Aries, *Western Attitudes Toward Death* (Baltimore: Johns Hopkins University Press, 1973). See also Robert Bernasconi's beautifully nuanced account of this Heidegger, Levinas, Derrida triangle in "Whose Death Is It Anyway? Philosophy and the Cultures of Death," in *Khoraographies for Jacques Derrida,* Tympanum 4, ed. Dragan Kujundzic, July 15, 2000.

17. I pursue this further in "Comment ne pas manger: Deconstruction and Humanism," in *Animal Others,* ed. Peter Steeves (Albany: SUNY Press, 1999),

and "Thinking with Cats," in *Animal Philosophy,* ed. Peter Atterton and Matthew Calarco (London: Continuum, 2004).

18. Of course, while this is literally true, it might be worth exploring the ways in which some do in fact mourn their own deaths in advance. This might perhaps allow one to think of Freud's account of mourning and melancholia, and the play between *eros* and *thanatos* within Heidegger's being-toward-death.

19. See section 53 of *Being and Time,* "Existential Project of an Authentic Being-toward-death."

20. In "Force of Law," in *Deconstruction and the Possibility of Justice,* ed. Drucilla Cornell et al. (New York: Routledge, 1992), 26, Derrida expresses his reservations about the concept of horizon (including Kant's regulative idea) "at least [on] their conventional interpretation" because of the incompatibility between the dimension of deferment (and idealization?) involved in the idea of horizon and the immediacy of the need for justice. It would have to be shown at greater length that what we are promoting as a virtue in both Heidegger's and Derrida's thinking is quite compatible with this immediacy of decision, the instant of which is, as Kierkegaard says, "madness."

21. Jacques Derrida, *The Other Heading: Reflections on Today's Europe* (Bloomington: Indiana University Press, 1992).

22. Kant, *Critique of Pure Reason,* A141/B180.

23. Compare the discussion of boundary operators in "Philosophy *as* Writing: The Case of Hegel," in my *Philosophy at the Limit* (London: Unwin Hyman, 1990).

24. Immanuel Kant, *Critique of Judgement,* trans. J. H. Bernard (New York: Hafner, 1972), section 49.

25. Ibid.

26. Søren Kierkegaard, *Concluding Unscientific Postscript,* trans. David F. Swenson and Walter Lowrie (Princeton, N.J.: Princeton University Press, 1968), 68–69.

27. Barrett, *Wittgenstein on Ethics.*

28. See Luther: "He who does not renew his quest loses what he has found, since one cannot stand still on the way to God!" (quoted by Van Buren, *Young Heidegger,* 198).

6. Glimpses of Being in Dasein's Development

1. The embedded quotation from Kant is from "Uber eine Entdeckung" [1790], in *Werke,* ed. Cassirer, VI, p. 71.

2. See Gadamer, *Truth and Method,* trans. William Glen-Doepel (London: Sheed and Ward, 1975), 238 ff., where he discusses Heidegger's development of the fore-structure of understanding, the Enlightenment's prejudice against prejudice, and the positive and negative values of prejudice.

3. Kant, *Critique of Pure Reason,* B371–72.

4. I say "experimental" despite Heidegger's own association of the experiment with *Machenschaft*. See, for example, *Contributions*, sections 77–80.

5. We may, as he puts it, "go to their encounter [*Entgegen gehen*]" or "go counter to them [*Dagegen angehen*]." See Heidegger, *What Is Called Thinking?* [hereafter *WCT*].

6. See Heidegger, "Language," in *Poetry, Language, Thought*, 190.

7. See *Contributions*, sections 217, 227. See also Heidegger, *What Is a Thing?* trans. W. B. Barton and Vera Deutsch (Chicago: Gateway, 1967), 244.

8. See Derrida's *Spurs/Eperons* (Chicago: University of Chicago Press, 1978), and also his "Choreographies" interview with Christie McDonald.

9. Of course, the situation is more complicated than this. In his *Contributions to Philosophy*, Heidegger begins in effect to identify Dasein with Nietzsche's *Ubermensch*, suggesting that ordinary adult existence is only on-the-way toward Dasein. I am also grateful to Lawrence Hatab for drawing my attention to section 15 of Heidegger's *Einleitung in die Philosophie*, Gesamtausgabe 27 (Frankfurt: Klostermann, 1996). This section is entitled "Entdeckendsein beim Fruhzeitlichen und fruhmenschlichen Dasein," discussing both primitive Dasein and childhood, albeit somewhat schematically. Heidegger does here seem to treat childhood, not as a state with its own positivity, but as a process of growing into the light.

10. On another occasion I would try to show (1) that philosophers ignore human cognitive and moral development at their peril; (2) that disagreements among developmentalists are no basis for setting aside this whole perspective; (3) that we can better understand both the cognitive and the moral in ontological terms—that is, in terms of constitutively relational possibilities (we would attempt to show this for developmental psychology as whole—Gilligan, Kohlberg, Piaget, Erickson, and Loevinger); and (4) that ontology is inseparable from economy—from ways of organizing inside/outside, self/other, time, risk, death.

11. Given Lacan's hostility to the very idea of development, to use him as an example might be thought rash. But it is precisely my point that development occurs by transformations that preserve discontinuities.

12. I believe that Freud's distinctions between oral, anal, and genital stages, as well as the stages identified by Melanie Klein and the fundamental distinction between what Kristeva calls the semiotic and the symbolic, can all be understood to mark out different economies of being. In saying this, I do not mean to underplay the differences between these different theoretical positions.

13. See "Comment ne pas manger," ch. 9 of my *Thinking After Heidegger*.

14. Freud's discussion in "Mourning and Melancholia" depends on this distinction. Heidegger's understanding of *Verwindung*, a twisting free that acknowledges the past (an advance on the naïveté of *Überwindung* [overcoming]), could perhaps be adapted to this third model.

15. See Derrida, *Aporias*. This responds, for example, to such remarks of Heidegger's as "Mortals are they who can experience death as death. Animals cannot do so" ("The Nature of Language," 107).

16. "What Is Metaphysics?" in Krell's *Heidegger: Basic Writings,* 103.

17. Husserl, *Ideas,* section 49.

18. See Maurice Blanchot, *The Writing of the Disaster,* trans. Ann Smock (Lincoln: University of Nebraska Press, 1986).

19. Heidegger makes this explicit, for example, in *Contributions,* section 98: "Time as what removes-unto and opens up is thus in itself simultaneously what *spatializes;* it provides 'space.' What is ownmost to space is not the same as what is ownmost to time, but space belongs to time—as time belongs to space."

20. In his essay "Language" (1950), Heidegger offers an astonishing interpretation of Georg Trakl's poem "Ein Winterabend" ("A Winter's Evening"), especially the line "Schmerz versteinert die Schwelle" / "Pain has turned the threshold to stone." Pain is understood as a marker of dif-ference, the rift, the mutual bearing/granting of world and things. See also "Language in the Poem" in the same volume (180–84, 189–90). Heidegger insists that this is not normal physical or psychological pain. But perhaps this is just what should be said about the pain, distress, and anxiety associated with transitions between one economy of being and another, and our residual memory of such transitions.

21. The original claim, Ernst Haeckel's biogenetic law (1866), may have been something of an exaggeration.

22. See, for example, "Performative Reflexivity," chapter 8 of my *Philosophy at the Limit* (London: Unwin Hyman, 1990); Karen Feldman, "The Performative Difficulty of Being and Time," *Philosophy Today* 44.4 (2000); and chapter 10, "The Performative Imperative," in my *Thinking After Heidegger.*

23. This is the central theme of Heidegger's "The Nature of Language," 57–108, and is clearly both thematized and practiced in *Contributions.*

24. *Of Grammatology,* 21.

25. "Le Facteur de la Verité," in *The Postcard,* trans. Alan Bass (Chicago: University of Chicago, 1987), 467.

26. This would add a temporally layered dimension to Nietzsche's remark (in the second preface to his *Gay Science*), when he asks himself "whether, taking a large view, philosophy has not been merely an interpretation of the body and a misunderstanding of the body" (34–35).

27. We do not need to retreat from beings to pursue being. A certain materialist history (I am thinking of Marx, Nietzsche, a certain reading of Lacan/Freud, and even aspects of Derrida in "Eating Well") is still perhaps both possible and necessary. In each case we find a logic of materiality, or (perhaps) different economies or organizations of beings. Must the question of being be lost sight of if we pursue beings? Perhaps it is precisely in seeming to be willing to give up the question of being that it can be returned to us!

28. See, for example, Scott, *The Time of Memory* (1999).

29. The work of Paul Ricoeur and Richard Kearney is most significant here. My treatment of Kearney's narrative imagination can be found in "Double Trouble: Narrative Imagination as a Carnival Dragon," in *Transversing the*

Imaginary: Richard Kearney's Postmodern Challenge, ed. Peter Gratton and John Manoussakis (Evanston: Northwestern University Press, 2005).

30. I allude here, of course, to Kant's remark in the *Critique of Pure Reason* that the "schematism of our understanding . . . is an art concealed in the depth of the human soul, whose real modes of activity nature is hardly likely ever to allow us to discover" (B180).

31. See "The Performative Imperative: Reflections on Heidegger's *Contributions to Philosophy,*" chapter 10 in my *Thinking After Heidegger.*

32. There is a particular move that Heidegger makes that leads him to abjure beings, a move that reflects his sense of the limits of transformative movement present *within* beings and his sense that what is not there or at the beginning cannot be there later. All discovery is an uncovery or recovery. This may be an unhelpful generalization of the claim that there can be no linear departure from the logic of the beginning. But everything depends on how we proceed. It is true that attempts at recovery often lead to blind repetition—a reawakening of the same mistake! This is a vital insight when thinking about renewal and the force of the new, and it suggests the need for a systematic engagement with Deleuze, who understands philosophy to be in the business of creating concepts; Derrida, who champions invention and chance; and indeed, Donna Haraway, who seems to have found a way of undermining Heidegger's claim that science does not think. Finally, Lyotard's complex position on the inhuman suggests that far from technology being essentially repressive, it is contradictory; and the contradictions need feeding to be creative. See Lyotard, *The Inhuman: Reflections on Time* (Cambridge: Polity Press, 1993).

7. The Event of Philosophy

1. The epigraphs to this chapter are from Michel Foucault, "Nietzsche, Genealogy, History," in *Language, Counter-Memory, Practice: Selected Essays and Interviews,* ed. Donald Bouchard (Ithaca, N.Y.: Cornell University Press, 1977), 139–64, [hereafter *LCMP*]; Gilles Deleuze, "What Is an Event?" in *The Deleuze Reader,* ed. Constantin V. Boundas (New York: Columbia University Press), 45 (originally from *The Logic of Sense*); and Catherine Keller, *Face of the Deep: A Theology of Becoming* (London: Routledge, 2003), 3.

2. See "The Origin of the Work of Art," in *Poetry, Language, Thought,* trans. A. Hofstadter (New York: Harper and Row, 1971).

3. Michel Foucault, *Madness and Civilization* (London: Tavistock, 1967), xi.

4. This suggests a strong line of defense on behalf of Merleau-Ponty to Derrida's critique (in *Speech and Phenomena*) that "there has never been any perception."

5. See "A Preface to Transgression" (1963) in *LCMP,* 29–52.

6. The reference is to his book *Repetition* (1843), in which Constantin Constantius ponders the impossibility of returning to Berlin, recapturing its past reality.

7. Heidegger, *An Introduction to Metaphysics* [1935] (New York: Anchor, 1961).

8. Derrida once remarked that we have yet to properly read his contemporaries.

9. In Foucault, *LCMP,* 165–96.

10. Françoise Dastur, "Heidegger's Concept of World after *Being and Time,*" in *Proceedings of the Annual Heidegger Conference,* De Paul, 1999.

8. Political Openings

1. Martin Heidegger, "The Rectorate 1933/34: Facts and Thoughts," trans. K. Harries, *Review of Metaphysics* 38 (March 1985): 485.

2. Martin Heidegger, "Hölderlin and the Essence of Poetry" [1936], trans. D. Scott, in *Existence and Being,* ed. W. Brock (Chicago: Gateway, 1949), 290.

3. Martin Heidegger, *An Introduction to Metaphysics* [1953; presented in lectures during 1935], trans. R. Manheim (New York: Anchor, 1961), 31; [hereafter *IM*].

4. G. W. F. Hegel, *Phenomenology of Spirit,* trans. A. V. Miller (Oxford: Oxford University Press, 1977), 7.

5. Friedrich Nietzsche, *Thus Spoke Zarathustra* (Harmondsworth: Penguin, 1975), part 2, chapter 42.

6. Heidegger, *Being and Time,* §6. Section 6 is the celebrated section entitled "The Task of Destroying the History of Ontology."

7. Martin Heidegger, "The Self-Assertion of the German University," trans. K Harries, *Review of Metaphysics* 38 (March 1985): 473; [hereafter SA].

8. Compare Hegel's account of Spirit falling into time (*Phenomenology of Spirit,* §§800–808), and Nietzsche's "Become what you are!" (see Nietzsche's *Ecce Homo,* subtitled "How One Becomes What One Is").

9. See Immanuel Kant [1796], "On a Newly Arisen Tone Recently Adopted in Philosophy," in *Raising the Tone of Philosophy: Late Essays by Immanuel Kant, Transformative Critique by Jacques Derrida,* ed. Peter Fenves (Baltimore: Johns Hopkins University Press, 1993).

10. See Hegel's Preface to *Philosophy of Right,* trans. T. M. Knox (Oxford: Clarendon, 1952), 5.

11. See Emmanuel Levinas, "Useless Suffering," trans. Richard Cohen, in *The Provocation of Levinas: Rethinking the Other,* ed. Robert Bernasconi and David Wood (London: Routledge, 1988), 161 ff.

12. Kant explains the way some find "omens of Doomsday . . . in extraordinary changes in nature, in earthquakes, storms, and floods, or comets and atmospheric signs" by reference to their belief in humans' innate depravity, for which only such an end is appropriate. For Kant, the explanation is more prosaic—that morality hobbles behind the cultivation of talents, needs increase faster than the power to meet them, and so on. Kant anticipates, not the end of the world, but the catching up of morality. See his "The End of All Things," in *Perpetual Peace,* trans. L. W. Beck (New York: Bobbs-Merrill, 1957), 74.

13. This citation and the next are from Martin Heidegger, "German Men and Women," trans. W. S. Lewis, in "Martin Heidegger and Politics: A Dossier," R. Wolin, ed., *New German Critique* 45 (Fall 1988): 103–104. These pieces appear in German in *Nachlese zu Heidegger*, ed. Guido Schneeberger (Bern: privately published, 1962).

14. See Søren Kierkegaard, *Sickness Unto Death*, trans. W. Lowrie (New York: Doubleday 1954), 147.

15. See Martin Heidegger, "Schlageter," trans. W. S. Lewis, in *New German Critique* 45 (Fall 1988): 96. Heidegger's memorial speech was given on May 26, 1933. Schlageter had been shot for sabotage against the French occupying army of the Ruhr ten years earlier.

16. See, e.g., Levinas's *Totality and Infinity*, trans. A. Lingis (Pittsburgh, Pa.: Duquesne University Press, 1969), 143–51; "I and Dependence," et passim.

17. See Habermas's important contributions: "A Kind of Settlement of Damages (Apologetic Tendencies)" and "Concerning the Public Use of History," in *New German Critique* 44 (Spring/Summer 1988). The problem of memory could be described as inaugural for Derrida. His first lengthy publication was a commentary on Husserl's *Origin of Geometry*, in which memory is central. More recently, see his *Mémoires for Paul de Man* (1986).

18. See Thomas Sheehan, "Heidegger and the Nazis," *New York Review of Books* 35, no. 10 (June 16, 1988): 38–47. John Caputo took up this challenge with vigor. His break with Heidegger begins with *Demythologizing Heidegger* (1993). Miguel de Beistegui's *Heidegger and the Political* (London: Routledge, 1998) redresses the balance somewhat by insisting we take Heidegger's thinking the political seriously.

19. See Lacoue-Labarthe, *Heidegger, Art and Politics* (1987).

20. See David Krell's excellent paper, "Heidegger's Rectification of the German University," in *Our Academic Contract: Mochlos in America*, ed. Richard Rand (Lincoln: University of Nebraska Press, 1990).

21. Martin Heidegger, "The End of Philosophy and the Task of Thinking," trans. J. Stambaugh, in *On Time and Being*.

22. Jacques Derrida, *Of Spirit: Heidegger and the Question*, trans. Geoffrey Bennington and Rachel Bowlby (Chicago: University of Chicago Press, 1991); *De l'esprit* (Paris: Galilee, 1987). A number of fine essays on the questions raised by Derrida's *Of Spirit* are assembled in *Of Derrida, Heidegger and Spirit*, ed. David Wood (Evanston, Ill.: Northwestern University Press, 1993).

23. Martin Heidegger, "Language in the Poem," trans. P. D. Hertz, in *On the Way to Language* (New York: Harper and Row, 1971), 159–198.

24. Derrida, *Of Spirit: Heidegger and the Question*, 91.

9. Following Derrida

1. This chapter began its life as a Chicago conference paper, and its performative dimension requires the style of that event context to be retained. I write

elsewhere (chapter 7, above) *about* the event. It thematizes and dramatizes the intimate connection between death and writing in Derrida. I have included it for that reason. Very much "of its time," it has an exemplary character that transcends its time. In this displaced *repetition*, I try to retain that sense. It is worth adding that the paper that followed on the program was Jacques Derrida's "Geschlecht II," which is why the auditorium was already packed for this paper.

2. Jacques Derrida, "Le retrait de la metaphore," in *Poesie* (Fall 1978); "The *Retrait* of Metaphor," trans. F. Gardner et al., *Enclitic* 2, no. 2 (Fall 1978): 5–33.

3. See John Searle, "Metaphor," in *Metaphor and Thought,* ed. A. Ortony (Cambridge: Cambridge University Press, 1979).

4. I have "dealt with" the question of strategy more fully in a number of other places. See, for instance, "Style and Strategy at the Limits of Philosophy: Heidegger and Derrida," and "Difference and the Problem of Strategy," part 4, chapter 3 of *The Deconstruction of Time,* 2nd ed. (Evanston: Northwestern University Press, 2001).

5. In Jacques Derrida, *Margins of Philosophy,* trans. Alan Bass (Chicago: University of Chicago Press, 1982), 1–27.

6. Ibid., 16–17.

7. Jacques Derrida, "Signature Event Context," in *Margins,* 307–30.

8. See, for example, "Violence and metaphysics," in *Writing and Difference,* trans. Alan Bass (Chicago: University of Chicago Press, 1978), 79–195 [on Levinas]; "Living On / Border Lines," in *Deconstruction and Criticism* (New York: Seabury Press, 1979) ["on" Blanchot (and others)].

9. Archibald Macleish, "Voyage West," in his *Collected Poems* (Boston: Houghton Mifflin, 1962).

10. Jacques Derrida, *The Postcard: From Socrates to Freud and Beyond,* trans. Alan Bass (Chicago: Chicago University Press, 1987); *La carte postale: De Socrate à Freud et au-delà* (Paris: Flammarion, 1980), 25.

11. I make no attempt to connect Austin's "sea-change" to either San Seriffe or to Macleish's "open ocean."

12. At the risk of seeming to celebrate the victory of metonymy over thought, I might add that the "Martini" possibility led me to thinking about Italian philosophers, and thence to Benedetto Croce's *What Is Living and What Is Dead in Hegel's Philosophy,* and to smile at the marvelous ease with which one might be able to draw that distinction in some less problematic space.

13. See Derrida, *Of Grammatology,* 25.

14. "Linguistics and Grammatology," ibid., 73.

15. See Derrida's "this dangerous supplement . . ." (on Rousseau) in *Of Grammatology.*

16. Jacques Derrida, *Positions,* trans. Alan Bass (Chicago: University of Chicago Press, 1981).

17. "Violence and Metaphysics," 80.

10. The Dark Side of Narrative

1. I draw here on various of Richard Kearney's philosophical writings, including *The Wake of Imagination* (London: Hutchinson, 1988); *Poetics of Imagining: From Husserl to Lyotard* (London: Harper Collins, 1991); *Poetics of Modernity* (Atlantic Highlands: Humanities, 1995); and "Narrative and the Ethics of Remembrance," in *Questioning Ethics: Contemporary Debates in Philosophy*, ed. Richard Kearney and Mark Dooley (London: Routledge, 1999).

2. This is a revised version of my "Double Trouble: Narrative Imagination as a Carnival Dragon," in *Transversing the Imaginary: Richard Kearney's Postmodern Challenge*, ed. Peter Gratton and John Manoussakis (Evanston, Ill.: Northwestern University Press, 2005).

3. Kearney, *Poetics of Imagining*, 248; [hereafter *PI*].

4. Richard Kearney, in *Questioning Ethics*, ed. with Mark Dooley (London and New York: Routledge, 1998), 18–33.

5. *Sam's Fall* (London: Sceptre, 1995); *Walking at Sea Level* (London: Sceptre, 1997).

6. See, for example, Roland Barthes's "Introduction to the Structural Analysis of Narratives," in *The Semiotic Challenge*, trans. Richard Howard (New York: Hill and Wang, 1988), 95–135.

7. See Lévi-Strauss, *The Savage Mind* (Chicago: University of Chicago Press, 1966); *Structural Anthropology* (New York: Anchor Books, 1968).

8. From Samuel Beckett, *The Unnamable* (1959), in *Three Novels by Samuel Beckett: Molloy, Malone Dies, the Unnamable* (New York: Grove Press, 1995).

9. Sigmund Freud, "The 'Uncanny'" [*Das Unheimliche*] [1919], in *Standard Edition*, Vol. 17, trans. James Strachey (London: Hogarth Press, 1955), 217–56.

10. Otto Rank, *The Double: A Psychoanalytic Study* (London: Karnac Books, reprint ed. 1989).

11. Ernst Theodor Hoffman, *Tales of Hoffmann*, trans. Stella Humphries, Vernon Humphries, and R. J. Hollingdale (Harmondsworth: Penguin, 1982).

11. Thinking Eccentrically about Time

1. Douglas Hofstadter, *Gödel, Escher, Bach: An Eternal Golden Braid* (New York: Basic Books, 1999).

2. See my *The Deconstruction of Time*, parts 2 and 3.

3. See Michel Foucault, *Discipline and Punish*.

4. More could be made of this reference to "two hands." See Derrida's "Geschlecht II: Heidegger's Hand," trans. John P. Leavey Jr., in *Deconstruction and Philosophy: The Text of Jacques Derrida*, ed. John Sallis (Chicago: University of Chicago Press, 1987).

5. Quotations are all taken from the Introduction to M. C. Escher, *The Graphic Work of M. C. Escher,* 2nd ed. (London: Oldbourne, 1961), 7 ff.

6. *Critique of Pure Reason,* A145. Kant summarizes these rules as relating "to the time-series, the time-content, the time-order, and lastly to the scope of time in respect of all possible objects."

7. Italo Calvino, *If on a Winter's Night a Traveller,* trans. William Weaver (London: Picador, 1982), 13. (Hereafter cited parenthetically in the text.)

8. See Heidegger, "The Origin of the Work of Art."

12. Art as Event

1. I include here those concerned with action, process, the moment, narrative, death, memory, etc. This list, truly endless, would include, for example: Salvador Dali, Wassily Kandinsky, Caspar David Friedrich, J. M. W. Turner, Yves Tinguely, Alexander Calder, Nicolas Poussin, Thomas Cole, John William Waterhouse, Umberto Boccioni, Piero della Francesca, Robert Smithson, Andy Goldsworthy, Bill Pye.

2. Assuming that reality consists of three spatial dimensions and time, painting is two dimensions short, and sculpture (superficially at least), one short. So we could say that part of the "art" of art is having to deal with the absence of time. Kinetic art is an exception. Obviously, the situation is complicated—does the lichen growing on a stone sculpture give it a temporal dimension? Is it a dimension of the *work* of art, or just the art object?

3. "Art, considered in its highest vocation, is and remains for us a thing of the past. Thereby it has lost for us genuine truth and life, and has rather been transferred into our ideas instead of maintaining its earlier necessity in reality and occupying its higher place" (*Hegel's Aesthetics: Lectures on Fine Arts,* trans. T. M. Knox [Oxford: Clarendon, 1975], 10). See Heidegger in the epigraph (below) from "The Origin of the Work of Art," 44.

4. Two key books here are *Six Years: The Dematerialization of the Art Object from 1966–1972* [1973], ed. Lucy Lippard (Berkeley: University of California, 1997), an extraordinary work of reference; and Pamela M. Lee, *Chronophobia: On Time in the Art of the 1960s* (Cambridge: MIT, 2004), very useful if somewhat misleadingly titled.

5. The Cole epigraph above comes from "Essay on American Scenery" [1936] in *Art in Theory: 1815–1900,* ed. Charles Harrison et al. (Oxford: Blackwell, 1998).

6. "Have you the courage to point to the stars . . . and say: it is our life that Wagner has set among the stars!" (Nietzsche, "Richard Wagner in Bayreuth" [1876], in *Untimely Meditations,* 253). Later he wrote, "He contaminates everything he touches—he has made music sick. I postulate this viewpoint: Wagner's art is diseased" (*The Case of Wagner* [1888], in *The Birth of Tragedy* and *The Case of Wagner,* trans. Walter Kaufmann [New York: Vintage, 1967]).

7. At the time of writing (fall 2005), an exhibition of Hudson River school

paintings (from the Wadsworth Atheneum Museum of Art) is being shown at the Frist Center for the Visual Arts in Nashville, Tennessee, and has aroused great public interest. The background must be the rise of environmental art generally, a growing awareness of our ecological crisis, and the disturbing growth of U.S. imperialism in world affairs, the seeds of which are arguably latent in early-nineteenth-century landscape painting: our God-given right to this land and the invisibility of its native inhabitants.

8. I have in mind, by analogy, Nietzsche's diagnosis of Socrates as a symptom of Greek decadence. Socrates asks after virtue only when it is no longer obvious to the citizens of Athens.

9. It is ironic that in the face of increasing public puzzlement about the point of space exploration, the latest justification is none other than the testing and refinement of the viability of the kind of self-enclosed human colony exemplified by a space station—as if the long-term viability of planet Earth were too immediate an issue.

10. See Heidegger's claim that "it was not German Idealism that collapsed; rather, the age was no longer strong enough to live up to the greatness, breadth and originality of that spiritual world" (*Introduction to Metaphysics* [1935]; amended translation). This is perhaps a special case, but the structure of untimeliness may be much more common.

11. A similar error occurs in Utopian thinking to the extent that it imagines *realized* utopias in which there are no longer any temporal horizons and in which no account of change is offered.

12. Clearly, there are situations in which blueprint projection of a new future works well—founding a city, building a home, establishing the rules of a new organization or board game. It may be that these success stories occur when what is representationally planned out ahead of time creates an order that was not there before. The imposition of such an order on existing functioning traditions and practices, where there is no festering problem to be solved, may be expected to succeed less frequently. See our discussion of Heidegger's confrontation with just this problem in the mid-1930s in chapter 8, "Political Openings."

13. This quote is from Heidegger, *Schelling's Treatise on the Essence of Human Freedom* [1936] (Athens: Ohio University Press, 1985), 4. The ambivalence of his entanglement with the language of spirit is taken up brilliantly by Derrida in his *Of Spirit: Heidegger and the Question* (Chicago: University of Chicago, 1989), 60 ff.

14. See W. J. T. Mitchell, ed., *Landscape and Power* (Chicago: University of Chicago, 1994).

15. See both Plato's cave, and Nietzsche's "workshop" in Nietzsche, *The Genealogy of Morals*, trans. Walter Kaufmann (New York: Vintage, 1969).

16. For Heidegger this tension is the fundamental strife between earth and world, between what will always be recessive, and the world in which a certain way of inhabiting "the truth of being" is set forth. At this level, tension is productive, creative, and necessary, not something to be eliminated.

17. Here Arthur Danto's work is exemplary, more in the Hegelian than Heideg-

gerian tradition, starting from *The Transformation of the Commonplace* (Cambridge, Mass.: Harvard University Press, 1981).

18. The point can be generalized even to philosophy.

19. This may explain why some works of art seem, or may come to seem, "great," even though they themselves are more innocently one-sided. Where they do not dramatize tensions as I have proposed, they may fuel our own dramatic constructions. Or they may be in conversation over just such deep matters in an ongoing art scene. It is hard not to think of this way of staging fundamental strife as second best.

20. The preceding epigraphs come from Lyotard's "Time Today," 68; and "Newman: The Instant," 88, both from *The Inhuman: Reflections on Time* [1988] (Stanford: Stanford University Press, 1992); subsequent page references are to this book.

21. Lyotard, "Time Today," in *The Inhuman*.

22. Ibid., 59.

23. Ibid.

24. He wrote a short monograph on phenomenology: Jean-François Lyotard, *Phenomenology*, trans. Brian Beakley (Albany: SUNY Press, 1991). This was originally published in French in 1954 and went through very many further revisions and editions.

25. Lyotard, "Time Today," 74.

26. Lyotard, "Newman: The Instant," 79.

27. Ibid.

28. Ibid., 82.

29. Lyotard quoting Newman in ibid., 86.

30. Ibid., 87.

31. Ibid., 88.

32. There is a remarkable parallel here to remarks by the mystic Jonathan Edwards quoted by Michael Fried at the beginning of his "Art and Objecthood" (1967): "It is certain to me that the world exists anew every moment; that the existence of things every moment ceases and is every moment renewed." It may be that there is a continuity between the idea that this renewal is the (almost magical) work of God, that it is work of a certain sublime painting, and that this renewal requires a complex material engagement with what the past has deposited in the present.

33. Lyotard, "The Sublime and the Avant-Garde," in *The Inhuman*, 90.

34. Ibid.

35. I am thinking of Smithson's "indifference" to Mayan ruins in his "Incidents of Mirror-Travel in the Yucatan." Or was that indifference precisely a kind of witnessing? See below.

36. Even as I write (summer 2005), a major retrospective on Smithson is being mounted by the Whitney Art Museum in New York.

37. Eugenie Tsai with Cornelia Butler, eds., *Robert Smithson* (Los Angeles: Museum of Contemporary Art, 2004); Ann Reynolds, *Robert Smithson: Learning*

from New Jersey and Elsewhere (Cambridge: MIT Press, 2003); Pamela M. Lee, *Chronophobia: On Time in the Art of the 60s* (Cambridge: MIT Press, 2004); Ron Graziani, *Robert Smithson and the American Landscape* (Cambridge: Cambridge University Press, 2004); and Jennifer L. Roberts, *Mirror-Travels: Robert Smithson and History* (New Haven, Conn.: Yale University Press, 2004). A few years earlier there was the excellent book by philosopher Gary Shapiro, *Earthwards: Robert Smithson and Art after Babel* (Berkeley: University of California, 1995). Jack Flam edited *Robert Smithson: The Collected Writings* (Berkeley: University of California Press, 1996).

38. For an excellent anthology, see Gregory Battock, ed., *Minimal Art: A Critical Anthology* (New York: Dutton, 1968).

39. Conceptual art, too, was not committed to realizing just *any* concepts, but in particular those that release us from grand narrative, from art being expected to offer ideological alibis for oppressive forms of power. See, for instance, the work of Joseph Kosuth, Terry Atkinson, David Bainbridge, and Michael Baldwin. Also Sol LeWitt. This hysterical exclusion of the temporal lies behind the title of Pamela Lee's excellent book about art in the 1960s, *Chronophobia*. The same general move away from the autonomous value of temporal significance and narrative was given classic form at this same period in Roland Barthes, "Introduction a l'analyse structurale des récits," in *Communications*, vol. 8 (Paris: Seuil, 1966); and Claude Lévi-Strauss, *The Savage Mind* (Chicago: University of Chicago Press, [1962], 1966).

40. Lyotard, *The Postmodern Condition*.

41. Jean-Paul Sartre, *Nausea* [1938] (Harmondsworth: Penguin, 1949).

42. An adventure can be understood in the future perfect, as something that will have been. This is what is promised by those offering Adventure Vacations, which offer the illusion of risk, and at least some assurance that you will come back alive and well.

43. See "Four Conversations Between Dennis Wheeler and Robert Smithson (1969–1970)" in *Robert Smithson: The Collected Writings*, ed. Jack Flam, 231; [hereafter *Writings*].

44. Smithson recorded his trip as a kind of photographic documentary art piece, published in September 1969 in *Artforum* as "Incidents of Mirror Travel in the Yucatan." See *Writings*, 119–33.

45. Compare the release of metallic chaff by an airplane to confuse any radar-guided missile that locks on to it.

46. "I actually value indifference. I think it's something that has aesthetic possibilities. But most artists are anything but indifferent; they're trying to get with everything, switch on, turn on" (Smithson, "What Is a Museum? A Dialogue Between Allan Kaplan and Robert Smithson" [1967], in *Writings*, 47). But while his Yucatán project seems a clear case of "indifference," the photographically illustrated essay "A Tour of the Monuments of Passaic, New Jersey" (1967), published in the same year as this interview, does not involve quite such indifference. Instead, there is an ironic transformation of the sites of industrial wasteland and urban blight with which he engages.

47. That this is not just a matter of theory is clear for those who say we cannot fight violence with violence. Obviously, it seems that we *can* respond to violence in the same currency, but if, when we reflect on it, it is violence we abhor, it may become clear that such a response is both immediately self-defeating and encourages more violence. And this is true even if we suppose that its legitimacy (security, police, law enforcement) makes it altogether distinct from the original violence. The importance of invisible frames in political discourse, and the ways in which we are drawn in to reaffirming them even as we think we are engaged in serious disputation, has been effectively promoted by George Lakoff. See, for example, his *Don't Think of an Elephant* (White River Jct., Vt.: Chelsea Green Publishers, 2004). See also his *Moral Politics* (Chicago: University of Chicago Press, 2002).

48. *Writings,* 127.

49. This position was advocated by Dilthey—see his *Weltanschaungtheorie*—and more recently by Rorty. It was most rigorously attacked by Husserl in his *Logical Investigations.*

50. See my review of *Art and Language,* ed. Paul Maenz and Gerd de Vries (Cologne: M. Dumont Schauberg, 1972), in *Studio International,* January 1973.

51. Fried's essay was published in *Artforum* in June 1967 (see "Art and Object-hood" in *Minimal Art: A Critical Anthology,* ed. Gregory Battcock [New York: Dutton, 1968]). Smithson's "Letter to the Editor" appeared in October 1967. See *Writings,* 66–67.

52. This is perhaps the point at which a Lyotard will say that postmodernism ("incredulity to metanarrative") is not so much opposed to modernism as its cutting edge. See his *The Postmodern Condition* (Minneapolis: University of Minnesota Press, 1979).

53. See Roberts's brilliant *Mirror Travels* (2004).

54. This was Smithson's own word. See "Ultramoderne" (1967), in *Writings,* 62–65.

55. Derrida, *Of Grammatology,* 153.

56. See my *Thinking After Heidegger,* ch. 10, "The Performative Imperative."

57. He died in a plane crash in 1973 at the age of 35 while surveying from the air the site of a projected earthwork, *Amarillo Ramp* (Texas), which was subsequently completed by his friends.

58. For a good broader survey, see Sue Spaid, *Ecovention, Current Art to Transform Ecologies* (Cincinnati: Contemporary Arts Center, 2002).

59. E.g., Michael Heizer's *City* and James Turrell's *Roden Crater.*

60. Of course, any such judgment is open to debate. *The Stations of the Cross* (1958–64) followed Newman's suffering a heart attack and is one of his most important projects. The series is subtitled "Why have you forsaken me?"—Christ's words on the cross. For Newman these words had a broad significance for his own time. The series can also be seen a memorial to the victims of the Holocaust.

61. *Writings,* 127.

62. Ibid.

63. In the course of promoting the value of permanence, he stumbles across the word *permeance,* which brings out an additional sense of connectedness with the past.

Selected Bibliography

Aries, Philippe. *Western Attitudes Toward Death*. Baltimore: Johns Hopkins, 1973.

Aristotle. *Poetics*. Trans. S. H. Butcher. New York: Hill and Wang, 1961.

Augustine. *The Confessions of St. Augustine*. Trans. Edward Pusey. New York: Collier, 1961.

Bachelard, Gaston. *The Poetics of Space*. Boston: Beacon Press, 1969.

Barrett, Cyril. *Wittgenstein on Ethics and Religious Belief*. Oxford: Blackwell, 1991.

Barthes, Roland. "Introduction a l'analyse structurale des récits," in *Communications*, vol. 8. Paris: Seuil, 1966.

———. "Introduction to the Structural Analysis of Narratives." In *The Semiotic Challenge*, trans. Richard Howard, 95–135. New York: Hill and Wang, 1988.

Battcock, Gregory, ed. *Minimal Art: A Critical Anthology*. New York: Dutton, 1968.

Beckett, Samuel. *The Unnamable* [1959]. In *Three Novels by Samuel Beckett: Molloy, Malone Dies, The Unnamable*. New York: Grove Press, 1995.

Beistegui, Miguel de. *Heidegger and the Political*. London: Routledge, 1998.

———. *Thinking With Heidegger: Displacements*. Bloomington: Indiana University Press, 2003.

———. *Truth and Genesis*. Bloomington: Indiana University Press, 2004.

Benjamin, Andrew, ed. *Complexity: Architecture/Art/Philosophy*. London: Academy Editions, 1995.

Benjamin, Walter. *Illuminations*. London: Fontana, 1977.

Bernasconi, Robert. "Whose Death Is It Anyway? Philosophy and the Cultures of Death." In *Khoraographies for Jacques Derrida*, Tympanum 4, ed. Dragan Kujundzic, July 15, 2000.

Blanchot, Maurice. *The Writing of the Disaster*. Trans. Ann Smock. Lincoln: University of Nebraska, 1986.

Boer, Karin de. *Thinking in the Light of Time: Heidegger's Encounter with Hegel*. Albany: SUNY, 2000.

Borges, Jorge Luis. *Labyrinths*. Harmondsworth: Penguin, 1970.

Borradori, Giovanna. *Philosophy in a Time of Terror.* Chicago: University of Chicago Press, 2003.

Buren, John van. *The Young Heidegger: Rumor of the Hidden King.* Bloomington: Indiana University Press, 1994.

Calvino, Italo. *If on a Winter's Night a Traveller.* Trans. William Weaver. London: Picador, 1982.

Caputo, John. *Demythologizing Heidegger.* Bloomington: Indiana University Press, 1993.

Casey, Ed. *The Fate of Place: A Philosophical History.* Berkeley: University of California Press, 1999.

Caygill, Howard. *Kant Dictionary.* Oxford: Blackwell, 1995.

Chanter, Tina. *Time, Death and the Feminine.* Stanford, Calif.: Stanford University Press, 2001.

Cole, Thomas. "Essay on American Scenery" [1936]. In *Art in Theory: 1815–1900,* ed. Charles Harrison et al. Oxford: Blackwell, 1998.

Courtine, J-F. "Phenomenology and/or Tautology." In *Reading Heidegger: Commemorations,* ed. John Sallis. Bloomington: Indiana University Press, 1993.

Danto, Arthur. *The Transformation of the Commonplace.* Cambridge, Mass.: Harvard University Press, 1981.

Dastur, Françoise. *Heidegger and the Question of Time.* Atlantic Highlands, N.J.: Humanities Press, 1998.

——. "Heidegger's Concept of World after *Being and Time.*" In *Proceedings of the Annual Heidegger Conference,* De Paul University, Chicago, Ill., 1999.

Davis, Bret. *Heidegger and the Will: On the Way to Gelassenheit.* Evanston, Ill.: Northwestern University Press, 2006.

Deleuze, Gilles, and Felix Guattari. *Anti-Oedipus: Capitalism and Schizophrenia.* New York: Viking Press, 1977.

——. "What is an Event?" In *The Deleuze Reader,* ed. Constantin V. Boundas. New York: Columbia University Press, 1993. Originally from *The Logic of Sense.*

Derrida, Jacques. *Aporias.* Trans. Thomas Dutoit. Stanford, Calif.: Stanford University Press, 1993.

——. "Choreographies" (interview with Christie McDonald). In *Feminist Interpretations of Jacques Derrida,* ed. Nancy Holland. University Park: Penn State University Press, 1997.

——. "The Deconstruction of Actuality" (interview). *Radical Philosophy* 68 (Autumn 1994).

——. *Edmund Husserl's Origin of Geometry.* Trans. John. P. Leavey. New York: Nicolas Hays, 1974.

——. *For a Justice to Come: An Interview with Jacques Derrida* for the BRussels Tribunal [*sic*], 2004.

——. "Force of Law." In *Deconstruction and the Possibility of Justice,* ed. Drucilla Cornell et al. New York: Routledge, 1992.

——. "Geschlecht II: Heidegger's Hand." Trans. John P. Leavey Jr. In *Deconstruction and Philosophy: The Text of Jacques Derrida,* ed. John Sallis. Chicago: University of Chicago Press, 1987.

——. *Ghostly Demarcations: A Symposium on Jacques Derrida's Specters of Marx,* ed. Michael Sprinker. London and New York: Verso Books, 1999.

———. *The Gift of Death*. Trans. David Wills. Chicago: University of Chicago Press, 1995.

———. *Given Time*, trans. Peggy Kamuf. Chicago: University of Chicago Press, 1992.

———. "Le Facteur de la Verité." In *The Postcard*. Trans. Alan Bass. Chicago: University of Chicago, 1987.

———. "Living On / Border Lines." In *Deconstruction and Criticism*. New York: Seabury Press, 1979.

———. *Margins of Philosophy*. Trans. Alan Bass. Chicago: University of Chicago Press, 1982.

———. *Mémoires for Paul de Man*. Trans. Cecile Lindsay et al. New York: Columbia, 1986.

———. "My Chances." In *Taking Chances: Derrida, Psychoanalysis and Literature*, ed. Joseph Smith and William Kerrigan. Baltimore: Johns Hopkins University Press, 1984.

———. "Marx and Sons." In *Ghostly Demarcations*, ed. Michael Sprinker. London and New York: Verso Books, 1999.

———. *Of Grammatology*. Trans. Gayatri Spivak. Baltimore: Johns Hopkins University Press, 1976.

———. *Of Spirit: Heidegger and the Question*. Trans. Geoffrey Bennington and Rachel Bowlby. Chicago: University of Chicago Press, 1991.

———. *The Other Heading: Reflections on Today's Europe*. Bloomington: Indiana University Press, 1992.

———. "*Ousia* and *Gramme*." In *Margins of Philosophy*. Trans. Alan Bass. Chicago: University of Chicago Press, 1982.

———. *Points . . . Interviews, 1974–1994*. Trans. Peggy Kamuf. Stanford: Stanford University Press, 1995.

———. *Positions*. Trans. Alan Bass. Chicago: University of Chicago Press, 1981.

———. *The Postcard: From Socrates to Freud and Beyond*. Trans. Alan Bass. Chicago: University of Chicago, 1987.

———. *Psyche: Invention of the Other*. Chicago: University of Chicago Press, 1993.

———. "The *Retrait* of Metaphor." Trans. F. Gardner et al. *Enclitic* 2, no. 2 (Fall 1978): 5–33.

———. "Signature Event Context." In *Margins of Philosophy*. Trans. Alan Bass. Chicago: University of Chicago Press, 1982.

———. *Specters of Marx: The State of the Debt, the Work of Mourning, and the New International*. London: Routledge, 1994.

———. *Speech and Phenomena*. Trans. David Allison. Evanston, Ill.: Northwestern University Press, 1973.

———. *Spurs/Eperons*. Chicago: University of Chicago Press, 1978.

———. "Violence and Metaphysics." In *Writing and Difference*. Trans. Alan Bass. Chicago: University of Chicago Press, 1978.

Escher, M. C. "Introduction," *The Graphic Work of M. C. Escher*, 2nd ed. London: Oldbourne, 1961.

Feldman, Karen. "The Performative Difficulty of *Being and Time*," *Philosophy Today* 44.4 (2000).

Flam, Jack, ed. *Robert Smithson: The Collected Writings*. Berkeley: University of California Press, 1996.

Foucault, Michel. *Discipline and Punish: The Birth of the Prison*. New York: Vintage, 1995.

——. *Madness and Civilization*. London: Tavistock, 1967.

——. "Nietzsche, Genealogy, History." In Michel Foucault, *Language, Counter-Memory, Practice: Selected Essays and Interviews*, ed. Donald Bouchard. Ithaca and London: Cornell University Press, 1977.

——. "A Preface to Transgression." In Michel Foucault, *Language, Counter-Memory, Practice*, ed. Donald Bouchard. Ithaca, N.Y. and London: Cornell University Press, 1977.

Freeman, Kathleen. *Ancilla to The Pre-Socratic Philosophers*. Oxford: Blackwell, 1966.

Freud, Sigmund. *The Interpretation of Dreams*. New York: Oxford University Press, 1999.

——. "The 'Uncanny'" [*Das Unheimliche*]. From *Standard Edition*, Vol. 17. Trans. James Strachey, 217–56. London: Hogarth Press, 1955.

Fried, Michael. "Art and Objecthood." In Gregory Battcock, ed. *Minimal Art: A Critical Anthology*. New York: Dutton, 1968.

Fukuyama, Francis. *The End of History and the Last Man*. Harmondsworth: Penguin, 1992.

Gadamer, Hans Georg. *Truth and Method*. Trans. William Glen-Doepel. London: Sheed and Ward, 1975.

Graziani, Ron. *Robert Smithson and the American Landscape*. Cambridge: Cambridge University Press, 2004.

Habermas, Jürgen. "Concerning the Public Use of History." In *New German Critique* 44 (Spring/Summer 1988).

——. "A Kind of Settlement of Damages (Apologetic Tendencies)." In *New German Critique* 44 (Spring/Summer 1988).

Hegel, G. W. F. *Aesthetics: Lectures on Fine Arts*. Trans. T. M. Knox. Oxford: Clarendon Press, 1975.

——. "The Anaximander Fragment." In *Early Greek Thinking*. Trans. David Farrell Krell and Frank A. Capuzzi. New York: Harper and Row, 1975.

——. *Phenomenology of Spirit*. Trans. A. V. Miller. Oxford: Oxford University Press, 1977.

——. *Philosophy of Right*. Trans. T. M. Knox. Oxford: Clarendon, 1952.

——. *Reason in History*. Trans. Robert S. Hartman. New York: Bobbs-Merrill, 1953.

Heidegger, Martin. *The Basic Problems of Phenomenology*. Trans. Albert Hofstadter. Bloomington: Indiana University Press, 1982.

——. *Being and Time*. Trans. John Macquarrie and Edward Robinson. Oxford: Blackwells, 1967.

——. *Being and Time*. Trans. Joan Stambaugh. Albany: SUNY Press, 1996.

——. *The Concept of Time*. Trans. William McNeill. Oxford: Blackwell, 1992.

——. *Contributions to Philosophy (From Enowning)*. Trans. Parvis Emad and Kenneth Maly. Bloomington: Indiana University Press, 1999.

——. *Einleitung in die Philosophie*. Gesamtausgabe 27. Frankfurt: Klostermann, 1996.

——. "The End of Philosophy and the Task of Thinking." Trans. J. Stambaugh. In *On Time and Being*. New York: Harper and Row, 1972.

——. "German Men and Women." Trans. W. S. Lewis. In "Martin Heidegger and Politics: A Dossier," ed. R. Wolin. *New German Critique* 45 (Fall 1988).

——. *The History of the Concept of Time.* Trans. Theodore Kisiel. Bloomington: Indiana University Press, 1985.

——. "Hölderlin and the Essence of Poetry." Trans. D. Scott. In *Existence and Being,* ed. W. Brock. Chicago: Gateway, 1949.

——. *Identity and Difference.* Trans. Joan Stambaugh. New York: Harper and Row, 1969.

——. *An Introduction to Metaphysics.* Trans. R. Manheim. New York: Anchor, 1961.

——. *Kant and the Problem of Metaphysics.* Trans. James Churchill. Bloomington: Indiana University Press, 1962.

——. "Language." In *Poetry, Language, Thought.* Trans. Albert Hofstadter. New York: Harper and Row, 1971.

——. "Language in the Poem." Trans. P. D. Hertz. In *On the Way to Language.* New York: Harper and Row, 1971.

——. "Letter on Humanism." In *Martin Heidegger: Basic Writings,* ed. David Farrell Krell. London: Routledge, 1977.

——. *The Metaphysical Foundations of Logic.* Trans. Michael Heim. Bloomington: Indiana University Press, 1984.

——. "The Nature of Language." In *On the Way to Language.* Trans. Peter Hertz. New York: Harper and Row, 1971.

——. "On the Essence of Truth." In *Heidegger: Basic Writings,* ed. David Farrell Krell. London: Routledge and Kegan Paul, 1978.

——. *On Time and Being.* Trans. Joan Stambaugh. New York: Harper and Row, 1997.

——. "The Origin of the Work of Art." In *Poetry, Language, Thought.* Trans. Albert Hofstadter. New York: Harper and Row, 1971.

——. *Pathmarks.* Trans. William McNeill. Cambridge: Cambridge University Press, 1998.

——. *The Question Concerning Technology.* Trans. William Lovitt. New York: Harper and Row, 1977.

——. "The Rectorate 1933/34: Facts and Thoughts." Trans. K. Harries. *Review of Metaphysics* 38 (March 1985): 485.

——. *Schelling's Treatise on the Essence of Human Freedom.* Athens: Ohio University Press, 1985.

——. "Schlageter." Trans. W. S. Lewis. In *New German Critique* 45 (Fall 1988).

——. "The Self-Assertion of the German University." Trans. K. Harries. *Review of Metaphysics* 38 (March 1985).

——. *What Is Called Thinking?* Trans. Fred Wieck and J. Glenn Gray. New York: Harper, 1968.

——. *What Is a Thing?* Trans. W. B. Barton and Vera Deutsch. Chicago: Gateway, 1967.

——. "What Is Metaphysics?" In *Heidegger: Basic Writings,* ed. David Farrell Krell. London: Routledge and Kegan Paul, 1978.

Hoffman, Ernst Theodor. *Tales of Hoffmann.* Trans. Stella Humphries, Vernon Humphries, and R. J. Hollingdale. Harmondsworth: Penguin, 1982.

Hofstadter, Douglas. *Gödel, Escher, Bach: An Eternal Golden Braid*. New York: Basic Books, 1999.

Holland, Nancy J. *Feminist Interpretations of Jacques Derrida*. State College: Penn State University Press, 1997.

Husserl, Edmund. *Analyses of Passive Synthesis* [1918–26], ed. Margot Fleischer. Trans. Anthony Steinbock. *Husserliana*, Vol. 11, 1966.

——. *Formal and Transcendental Logic*. Trans. Dorion Cairns. The Hague: Martinus Nijhoff, 1969.

——. *Ideas*. Trans. W. R. Boyce-Gibson. London: George, Allen and Unwin, 1931.

——. *Logical Investigations*. Trans. J. M. Findlay. London: Routledge and Kegan Paul, 1970.

——. *The Phenomenology of Internal Time-Consciousness*. Bloomington: Indiana University Press, 1964.

Janicaud, Dominique. *Chronos: Pour l'intelligence du partage temporal*. Paris: Grasset, 1997.

Kant, Immanuel. *Critique of Judgement*. Trans. J. H. Bernard. New York: Hafner, 1972.

——. *Critique of Pure Reason*. Trans. Norman Kemp Smith. London: Macmillan, 1964.

——. "The End of All Things." In *Perpetual Peace*. Trans. L. W. Beck. New York: Bobbs-Merrill, 1957.

——. *Lectures on Ethics*. New York: Harper and Row, 1963.

——. "On a Newly Arisen Tone Recently Adopted in Philosophy." In *Raising the Tone of Philosophy: Late Essays by Immanuel Kant, Transformative Critique by Jacques Derrida*, ed. Peter Fenves. Baltimore: Johns Hopkins University Press, 1993.

Kearney, Richard. *Poetics of Modernity*. Atlantic Highlands, N.J.: Humanities, 1995.

——. *Poetics of Imagining: From Husserl to Lyotard*. London: Harper Collins, 1991.

——. *Questioning Ethics: Contemporary Debates in Philosophy*, ed. Richard Kearney and Mark Dooley. London: Routledge, 1999.

——. "Narrative and the Ethics of Remembrance," in *Questioning Ethics*.

——. *Sam's Fall*. London: Sceptre, 1995.

——. *The Wake of Imagination*. London: Hutchinson, 1988.

——. *Walking at Sea Level*. London: Sceptre, 1997.

Keller, Catherine. *Face of the Deep: A Theology of Becoming*. London and New York: Routledge, 2003.

Kierkegaard, Søren. *Repetition*, New York: Harper and Row, 1964.

——. *Sickness Unto Death*. Trans. Walter Lowrie. New York: Doubleday, 1954.

Kirk, G. S., and J. E. Raven. *The Presocratic Philosophers*. Cambridge: Cambridge University Press, 1971.

Kisiel, Theodore. *The Genesis of Heidegger's Being and Time*. Berkeley: University of California Press, 1993.

——. "On the Way to *Being and Time* . . . ," *Research in Phenomenology* 15 (1985).

Kisiel, Theodore, and John van Buren. *Reading Heidegger from the Start*. Albany: SUNY Press, 1994.

Krell, David Farrell. *Architecture: Ecstasies of Space, Time and the Human Body*. Albany: SUNY, 1997.

———. "Heidegger's Rectification of the German University." In *Our Academic Contract: Mochlos in America*, ed. Richard Rand. Lincoln: University of Nebraska Press, 1990.

Lacoue-Labarthe, Philippe. *Heidegger, Art and Politics*. Trans. Chris Turner. Oxford: Basil Blackwell, 1990.

———. *La Fiction du Politique*. Paris: Christian Bourgeois, 1987.

Lakoff, George. *Don't Think of an Elephant*. White River Jct., Vt.: Chelsea Green, 2004.

———. *Moral Politics*. Chicago: University of Chicago Press, 2002.

Lee, Pamela M. *Chronophobia: On Time in the Art of the 1960s*. Cambridge: MIT Press, 2004.

Levinas, Emmanuel. *Otherwise than Being or Beyond Essence*. Dortrecht: Kluwer, 1974.

———. *The Provocation of Levinas: Rethinking the Other*, ed. Robert Bernasconi and David Wood. London: Routledge, 1988.

———. "Simulacra: The End of the World." In *Writing the Future*, ed. David Wood. London: Routledge, 1990.

———. *Totality and Infinity*. Trans. A. Lingis. Pittsburgh: Duquesne University Press, 1969.

———. "Useless Suffering." Trans. Richard Cohen. In *The Provocation of Levinas*, ed. Robert Bernasconi and David Wood. London: Routledge, 1988.

Lévi-Strauss, Claude. *The Savage Mind*. Chicago: University of Chicago Press, 1966.

———. *Structural Anthropology*. New York: Anchor Books, 1968.

Lightman, Alan. *Einstein's Dream*. New York: Vintage, 2004.

Lippard, Lucy, ed. *Six Years: The Dematerialization of the Art Object from 1966–1972*. Berkeley: University of California Press, 1997.

Llewelyn, John. *The Middle Voice of Ecological Conscience*. London: Macmillan, 1991.

Lowrie, Walter. *A Short Life of Kierkegaard*. Princeton, N.J.: Princeton University Press, 1970.

Lyotard, Jean-François. *The Inhuman: Reflections on Time*. Cambridge: Polity Press, 1993.

———. "Newman: The Instant." In *The Inhuman: Reflections on Time*. Stanford, Calif.: Stanford University Press, 1992.

———. *Phenomenology*. Trans. Brian Beakley. Albany: SUNY Press, 1991.

———. *The Postmodern Condition*. Minneapolis: University of Minnesota Press, 1979.

———. "The Sublime and the Avant-Garde." In *The Inhuman: Reflections on Time*. Stanford: Stanford University Press, 1992.

———. "Time Today." In *The Inhuman: Reflections on Time*. Stanford: Stanford University Press, 1992.

Macleish, Archibald. "Voyage West." In *Collected Poems*. Boston: Houghton Mifflin, 1962.

Marcuse, Herbert. *Eros and Civilization*. London: Alan Lane, Penguin Press, 1969.

———. *One-Dimensional Man*. New York: Beacon Press, 1964.

Mauss, Marcel. *The Gift*. New York: W. W. Norton, 1981.

McNeill, William. *The Glance of the Eye: Heidegger, Aristotle and the Ends of Theory*. Albany: SUNY, 1999.

Merleau-Ponty, Maurice. *The Visible and the Invisible.* Trans. Alphonso Lingis. Evanston, Ill.: Northwestern University Press, 1968.

Mitchell, W. J. T., ed. *Landscape and Power.* Chicago: University of Chicago Press, 1994.

Nietzsche, Friedrich. *The Case of Wagner* [1888]. In *The Birth of Tragedy* and *The Case of Wagner.* Trans. Walter Kaufmann. New York: Vintage, 1967.

———. *Ecce Homo.* Trans. Walter Kaufmann. New York: Random House, 1967.

———. *The Gay Science.* Trans. Walter Kaufmann. New York: Vintage, 1974.

———. *The Genealogy of Morals.* Trans. Walter Kaufmann. New York: Vintage, 1969.

———. "Richard Wagner in Bayreuth." In *Untimely Meditations.* Trans. R. J. Hollingdale. Cambridge: Cambridge University Press, 1983.

———. *Thus Spoke Zarathustra.* Harmondsworth, England: Penguin, 1975.

Rank, Otto. *The Double: A Psychoanalytic Study.* London: Karnac Books, repr. ed., 1989.

Rapaport, Herman. *Heidegger and Derrida: Reflections on Time and Language.* Lincoln: University of Nebraska Press, 1989.

Reynolds, Ann. *Robert Smithson: Learning from New Jersey and Elsewhere.* Cambridge: MIT Press, 2003.

Ricoeur, Paul. *Freud and Philosophy: An Essay on Interpretation.* New Haven, Conn.: Yale University Press, 1970.

———. *Oneself as Another.* Chicago: University of Chicago Press, 1992.

———. *The Rule of Metaphor.* Toronto: University of Toronto Press, 1981.

———. *Time and Narrative,* Vols. 1–3. Chicago: University of Chicago Press, 1990.

Roberts, Jennifer L. *Mirror-Travels: Robert Smithson and History.* New Haven, Conn.: Yale University Press, 2004.

Ryle, Gilbert. *Concept of Mind.* Chicago: University of Chicago Press, 2002.

Sallis, John. "Another Time." In *Appropriating Heidegger,* ed. James Falconer and Mark Wrathall. Cambridge: Cambridge University Press, 2000.

Sartre, Jean-Paul. *Nausea.* Harmondsworth, England: Penguin, 1949.

Scott, Charles. "The Middle Voice of Metaphysics." *Research in Phenomenology* 42 (June 1989): 743–64.

———. *The Time of Memory.* Albany: SUNY, 1999.

Searle, John. "Metaphor." In *Metaphor and Thought,* ed. A. Ortony. Cambridge: Cambridge University Press, 1979.

Shapiro, Gary. *Earthwards: Robert Smithson and Art after Babel.* Berkeley: University of California, 1995.

Sheehan, Thomas. *Heidegger: The Man and the Thinker,* ed. Thomas Sheehan. Chicago: Precedent, 1981.

———. "Heidegger and the Nazis." *New York Review of Books* 35, no. 10 (June 16, 1988): 38–47.

———. "Heidegger's Early Years: Fragments for a Philosophical Biography." In *Heidegger: The Man and the Thinker,* 1981.

Shell, Marc. *Money, Language and Thought.* Berkeley: University of California Press, 1982.

Smithson, Robert. "Four Conversations Between Dennis Wheeler and Robert Smithson. 1969–1970." In *Robert Smithson: The Collected Writings,* ed. Jack Flam. Berkeley: University of California Press, 1996.

——. "Incidents of Mirror Travel in the Yucatan." *Artforum,* September 1969. Also in *Smithson: The Collected Writings,* along with "What Is a Museum? A Dialogue Between Allan Kaplan and Robert Smithson," "A Tour of the Monuments of Passaic, New Jersey," and "Ultramoderne."

Spaid, Sue. *Ecovention, Current Art to Transform Ecologies,* Contemporary Arts Center, Cincinnati, Ohio, 2002.

Tsai, Eugenie, with Cornelia Butler, eds. *Robert Smithson.* Museum of Contemporary Art, Los Angeles, 2004.

Vanhooser, Kevin J. "Philosophical Antecedents to Ricoeur's *Time and Narrative."* In *On Paul Ricoeur: Narrative and Interpretation,* ed. David Wood. London: Routledge, 1991.

Wittgenstein, Ludwig. *Notebooks 1914–16,* 2nd ed. Edited by G. E. M. Anscombe and G. H. von Wright. Chicago: University of Chicago Press, 1984.

Wood, David. "The Artefactuality of God: Reply to Caputo." In *Styles of Piety: Practicing Philosophy After the Death of God,* ed. Clark Buckner and Matthew Statler. New York: Fordham University Press, 2006.

——. "Comment ne pas manger: Deconstruction and Humanism." In *Animal Others,* ed. Peter Steeves. Albany: SUNY Press, 1999.

——. *The Deconstruction of Time,* 2nd ed. Evanston, Ill.: Northwestern University Press, 2001.

——. "Double Trouble: Narrative Imagination as a Carnival Dragon." In *Transversing the Imaginary: Richard Kearney's Postmodern Challenge,* ed. Peter Gratton and John Manoussakis. Evanston, Ill.: Northwestern University Press, 2005.

——. "Heidegger and the Challenge of Repetition." In *Thinking After Heidegger.* Cambridge: Polity, 2002.

——, ed. *Of Derrida, Heidegger and Spirit.* Evanston, Ill.: Northwestern University Press, 1993.

——, ed. *Paul Ricoeur: Narrative and Interpretation.* London: Routledge, 1991.

——. "The Performative Imperative: Reflections on Heidegger's *Contributions to Philosophy."* In *Thinking After Heidegger.* Cambridge: Polity, 2002.

——. "Performative Reflexivity." In *Philosophy at the Limit.* London: Unwin Hyman, 1990.

——. *Philosophy at the Limit.* London: Unwin Hyman, 1990.

——. "Philosophy *as* Writing: The Case of Hegel." In *Philosophy at the Limit.* London: Unwin Hyman, 1990.

——. *The Step Back: Ethics and Politics after Deconstruction.* Albany: SUNY Press, 2005.

——. "Style and Strategy at the Limits of Philosophy: Heidegger and Derrida," and "Difference and the Problem of Strategy," in *The Deconstruction of Time,* 2nd ed. Evanston, Ill.: Northwestern University Press, 2001.

——. *Thinking After Heidegger.* Cambridge: Polity, 2002.

——. "Thinking God in the Wake of Kierkegaard." In *Kierkegaard: A Critical Reader,* ed. Jonathan Rée and Jane Chamberlain. Oxford: Blackwell, 1998.

——. "Thinking with Cats." In *Animal Philosophy,* ed. Peter Atterton and Matthew Calarco. London: Continuum, 2004.

——, ed. *Writing the Future.* London: Routledge, 1990.

Index

Page numbers in italics indicate illustrations.

a priori, 60, 63; assumption, 34; condition of experience, 12
Abraham and Isaac, 55–56, 209n35
abyss, 23, 100–101; abyssal, 120; of difference, 23; in the soul, 51
accident, 15, 126
acting, 139
action, 34; self-defining creative, 90
active/passive, 43, 94. *See also* activity; passivity
activity, 22, 39, 93; as something taking place in time, 38; and passivity, 40, 45, 90, 208n7
addiction, 21
adults, 13, 18, 217n9; Dasein, 108; human experience, 110; maturity, 19. *See also* maturation; maturity
adventure, 149–150, 193, 227n42
aesthetic: distance, 28; unity, 35
affirmation, 4, 21–22, 165; of eternal return, 111. *See also* recurrence; return
aging, 16. *See also* adults; maturation; maturity
algorithms of accountancy, 17, 73
allegory, 23, 99. *See also* metaphor
all-or-nothing alternative, 11, 21. *See also* binaries; either/or; opposition
always already, 2, 125, 212n30
anamnesis, 63, 110

Anaximander, 24–26, 29, 36
Angst, 5, 110–111, 114, 146
animal existence, 109–110; impoverishment of world, 109
animality, 141–142
anthropologism, 71
anticipating, 27, 97
anticipation, 52–53, 158; of death, 110. *See also* expectation
anxiety, 18, 20, 90, 93, 218n20; in the face of the animal, 109; infantile, 16; of influence, 6
apocalyptic, 9, 36, 80, 132, 134–135
aporetic: consequences, 48; logic, 47; spaces, 97
aporia, 22, 31–33, 36, 55, 101; immanent, 122; narrative time heals, 31–32, 34–35
apparent, 151. *See also* real
appearance, 27; appearing within, 89; of things, 130; of unity, 19
application, 99, 138–139, 142; of rules, 100
architecture, 25
Aristotle, 15, 30–31, 34–35, 47
art, 4–5, 28, 182, 184–187, 189, 191, 194–196, 200–201; always thinking, 189; as a thing of the past; 182; as didactic, 199; as event, 197–202; as

241

question, 191; conceptual, 196, 227n39; counteracts habituation, 198; death of, 11; dimensions in, 224n2; earth, 192; end of, 182, 184, 200; institutionalized, 195; modern, 10, 196; opens a world, 187, 200; repetition in, 191; significance of, 185; temporality, 188, 199; transcends representation, 186; virtual horizon, 187

artefactual problems, 92

artefactuality, 89

artist, 173, 182, 197, 202

artistic: creativity, 198; exploration, 197; innovation, 195; practice, 198–202; temporal forms, 25

A-series. See time, cosmic (B-series)

audience, 145–146, 157, 196

Augustine, 10–11, 30–31, 33, 211n22

Auschwitz, 14, 134, 138. See also Final Solution; genocide; Holocaust; Nazi; Third Reich

authentic: being-toward-death, 114 (see also being-toward-death); historicality, 136, 139 (see also historicality [Geschichtlichkeit]); time, 31, 66, 90, 136 (see also time); and inauthentic temporality, 61; shape of engagement, 94

authentically, 136

authenticity, 39, 61, 106–107, 135

author, 177; death of, 11; intentions of, 104

autonomous: economies of space and time, 26, 28, 30; identity, 21; semi-, 26

autonomy, 28, 38, 72, 94

auto-reflection, 123

avant-garde, 191

Bachelard, Gaston, 25–26

Barthes, Roland, 167, 172, 193, 227n39

Bataille, Georges, 124

Baudelaire, Charles, 48

bearing in mind, 54–55

Beckett, Samuel, 165, 168

becoming, 191

before and after, 11

being, 22, 26, 35, 38, 44–45, 47, 60, 67, 70, 82, 88; as a thing: 42; as destiny, 77 (see also destiny, of Being [Geschick des Seins]); as historical, 107; call of, 153; constitution of, 26; creative movement of, 190; dehiscence of, 72; economy of, 108–109, 112; epochality of, 78, 109; question of, 67–68, 84, 107–108, 110; temporally dramatized, 5, 25–26; ways of, 5; what has been, 200

being-carried-away, 64

being-in-the-world, 130, 135, 171

being-in-time, 25, 130. See also time

being-temporal, 130

being-toward-death, 40, 55, 90, 95–97, 105–106, 114, 167, 171, 197, 216n18

being-with-others, 135, 137–138

being whose being is dramatized temporally, 25

beings, 29, 43; complex living, 18; living, 12, 26, 169; that manage fragile and permeable boundaries, 36; vulnerability of, 36

belonging, 69, 70–72, 93

betrayal, 184

beyond language, 181

binaries, 20, 124, 126, 167. See also all-or-nothing alternative; either/or; opposition

biography, 22

birth, 2, 12; of Christ, 13, phenomenology, 114; of something new, 132

black holes, 26–27

Blanchot, Maurice, 110

body, as traditional symbolic boundary, 17

body rhythms, 17–18, 28. See also cycles

boredom, 49, 51, 157

Borges, Jorge Luis, 2

bound signification of narrative, 171. See also unbound signification

boundaries, 17, 26, 27, 35, 123 (see also inside, outside); absolute, 27; economic, 29; elastic or permeable, 20, 27, 29; internal, 26; managing, 26–27, 29, 32, 207n23; mark out beings from one another, 26; of norms and names, 17; of self, 16, 19, 32; staked out and defended to the death, 20; traditional symbolic, 17 (see also family; life, and death; nation; self; species); vulnerability to breaching, 29

boundary: crossing, 27; dissolutions, 111; feelings as, 18; procedures for the management of otherness, 26–27

bracketing out, 27, 89. See also suspend

break, 15, 19, 33; in the shape of experience by dreaming, 19; with my past, 180

breakdown, 6, 10, 185; of capacity to project and envision a future, 5; of myth, 9; of narrative, 33; of time, 10, 20; of traditional models of time, 5

broadcasting, 10

B-series. *See* time, cosmic (B-series); time, lived experience; time, phenomenological

Cage, John, 28

calculation, 27, 73

calendar, 13, 40, 51, 98

call, 152–155; of Being, 153; of conscience, 153; of death, 153

calling on the gods to return, 6

Calvino, Italo, 5, 170, 172–181

capital, 10

capitalism, 12, 17, 207n10; penetrates boundaries, 17

capitalist: development, 17; expansionism, 12

care, 69, 72

caress, 109

carnival, 127–128

Carpocratian, 168–169

Cartesian subjectivity, 40, 42

castration: fear of, 110; new site of truth, 113

category mistake, 16

category rigidity, 20

Catholicism, 87

causality, 35. *See also* time, lived experience; time, phenomenological

Cervantes, Miguel de, 2

chance, 79, 126, 128, 218n32; economy of, 52; meeting, 15

change, 12, 27; inability to accept, 20

chaos, 13. *See also* disorder; entropic; entropy; negentropic; order

chiasm, 122

childhood, 5, 108–110, 217n9. *See also* adults

chimera, 2

Christian, 12, 92; faith, 204n6; mysticism, 65; significance, 141; theologians, 142; thinkers, 91, 93; tradition, 141. *See also* salvation

Christianity, 12–13, 17, 87, 91

chronological task, 190

chronological truth, 191

Chronos, 55, 209n33

Church, Frederic, 183–186

circle, 45, 47, 51, 87, 100–101, 133, 175; circling back, 214n56

circling, 86

circularities, 187

Civil Rights Movement, 16

clearing, 69

clock, 10, 27–28, 51, 98

closed system, 198, 201

closure, 33, 64, 88, 114, 138, 152, 198; humanistic, 36; of metaphysics, 151; of philosophy, 150, 158. *See also* disclosure; truth, as living in relation to disclosure; worldly, enclosures

cognitive restructuring, 4

Cole, Thomas, 183–184, *186*

commercialization, 191

commodified lives, 22

commodity: consumption, 17; fetishism, 40, 44, 89

community, 5, 135, 137, 159; historical reflection of a, 75; of nations, 136

completeness, 107, 179

completion, 47

complexity, 10, 26

concealment, 43, 98, 209n8. *See also* unconcealment

concept, 23, 91, 94; orders according to a rule, 49

conceptual art, 196, 227n39

conceptualization, 51

conceptualize ontologically, 87; non-conceptual within the conceptual, 99

conditions of possibility, 40, 66, 196, 198

confession, 22, 33–34

constitution, 87; auto-, 46; of beings, 26

constitutive, 12, 115; not regulative, 15

constraints, 17, 198

consumerism, 17. *See also* commodity

continuity, 2, 12, 15, 21, 29, 31, 56, 169, 172, 180; illusion of narrative, 5; of life, 180

conversation, 22

cooperation, 15, 28; well-managed strategies of, 19

coping mechanism, 115

corruption, 27, 29

counter-memory, 128. *See also* memory

counter-narrative, 164–165. *See also* narrative

counting, 13

create, 6, 13, 30; re-create, 6
creative, 151, 198; force, 17, 37; of interruption, 34; movement of being itself,
190; opening, 4, 198; response, 202
creatively move on, 98
creativity, 5, 120; norm of, 2
crippling psychologies, 111
crisis, 77, 132, 147; ecological, 225n7 (*see
also* environmental meltdown; global
warming)
critical, 120; destructive resource, 91; dispositions, 100; spirit, 141
criticism, 158. *See also* going counter to a
thinker
critique, 25
cycle of life (birth, growth, decline,
death, rebirth), 12
cycles, 16, 172; destructive, 4; diurnal
metabolic, 16; economic, 28; interwoven, 16; menstrual, 16; natural,
40; of repetition, 101. *See also* body
rhythms

danger, 19, 146; of narrative totalization, 193
dark: ages, 12; forces, 167; side, 164;
darkness, 98
das Man (one, They), 39–40
Dasein, 18, 38, 43, 63, 94, 108, 135–
136, 141, 217n9; as a whole, 61;
Dasein's ecstatic temporality, 42,
75; Dasein's existence, 110; Dasein's
temporality, 110–111; Daseins, individual, 31; is its time, 97–98; is outside itself, 39
dawn of man, 18
deadening repetitions of everydayness, 119
death, 11–13, 39, 90, 110–111, 114,
119, 130, 135, 145, 154–159, 168,
201; as an accounting question, 18;
as such, 95; connection with writing, 222n1; drive, 19, 197, 206n7;
economy of, 16; final heat, 201; inevitability of, 180; my own, 40, 96–97,
216n18; not my, 94; of a family member, 51; of God, 21, 51; of love, 51; of
the other, 96 (*see also* mortality). *See
also* being-toward-death
debt, 17, 46
decay, 13, 192, 198, 201; cosmic, 192.
See also decline; ruin

deception, 168
decide responsibly, 54
decision, 32, 51
decline, 12, 132. *See also* decay; ruin
deconstruct, 5, 103
deconstruction, 25, 157–159; of the subject and of identity, 16
dedifferentiation, 197
deferment, 52, 62
deferral, 159
deferring, 20
dehiscence, 29, 70, 71; of Being, 72; of
selfhood, 137; of substantialist identity, 136
delay, 19, 111
Deleuze, Gilles, 4, 114, 122, 129–130,
207n10, 225n32
democracy to-come, 52, 88, 96
dependence, 19, 93, 136 (*see also* receptivity); of B-series on A-series, 32.
See also independence
dependency, 21, 94, 108, 136
depression, 21, 132
Derrida, Jacques, 2, 6, 12, 14, 22, 38, 45–
49, 52–56, 59, 72, 75, 78–79, 88, 90,
94–97, 108, 110, 113–114, 121, 141–
142, 146–149, 151–159, 171, 189,
198, 204n2, 215n4, 221n17, 222n1,
225n32
desire, 2, 15, 17, 178–179, 181; for significance, 13; guiding, 15; instinctual,
16; metaphysical, 119; satisfaction of,
17; to overcome, 106, 111
despair, 4, 21, 132; despairingly willing
to be oneself, 20
destiny (*Geschick*), 5, 15, 29, 64, 68,
75–77, 79–80, 135–138, 184,
214n60; of Being (*Geschick des
Seins*), 47, 54, 60, 75, 77–79. *See
also* fate (*Schicksal*)
destiny's gift of presence, 47
destroy the tradition, 103
destruction, 27
destructive, 158; cycles, 4; spirit is, 141
devastation of the earth, 5, 184. *See also*
environmental meltdown; global
warming
development, 26, 29, 102, 106, 108–
109, 110, 111, 113–115, 217n11; arrested, 100; capitalist, 17; history, 18;
human (*see* human, development); incomplete, 5, 18; narrative, 178; of an

inner principle, 15. *See also* growth; maturation
developmental identity transitions, 110, 114
developmental path of Spirit, 12
différance, 52, 81, 121, 147–148, 154, 171
difference, 60, 62, 71, 108, 121, 147, 154; as opposed to identity, 126; ontological, 82, 108; sexual, 108; singular, 130
differential forces, 128
Dilthey, Wilhelm, 71. *See also Weltanschauung*
dimensional understanding, 97
dimensionality, 88, 107, 111. *See also* opening; presencing
dimensions, 28, 37, 121, 182, 224n2; multiplicity of, 39
directive idea. *See* guiding idea
disaster, 110
disclosure, 115, 128; events as, 123; truth as, 115
discontinuity, 15, 27, 180. *See also* continuity
discover, 15, 198
disengagement, 11. *See also* engagement
disintegration, 132. *See also* integration, experiential and reflective
dislocation, 2
disorder, 13, 201. *See also* entropic; entropy; negentropic; order
disorganization, 26
dispersion, 63, 65, 121, 201
displacement, 19, 21, 120, 123, 157
disruption, 48, 56, 169; radical, 11
dissemination, 113
dissociation, 126, 128
distress, 111, 115
distribution, 17, 108, 121
doing, 22, 139
Don Quixote, 2
double, 167–169; cross, 168; duties, 97; mapping, 28, 35; movement, 82; withdrawal, 44
dream, 19, 27, 50; dreaming as a break in the shape of experience, 19; illusory, 159; sequentiality of dreams, 19. *See also Einstein's Dream*
Duchamp, Marcel, 189, 190–191
dwell awhile, 112
dwelling, 69, 71–72
dynamic, 11, 22

earth: art, 192; devastation of, 107; life on, 107. *See also* strife between earth and world
ecologists, 76
economic: boundaries, 29; cycles, 28; management, 134; relations, 114
economies, 15, 19; of autonomous space and time, 26, 28, 30; human subjects in, 16; of relation, 43; shifting, 19
economists, 76
economy, 17, 26, 38, 52, 71, 111; of being, 25, 108–109, 112; of chance, 52; of death, 16; of exchange, 47; of language, 26; of narrative, 36; of production; 48; of the event, 54; of thinking, 123; of time, 25–26, 28, 38, 51, 111, 119; primitive, 70–71
ecstases, 65
ecstasies, 64, 106
ecstasy, 49, 111, 157, 198
ecstatic: being-toward-death, 110; temporality, 42, 62, 64, 75, 94, 97, 105, 137; unity, 64
education, 23, 111; re-educate, 40. *See also* learn
Einstein's Dream, 10, 23
either/or, 20–21. *See also* all-or-nothing alternative; binaries; opposition
emancipation, 100
emancipatory point of philosophy, 138
embodiment, 16, 28, 35; phenomenology of, 25
emergence into persistence, 25
empty repetition. *See* repetition, empty
end, 107, 134; achieved, 188; of all absolute grounds, 21; of art, 182, 184, 200; of theodicy, 134; of time, 13, 22, 197; of the world, 208n23, 220n12; point, 101; ulterior, 165
ends, 34. *See also* teleology; telos
enframing, 140, 213n35. *See also* Gestell
engaged: interrogation, 91; structurally or dynamically, 101
engagement, 86, 90, 97; authentic shape of our, 94; with language, 122; with phenomena, 25; with the world, 97
enigma, 43. *See also* intelligibility
Enlightenment, 9, 12–13; idea of progress, 12
entities, 15, 43
entropic, 26; decay, 192, 202; slope, 202;

stasis, 197. *See also* chaos; disorder; entropy; order
entropy, 13, 197–198, 201. *See also* entropic; negentropic; order
environmental meltdown, 9. *See also* devastation of the earth; global warming; industrialization, toxic
envoi, 78–79. *See also* epochs; sending
epochality of being, 78, 109
epoché, 31, 148
epochs, 78, 109
equality, 9. *See also* justice
equiprimordiality, 86
Ereignis, 22, 46–47, 62, 115, 120, 141. *See* also event
eroticism, 124
error, 17, 43, 124
eruption, 16, 19
es gibt, 43–47, 64, 69, 73, 93; *Sein*, 42, 43, 78
es gibt Zeit, 42
Escher, M. C., 5, 49, 101, 170, 172–175, *176*, 181
esotericism, 87
eternal recurrence. *See* recurrence, eternal
eternal return. *See* return, eternal
ethical, 35; engagement with the world, 97; issue, 169; moment, 169; opposition between ontological and, 106; responsibility, 114, 164–165
ethico-political, 88
ethics, 36, 99–100; of communication, 144
event, 3–4, 13, 19, 21–22, 47, 119–120, 123, 126, 128–130, 188, 190–191, 198, 202; art as, 197–202, discontinuity, 27; economy of, 52, 54; horizon, 26–27; of inauguration, 143; of philosophy, 121, 123, 129; original, 3, 171; originary, 47, 141; philosophy as, 125, 129; real-time, 23; response to what has been, 188; successive, 31; that opens, 199; time, 22, 129, 189, 201; unfold, 14
eventuate, 115
eventuation, 4, 129, 189, 191, 197
everyday, 12, 21, 66–67, 134
everydayness, 89, 134–135
exchange, 27, 48
existence, 5, 24
existential: analytic, 40; historicity, 22; responses, 4; salvation, 20; temporal forms, 25; time, 66; trajectory, 5

existentiell, 63
expectation, 15, 21, 28, 97, 187. *See also* anticipation
expedition, 193. *See also* adventure; exploring unknown territory
experience, 14–15, 19–20, 47, 52, 55–56, 74, 93, 109, 171, 178; death, 110; human, 13, 110; lived, 10, 11, 31; of shifting from one economy to another, 19; social and historical, 16; unity of, 13
experiences, 11; in time, 24; of our bodies, 10; temporal, 49
experiencing, 44
experiment, 2, 20, 217n4
exploring unknown territory, 193, 196
external dimension, 28, 37

failure, 11, 77, 105, 154; of the tradition, 31
fairy tale, 22. *See also* stories
faith, 5, 106
fall, 12; into illusion, 13
fallibility, 168
false hope. *See* hope, false
family, 17, 49–51
fate (*Schicksal*), 5, 64, 75, 135–137, 214n60; of public speech/writing, 156. *See also* destiny (*Geschick*)
feeling, 93. *See also* intuitions
femininity, 189. *See also* sexual difference
fiction, 151–152
film, 37. *See also* movies
Final Solution, 140. *See also* Auschwitz; genocide; Holocaust; Nazi; Third Reich
finite, 24, 90. *See also* infinite
finitude, 9, 22, 24, 30, 55, 137
fixity, 88
flexibility, 164
flux, 27, 215n14
forget, 30, 50; forgetting, 138, 187; active forgetting, 125, 127; forgive but not forget, 50; philosophy as forgetting, 66
forgiveness, 50, 168
form, 12; formal assurances, 12; formally describing, 26
Foucault, Michel, 14, 122, 124–130, 172
foundation, 73; foundational prejudices, 149
four-dimensional time-space, 121
fracticity, 82, 214n58
fragile, 15, 200; boundaries, 36; mortality, 36

fragility, 29, 36, 94

fragmentation, 17, 22, 179

frame, 26, 183, 194–195, 228n47

frameworks, 10–11, 14–15, 20

freedom, 24, 76, 106, 193; as teleological structure, 14

Freud, Sigmund, 13, 18–19, 32, 109–110, 197; critique of religion, 204n6; father principle, 20; Freudian displacement, 20; pleasure principle, 19, 206n7; reality principle, 19, 206n7

friends, 17, 22

Führer, 136. *See also* Hitler, Adolf; Nazi; Third Reich

fundamental ontology, 60, 62–63, 66–67, 92, 211n16

future, 4–5, 11, 18, 20, 21, 52, 56, 77, 94, 185, 186, 187; alternative, 134; foreseeable, 4; openness to, 4; pleasure, 20; predicated on the past, 172; present, 11, 13, 97, 107; shared community, 5, 76; synthesis with past present, 4; unrepresentable, 97

gap, 23, 99, 101

gateway, 98, 100

gathering, 54

genealogy, 125–127; genealogical problems, 92

generation, 120

generosity, 53, 198, 209n28

genetic fallacy, 18

genocide, 9, 184. *See also* Auschwitz; Final Solution; Holocaust; Nazi; Third Reich

geometry, 86, 121

German Idealism, 129, 225n10

Germany, 131–132, 134–138, 140, 142

Gestell, 109, 140, 213n35

gift, 38, 44–48, 56, 69; of death, 55; impossible, 47; pure, 52

giving, 43, 45, 47, 69, 70–71, 77

global warming, 28. *See also* crisis, ecological; devastation of the earth; environmental meltdown

God, 9, 43, 55, 92–93, 107, 136, 211n22; death of, 11

gods, 6

going counter to a thinker, 104, 120. *See also* criticism; polemics

going to the encounter, 104, 120. *See also* thinking

good and evil, 167

grand narratives, 11, 13, 15, 192–193, 227n39; as regulative ideas, 13; demise of, 22. *See also* narrative

gratitude, 47. *See also* thanking

grid, 172, 180

ground, 20–21, 73; middle (*see* middle, ground)

growth, 12, 27. *See also* development; maturation

Guattari, Felix, 114, 207n10. *See also* Deleuze, Gilles

guiding desires, 15

guiding idea, 3, 104, 106, 112, 115

guilt, 39

habit, 2, 21

healed, 32, 35. *See also* narrative

health, 11, 17

hear, 28, 69

heart, 46

Hebrew, 50, 142

Hegel, G. W. F., 5, 47, 55, 59, 132–133, 141, 182, 188, 198, 200–201; model of time, 12

Heidegger, Martin, 3, 5–6, 14, 18, 21–22, 31–32, 38–39, 41–48, 54–56, 59–79, 81–82, 84, 86–97, 100–108, 110–115, 120–121, 123, 128–137, 139, 140–143, 150, 152–155, 167, 171, 185, 189, 197–200, 206n8, 212nn34,35, 214n56, 219n32, 225n16; as theologian, 88; logic of thinking, 69, 72; optimism, 48; political involvement, 5, 131, 140; reading, coming after, 6; Rectoral Address at Frieburg, 131, 133, 136, 138–139, 141; time-driven re-reading of, 6; transformative inhabiting of, 111

Heideggerian hope, 154

(mock-)Heideggarian idiom, 31

helplessness, 13. *See also* development; infant

hermeneutic, 28, 29, 86, 100, 163, 165

hesitate, 10, 11, 23

hesitation, 23, 137, 141

heterogeneity, 25, 163–167

hidden law, 71, 73

Hiroshima, 14

historical: beginnings, 125; being (*see* being, as historical); corruption, 2; exhaustion, 3; experience, 16; pessimists, 14; sense, 127; thrownness, 137; time (*see* time, historical)

historicality (*Geschichtlichkeit*), 61, 75, 78, 89
historically: delimited, 9; determined discourse, 23; engaged existence, 5; significant human practice, 171
historicism, 129
historicity, 22; of boundaries of self, 16
historizing (*Geschehen*), 61
history, 1–2, 11, 14, 18, 22, 28, 31, 77, 98, 108, 125, 128–129, 133, 134, 142, 155, 159, 192, 202; as a discipline, 22; as organized, 13; as product of chance and accident, 126; complex of development and maturation, 18; effective, 126; human, 112; metaphysical, 126; monumental, 127; of being, 111; of ontology, 78; of the world, 14; providential, 12, 14; unity of, 33; universal and directional, 14; weight of, 197
Hitler, Adolf, 137, 142; his applications of Nietzsche, 139. *See also* Führer; Nazi; Third Reich
Hofstadter, Douglas, 170
Hölderlin, Friedrich, 132
Holocaust, 138, 228n60. *See also* Auschwitz; Final Solution; genocide; Nazi; Third Reich
hope, 3, 20, 53, 185, 187, 200; false, 150, 152; framework of, 20; Heideggerian, 154; provisional, 14; springs eternal, 179
horizon, 11, 21, 64, 86, 97, 111, 216n20; event, 26–27; of beings, 62 (*see also* being); of engagements, 91; of expectation, 53; of my mortality, 89; of response, 22; transcendental, 68; virtual horizon of art, 187
horizonal thinking, 91
horizonal unity ecstematic, 64–65
horizonality, 11, 14, 21; of time, 120
horizonlessness, pathological expressions of, 21
horizons of significance, 36
hospitality, 54
hubris, 92–93; humanistic, 185
Hudson River school, 183, 224n7
human, 13, 16, 26, 110, 163, 171; and the animal, 95; development, 5–6, 18–19, 108–110, 113, 115, 217n10; experience as resistance to entropy, 13; finitude, 171; history, 112; mortality, 29; not closed systems, 198

humanistic closure, 36
hunger, 28
Husserl, Edmund, 18, 29, 31, 38, 60, 89, 95, 110, 121, 132, 148, 155–156, 171, 208n23, 215n14; account of inner-time consciousness, 27; Husserlian phenomenology, 26, 37, 87

iconoclasts, 14
idea, 12, 104; of horizon, 64; of providence, 14; of universal history, 14
ideal possibility, 53
idealist myth, 90
ideality, 126, 128; continuist model of, 19
idealization, 23
idealizing unification of history, 128
ideas, 13, 174
idée fixe about time and history, 192
identification, 17
identity, 10, 15, 24, 26, 28–29, 126, 135–137; achievement of cooperation, 15; autonomous, 21; constructing a personal, 32; consumer, 17; deconstruction of, 16; logic of, 47–48; management of boundaries, 17; narrative, 31, 35, 164, 166; projectable, 21; stratified, 19; substantial, 15; the *is* of, 70–71; through naming, 109; wars, 15
ideological mystification, 196
ideology, 131, 137
illuminative idea. *See* guiding idea
illusion, 13, 77, 150–151, 167, 186–187; of narrative continuity, 5; of risk, 227n42; opposed to truth (*see* truth, illusion of); religious, 13
illusory dreams, 159
image in thought, 98–100
image-words, 100
imaginary world, 19, 187
imagination, 66, 167; disruptive, 169; experiments with time, 10; organizing power of, 32; productive, 22, 34; rule-governed, 31. *See also* narrative, imagination
imagine, 27, 50, 164
immanent basis for transcendence, 107
immediate gratification, 111
impossibility, 45–46, 51, 97, 106
inadequacies, 11, 173
inaugural, 3, 133–134, 137, 191, 221n17
incompleteness, 196
independence, 108. *See also* dependence
indirect communication, 99

Index

indirect speech, 154
individual: life, 12, 31; memories, 19; psyches, 16. *See also* human
individualism, 17, 204n11
industrialization: of the day, 10; toxic, 184 (*see also* global warming)
infant, 108–109. *See also* childhood
infantile, 19–20, 204n6; sense of helplessness, 13
infinite, 11, 22, 112
injustice, 15
inner, 15, 26, 37
inner time-consciousness. *See* phenomenology of inner time-consciousness
inorganic existence, 18
inside, 27, 29
insight, 15, 149
institutions, 10, 26
integration, experiential and reflective, 12
integrity, 3, 5–6
intellectual shift, 15
intelligibility, 12, 13, 15, 41, 87, 169, 180, 193, 200; attacks on, 20; fundamental grounds of, 10; that is unintelligible, 43; umbrellas of, 13
intelligible, 32, 201
intensification, 65
intention, 38, 54
interconnectedness, 86
interests, 15, 19
interpersonal nexus, 21
interpretation, 2, 15, 20, 25–26, 36, 56, 99, 103. *See also* reinterpretation
interpretive violence, 104
interrupting, 22–23, 34, 190
interruption, 15, 19–20, 27, 52
intersubjectivity, 18–19
interweaving, 28, 62; of language and time, 171
intuition, 24, 28, 31
intuitive, 27, 28, 88
invitation, 23, 146
inviting, 144–145
invulnerable discourse, 158. *See also* vulnerability
Irigaray, Luce, 108–109
irresponsibility, 16
islands, 149–152, 159. *See also* Macleish, Archibald

Jacob/Israel, 142
Jewish space, 190

Jewish tradition, 142
joke, 151–154
jouissance, 111, 157. *See also* pleasure
justice, 9, 15, 52, 56, 88, 211n16

kairological temporality, 87
Kant, Immanuel, 6, 12–13, 22, 31, 35, 37, 66, 93, 98–99, 104–105, 174, 179, 220n12; Analytic of Principles, 31; conception of the transcendental, 62; Kantian worries, 65
Kearney, Richard, 5, 114, 163–169, 218n29
Kierkegaard, Søren, 3, 14, 20, 55, 71, 93, 99, 106, 137, 198, 211n16
Kiekegaardian sense, 97

Lacan, Jacques, 108–109, 113–114, 177, 217n11
lacuna (gap), 29
landscape, 83; painting, 183, 196, 225n7
language, 24, 30, 70, 93, 107, 109, 113, 122, 146–147, 148, 150–152, 171, 175, 177–178, 180–181, 196, 198; as *poesis*, 30; conceptual resources of, 31; inadequate, 174; limits of, 99; of economy, 26, 206nn7,8; ordinary, 147, 148; privileged, 69; protects, 30; relation to, 109; theory of, 109; time and, 30, 33; undergoing an experience with, 74
last analysis, 127, 134–135
leap, 101
learn, 21. *See also* education
legitimacy, 22
legitimation, technological, calculative modes of, 115
letting, 45. *See also* presencing
Levinas, Emmanuel, 22, 32, 54, 88, 94, 96, 134, 208n23, 212n30
Levi-Strauss, Claude, 167, 172, 193, 227n39
liberal, 14
liberalism, modern, 17
life, 96, 155–156; affirmation, 125; after death, 107; and death, 11, 17, 156, 167; and death struggle, 13, 55; on earth, 107
lifetime: projects, 199; our own, 14
Lightman, Alan, 10
limits, 99–101, 198; of conceptuality, 56; of language, 99; of validity, 32
linear time. *See* time, linear

linguistic: mediation, 173; synthesis, 33–34
listening, 74, 79, 157
literature, 22, 37
lived experience, 10, 11, 31
living beings, 13, 26, 169
logic, 19, 20, 43, 47, 74, 198; circle, 85–86; conflicting, 28; of Heidegger's thinking, 69, 72; space, 65
logocentrism, 53
logos, 43, 79
loss, 10, 111, 136, of foundation, 101; of meaning, 157; of origin, 132
luck, 19. *See also* chance
luminotopological discourse, 69
Lyotard, Jean-François, 22, 188, 190–192, 197, 200, 202, 219n32, 228n52

Macleish, Archibald, 149–152, 159
madness, 122, 216n20
man, 35, 106–107, 136, 183
management, 19, 26–27; boundaries of inside and outside, 27; of otherness, 26–27; the world (economic and technological), 134
maps, 62, 123, 152, 193
mastery, 114, 124, 130, 158
material, 16, 126, 198
maturation, 16, 18, 102. *See also* development; growth
maturity, 19, 111
Mauss, Marcel, 47–48
meaning, 15, 24, 110, 155, 156; bestowing function of ideal acts, 121 (*see also* Husserl, Edmund); closure of, 33; of Being, 62
memories, 98; buried, 18; lost, 10
memory, 10, 15, 22, 28, 31, 46, 49, 56, 109, 128, 130, 134, 138, 203n1, 221n17; artificial, 72; impossibility of adequate, 23; nonlinear, 114; problem of, 54, 114; recollective, 91; technology of, 72; town without, 23 (*see also Einstein's Dream*). *See also* recollection
mercy, 88
Merleau-Ponty, Maurice, 20, 25, 112, 122
messiah, 22–23, 142
messianicity without messianism, 52
metaphor, 33–34, 65, 99, 146–147
metaphysical, 15; concept, 41; desire, 119, 177; distortion, 88; frame, 202; history, 126; illusion, 126; lure, 128;

neutrality, 26; prejudice, 47, 65; thinking, 147; umbrella, 200
metaphysics, 17, 63, 67, 141; closure of, 151; of ruination, 201; overcoming, 111; revisionary, 25. *See also* post-metaphysical
metontology, 63, 211n16, 214n56
metonymy, 33, 222n12
middle: ground, 21, 28; voice, 43, 94
mirror stage, 108–109
mirrors, 194, 201
misrecognition, 16. *See also* recognition
misunderstandings, 3, 157
Möbius strip, 82, 209n27, 212n27
modality, 100–101
mode, 26, 100, 109
model, 15, 28; of action, 77; of identity, 19; of time, 5, 66–67, 85; of world as a homogeneous unity, 26
modernist, 10, 196–199, 228n52. *See also* postmodernist
momentary flash, 202
monument, 202; monumental history, 127
morality, 12, 16, 55
mortality, 22, 94, 96, 130
mourning, 96, 114, 216n18
move forward, 185–187
movement, 82
movies, 10. *See also* film
multiplicity, 15–16, 19, 81
music, 28–29, 37
musical: ecstasy, 51; instruments, 26; performances, 27
mysteries, 2
myth, 9, 90, 172; of Sisyphus, 21
mythic heroism, 184

names, 17, 30, 138
narrative, 5, 10, 13, 22, 31–34, 114, 138, 171, 172, 175, 192–193; activity, 22; counter-, 164–165; dark side of, 5; development, 178; economy, 36; frame, 167; grand (*see* grand narratives); guardian of time, 31; heals aporia, 31–35; identity, 31–32, 35, 164, 166; illusion of continuity, 5; imagination, 5, 22, 114, 163, 165–166, 169, 218n29; indirect discourse of, 31; intelligibility, 35, 193; minority, 165; of restructuring, 6; organization, 207n20; play, 23; poetics, 34; power to tame time, 33; question of, 193; socially integrative, 115; subversive, 165

narrativity, 10, 164, 167, 193; as democratic activity, 22; as sense-making,
22; local, 5; power of proliferating, 22
nation, 15, 135, 137–138, 154, 164; traditional symbolic boundary, 17
nationalism, xenophobic, 164
nationality, 135
natural: attitude, 89; phenomena, 28; settings, 184
nature, 107
Nazi, 134, 140. *See also* Auschwitz; Final
Solution; Führer; genocide; Hitler,
Adolf; Holocaust; Third Reich
necessity, 79, 128; of philosophy, 106
negentropic, 26. *See also* chaos; disorder;
entropy
nestedness, 112, 175
neurosis, 109
new, 133, 191, 219n32; beginning, 112,
140. *See also* renew
Newman Barnett, 5, 189–191, 197, 200,
202, 228n60
Nietzsche, Friedrich, 3–6, 9, 14, 17, 21,
65, 75–76, 80, 87–88, 101, 105–106,
111–112, 115, 125–129, 132–133,
139, 151, 184, 202; refusal of followers, 6
nihilism, 196
nostalgia, 185, 187
novel, 166–168, 176–179; postmodern,
180

obedience, 55, 139
object, 23, 28; pole, 26; opposed to appearance, 196; proper research, 24;
silent, 157
objectification, 189
objective time. *See* time, objective
obligation, 190
offering, 144–145
old, 133
one and the many, 29, 33, 137. *See also*
time, one and many
ontic, 28, 44, 47, 53, 65, 82; discourse,
69, 82; meaning, 65; orientation, 63;
roots, 72; time, 9. *See also* ontological
ontogeny recapitulates phylogeny, 111–
112
ontological, 10, 28, 30, 44, 47, 53, 60,
68, 82, 87; adumbration of, 29; decay,
202; difference, 62, 82, 108; failure,
201; limits of representation, 189; neutrality, 26, 29, 88, 94; presuppositions

of logic, 62; task, 190; time, 62 (*see*
time, ontological); truth, 191. *See also*
ontic
ontology, 29, 36, 75; as such, 62; general,
44; regional, 44
open possibilities, 23, 140, 185
open-ended interrogation, 196
opening, 3, 68–69, 76, 100–101, 143; a
new beginning, 112, 140; a world,
180; onto the day, 4; to the gaze, 174
openness, 22, 56, 146, 180; indefinitely,
13; recursive, 88, 96; to future, 4 (*see
also* time, openness); to interruption,
96; to the other, 52, 54
opposition, 32, 127, 194, 196. *See also*
all-or-nothing alternative; binaries;
either/or; time, cosmic (B-series);
time, phenomenological
order, 29, 180; of flux, 27; that holds
sway, 35. *See also* chaos; disorder;
entropic; entropy; negentropic
ordinary language, 147; philosophy, 148
organization, 19, 24, 26–27, 32, 37; narrative, 207n20
orientation, 91, 195
origin, 120–122, 125, 134, 143, 147,
191; of time-shelters, 30; pure, 126–
127; reactivation of, 123
original, 171; event, 3, 171; primordial
temporalization, 141; thanking, 54;
time, 90; unbroken relation, 177
originality, 1–3, 6
originary event, 47, 141
oscillation, 64–65
the other, 22, 88, 98, 149, 153–155, 157,
212n30; exclusion of, as other, 88; the
other's fragile mortality, 95
otherness, 143
out of time, 52, 191
outside, 26–27; within, 27
overcoming, 85, 112; cease all, 107, 112;
metaphysics, 111; representation, 99;
structure of concealment, 43
overman, 23, 101, 217n9

painters, 182, 186
painting, 187, 189, 191; landscape, 183,
196, 225n7; present to itself, 190
paradox, 3, 165, 167, 173
paranoid stance, 20
parodic, 126
parody, 127–128
passing away, 30

passion, 28, 37
passive synthesis, 38, 87, 93
passivity, 39, 158. *See also* activity
past, 4, 6, 10, 11, 18, 91, 165, 172, 180,
    182, 184, 188; adumbration of, 106;
    as resource, 21; errors, 124; fidelity to
    the, 125; keeping alive the, 4; present
    future, 11, 33; settling accounts with,
    11; stuck in the, 98; things of the, 5;
    transforming the, 5; veneration of the,
    127. *See also* synthesis
pathological, 5, 15, 21
pathos, 22; cosmic, 25; of writing, 149
peace, 164
peasant life, 71–72, 74, 153, 212n34
people (*des Volkes*), 28, 135, 138. *See also*
    nation
performativity, 107, 112–113, 115,
    165, 198
person, 24, 26, 28, 32
pessimism, 21
phenomenological: account of language,
    148; consciousness, 155; lament, 121;
    theory, 28; time (*see* phenomenology,
    internal time consciousness; time,
    lived experience; time, phenomeno-
    logical)
phenomenology, 38, 53, 63, 122; internal
    time consciousness, 27, 31, 171; of
    embodiment, 25; of religion, 92
phenomenon, 43; of having a name, 17;
    of sheltering, 27
philosophers, 10–12, 21, 124, 134, 166,
    196; -kings, 76, 139
philosophical: dangers, 60; fiction, 12;
    mentor, 6; method, 65; nationalism,
    143; practice, 25; prescription and
    legislation, 5; problems, 89; progress,
    120; questioning, 59; reflection, 198;
    transgressions, 124; truth, 100
philosophy, 6, 54, 59, 95, 99–100, 102–
    103, 106, 123–124, 131, 138, 140,
    159, 189, 195, 226n18; as an event,
    125, 129; as forgetting, 66; as a prepa-
    ration for death, 130; closure of, 150,
    158; confronts its own limits, 200;
    death of, 11; event of, 129; fate of,
    22; instrumentalization, 196; neces-
    sity of, 106; of event, 121, 123, 129;
    of feeling, 67; ordinary language, 148;
    pervasiveness of time in, 24, 129; to
    complete, 107
photograph, 49–51

phronesis, 16, 163
Plato, 6, 28, 104, 110, 122, 130
play, 128; of limitations, 124; playing vic-
    tim, 147
pleasure, 4, 21, 111, 157; future, 20;
    immediate, 19; principle (*see* Freud,
    Sigmund, pleasure principle)
poetic eschatology, 76
poetics, 25, 31, 34; becomes ethics, 36;
    for speculative and practical ends, 34;
    of space, 25; of time, 25–26, 173
poetry, 30, 132, 134, 141, 149–150, 159
polemics, 15, 165. *See also* going counter
    to a thinker
possibility, 97, 152, 186; and neces-
    sity, 90; of my death, 97; of my
    possibility, 95
postmetaphysical, 156
postmodernism, 114, 158, 197, 199,
    228n52
postmodernist, 17, 196, 198; nihilistic,
    17. *See also* modernist
power, 21, 137, 157–158; constituting,
    71; of the original, 3; -play, 157
prayer, 3
preparation, 140
presence, 30, 41, 45, 47, 71, 74, 144,
    147, 155–156, 190; and presencing,
    44–45, 89; apotheosis of presence, 41;
    of the speaker, 146; of the writer to
    the reader, 144; privilege of, 59, 111;
    self-, 144, 155
presencing, 82, 89, 200, 202, 214n57
present, 4, 11, 53, 54; age, 20; deviations
    from present, 17; eternal, 27; present-
    ness itself, 64; synthesis with past and
    future, 4. *See also* future; past
presentation, 90
preservation, 125
preserve, 26, 30, 123
presuppose, 9, 25–26
primal, 92, 197
primitive, 18, 72; economy, 70–71,
    212n30; principle of succession, 12;
    strife, 122
primordial: temporality, 142; time, 66, 81
primordiality, 60
principles, 13, 28
problems, 49; of philosophy, 54; of time
    and temporality as such, 60
productive, 2, 22, 23, 150
productivity, 172
progress, 9, 68, 105, 183–184, 193, 199,

203n1; Enlightenment, 12; philosophical, 120
progressive modernist, 196
progressive series of stages, 197
promise, 53, 93, 184–185; of deconstruction, 150; making, 16; promised ends of teleology, 14; promising, 32, 163; promises, 144
prosperity, as teleological structure, 14
Protestantism, 87
"proto-SZ" (Heidegger lecture), 61
provisional, 61, 111, 148
psychic, 18–19, 32
psychoanalysis, 113–114. See also talking cure
psychologism, 71
purification, 72
purified: event, 190; experience, 171

quasi-transcendental, 65
question, 23, 49, 99, 155, 185, 195; of art's relation to time, 196; of Being, 67–68, 84, 107–108, 110; of knowledge, 105; of narrative, 193; of Time, 59, 64, 67
questioning, 137, 191

rational, 20
reactivation, 121, 123, 142. See also reanimate
read, 82; another thinker, 120
reader, 40, 157, 177–178
reading, 20, 25, 56, 98, 100, 105, 146, 148–149, 158, 178–179; after Heidegger, 6; philosophy, 102; risks, 78
reaffirmation, 20. See also affirmation
real, 23, 27, 30, 35, 99, 104, 127–128, 151; radical reduction of, 28; vacation from, 21; world, 19, 23. See also memory
realignment, 39–40
reality, 23, 126, 196; adjustment to, 16; noumenal, 30; principle (see Freud, Sigmund, pleasure principle); subordinate fantasy to, 169
reanimate, 3, 184; the tradition, 111
rearrangement, 123
reason, 14, 24
reasoning, 73, 196
rebirth, 12
recapitulation, 28, 103
receptivity, 93, 106
recognition, 6, 15–17, 23, 50, 53, 55,

164; demand for, 16; ethnic, 16; historic failure of, 15
recollection, 91, 119. See also memory
reconciliation, 35, 164
recover, 12, 82, 133
recurrence: eternal, 65, 129. See also return, eternal
redemption, 12, 194
re-emergence, 109, 125
reflection, 10, 30
regressive, 4, 15, 19–20
regularities, 16, 27
regulative, 12–13, 15, 26, 100; ideas, 13, 88, 215n4, 216n20 (see also grand narratives; Kant, Immanuel); value, 29
reinterpretation, 2, 105. See also interpretation
relation, 26, 53, 89; between past, present, future, 11; between Time and Being, 44, 61, 102; of writer to reader, 149; to the other, 10, 94, 149, 154, 156, 159, 163; to the world, 105
relationality, 27
relativism, 14, 196
religion, 13, 204n6; neutral discourse, 87. See also Catholicism; Christianity
religious, 88, 197, 199; partition of temporal and eternal, 107; thinking, 92
remember, 27, 130, 138
reminders, 100
renew, 82, 196, 219n32; renewal, 4, 22, 133; spiritual renewal, 143. See also new
repeat, 133; repeated invocation, 6; repeating, 171; repeats and reworks, 199
repetition, 1–3, 4, 6, 15, 21, 28, 74, 82, 86, 88, 105, 120, 125, 128–129, 137, 168, 171; as surface imitation, 3; banal, 3; blind, 198, 219n32; -compulsion, 168; empty, 4, 11, 120–123, 127, 128–129; in art, 191; mysteries of, 2; necessary, 101; of origin, 132; of repetition, 102; of the tradition, 75, 90; regressive, 4. See also Wiederholung
representability, 21–22
representation, 11–12, 22–23, 72, 84–85, 88, 99, 172, 175, 187, 196; analogical, 190; itself, 78; betrayal by, 98; representational sclerosis, 11; representational space, 86; representational thinking, 87; representational time,

91, 94; representations of impossible projects, 179

representing, 27; dangers of the past, 165

resistance, 22, 27, 193

resoluteness (*Entschlossenheit*), 40, 139, 171

respect, 36, 106

responding, 11, 188

response, 5, 22, 202

responsibility, 16, 54, 107, 115, 204n12

ressentiment, 111, 202

restitution, 47, 51–53, 56

return, 19, 47, 82, 121–122, 184; eternal, 4, 21; inevitable, 34; of the repressed, 19, 32; to origin, 138. *See also* recurrence

revenge, 106, 111

reversal, 120, 126

revolution, 15, 90, 135, 204n11

revolutionary, 6; thinker, 76, 90; times, 77

rhythms, 19, 27–28, 36; rhythmic interlacing, 28; within rhythms, 82

Ricoeur, Paul, 22, 30–36, 172, 207n23, 218n29

risk, 19, 76–78, 103, 113, 146, 149, 157, 193, 195, 214n60; illusion of, 227n42; risking myself, 144–145

rosemary, 149–150, 159

ruin, 5, 14, 197, 201–202; cosmic, 192. *See also* decay

rules, 27–28, 31, 77

ruptures, 15

sacrifice, 126, 128

safety, 13. *See also* security

salvation, 12; as a teleological structure, 14

sanity, 19

Sartre, Jean-Paul, 95, 146, 186, 193, 198

satiation, 28

satisfaction, 20

saying, 73–74, 79

schema, 11, 22–23, 26, 31, 91, 105, 174; of a pure concept of understanding, 98, 174; of a sensible concept, 98, 174; of space and time, 26; of time and identity, 16

science, 23, 34, 72, 100, 132; positive, 63; temporal or transcendental, 63; vocation of, 133

scientific mind, 25

secular theodicy, 9. *See also* theodicy

secular translations of religious phenomena, 92

security, 151, 156, 228n47. *See also* safety

seduction, 146–147, 154

selectivity, 28

self, 16, 19, 24, 28, 101, 135, 137, 180, 188, 196; as unity, 108; -blind dependency, 19; constituted by another, 137; -containment, 19, 135; -determination, 16; fracturing of, 94; -fulfillment, 110; integrated, 16–17; -legislation, 35 (*see also* time, phenomenological); -presence, 144, 155; -relatedness, 55, 89, 94; -satisfaction, 47; -situatedness, 89; traditional symbolic boundary, 17; -transformation, 115; -understanding, 22, 28, 35

selfhood, 19, 137, 163, 207n23

selflessness, 47

sending, 77–78; of being, 137. *See also* destiny (*Geschick*)

sequence of sentences, 73–74

series, 13, 18, 191

seriousness, 126–127, 151, 153, 156. *See also* parody

sexual difference, 108

sexual factuality, 63

sexuality, 124

shattering, 64

shelter, 27, 30, 142, 206n6; sheltering, 27, 30, 200

showing, 81–82, 189

sickness of the soul, 132

significance, 2, 13; of art, 185; of time, 189

signification, 173, 175

signifiers, 19

signs, 48; of signs, 179

simple, 65; succession, 170–171, 175

simplifying representation, 45

simulacra, 77

singularity, 4, 128–129

situations, 14

slaughter, 14

slavery, 16

sleeping and waking, 16, 28

smell, 150

Smithson, Robert, 5, 182, 191–194, *195*, 196–202, 227n46

social, 5, 16–18

solve problem by eliminating possibility, 49

songs, 22

Sorge. See care

sound, 26, 28, 66

space, 25, 28, 76, 85, 123, 196

spatial, 27; spatialization, 85

speak, 22, 144, 146
species, 17–18
spirit, 12, 141–142, 155, 186; of responsibility, 125; of seriousness, 125
state, 138. *See also* nation
stories, 10, 12, 96, 170, 193; about stories, 179; of one's life, 12; tall, 22
strange loops, 170
strangeness, 112
strategy, 124, 147–148, 157, 222n4
strength, 139
strife between earth and world, 121–123, 199, 225n16
structuralist, 167, 193
struggle, 6, 13, 15, 19, 76, 80, 104, 156
subject, 28, 30, 34, 37, 41, 46, 88, 124, 188, 204n11; as inner principle, 15; boundary, 109; death of, 11; deconstruction of, 16, 37; naïve unchanging, 39; pole, 26; subjective time, 170. *See also* object
sublime, 183, 190, 202; witness to the moment, 5
submission of the will to a community, 136
substance, 136; as inner principle, 15
substantive, 101
substitutes, 25
succession, 11, 12, 13, 170–171, 175, 193; numerical, 172
suffering, 90
suicide, 154
surging forward, 4
surplus, 131
survival, 27, 35–36, 150
suspend, 20, 26, 29, 50, 54, 193
suspicion, 165
symbolic, 3, 16, 21, 99, 108
synagogue, 190
synthesis, 4, 26, 28, 32, 169, 175, 188; linguistic, 33–34; objective, 194; of heterogeneity, 163–167; passive (*see* passive synthesis); temporal, 51, 189
synthetic activity, 22
synthetic power, 108, 167
systems, 13, 15, 17–18, 198, 201

talking cure, 32. *See also* psychoanalysis
technicity, 140
technology, 41, 72, 114, 140–141; of memory, 72; pervasiveness of, 41
teleological, 13, 109
teleology, 21, 78
telos, 111, 123. *See also* ends

temporal, 5, 13, 20–21, 27, 29, 61, 82, 85, 86, 105; constitution, 28, 191; continuity, 20, 200; dimension of the practice of art, 182; duality, 168; dwelling, 20; ecstasies, 64; experiences, 49; forms, 25; integrity, 35; openness, 70; organization, 27–28; presencing, 202; repetition, 60; structures, 27, 34, 59; succession, 11–12, 193; synthesis, 51, 189; temporalization, 51; unity, 9. *See also* category rigidity; change, inability to accept
Temporalität, 62–63, 66, 71. *See also* *Zeitlichkeit*
temporality, 6, 11, 22, 27, 90–91, 107; constitutive, 90; nonlinear, 6, 133; of the painting itself, 190; regressive, 19
temporally dramatized being, 5, 25–26
temporary, 61. *See also* present
terminus ad quem, 75
testimony of the dispossessed, 22
texts, 28
Thanatos. *See* death, drive
thanc, 46, 54
thanking, 22, 46, 56, 79, 93
theodicy, 134; secular, 9
theories, 12, 20, 21, 23
thermodynamic law. *See* entropy
things, 26–27
think, 46, 104, 113; Being in terms of giving, 44; Being without beings, 41; of time, 25; the unthinkable, 72
thinkers, 21, 24, 124
thinking, 21–23, 41–42, 47, 68–69, 72–74, 85, 92–93, 111, 121, 134, 140, 189, 191, 196, 198; about time, 11, 26, 33, 42, 206n8; anew, 113; as creative opening, 4; as event, 120; eccentrically about time, 170, 172–173, 177; from *Ereignis*, 115; impurity, 69; of Being, 87; reflective practice of, 23; time and the other, 53
Third Reich, 5, 135. *See also* Hitler, Adolf; Holocaust; Nazi
this-timeness, 4
thrownness, 30, 135, 137
timbre, 28
time, 1, 9, 11–14, 20–24, 27–30, 32–34, 36, 49, 51, 89, 107, 123, 167, 169, 172, 196; accurately accounting for, 97; acquiescing, 33; affectivity of, 20; agricultural, 171; aporias of, 22, 34; as a circle, 45; as a diverting topic, 24; as a homogeneous condition, 25;

began when the world was created, 31; breaks down, 5, 10, 14–15, 19, 33; causal, 32; central to philosophy, 24, 129; charming, 26; chronological, 78, 133; conflicting, 28; constituted, 171, 173, 175; cosmic (B-series), 14, 30, 32–34 (see also time, lived experience); cosmological (see time, cosmic [B-series]); destroyer of all we are proud of, 24; detached from space, 13; directional, 13; disciplinary, 171; dramatization of, 28; economy of, 25–26, 28, 38, 51, 119; end of, 13, 22, 197; event, 22, 129, 189, 201; folding back onto itself, 62, 66; historical, 98, 142; horizon, 11, 21, 111; horizon of the question of Being, 38, 63, 86, 97, 115; imaginative experiments with, 10; innocent sense of, 6, 37 (see also Augustine); inscrutability of, 33, 36; institutional, 172; intentional, 32; interruption of sameness, 94; is dead, 12; is out of joint, 11, 204n2; is pervasive, 31; linear, 9, 11, 19, 22, 34, 78, 107, 124, 129, 134; lived experience, 10, 18, 30–32, 56, 98 (see also time, phenomenological; time, cosmic [B-series]); management of, 17; metaphysical concept, 12, 90; narrative, 13, 31, 33; necessary backdrop, 37; nonlinear creative interruption, 34; objective, 27, 31, 84, 170; of art, 202; on our side, 9; one and many, 29, 33; ontic, 9; ontological, 62, 133; openness, 10; ordinary, 46, 51, 68; organization in and of, 27; original, 90; outwits consciousness, 190; passage of, 10, 27, 51; personal, 98; pervasiveness of, 25; phenomenological, 30, 32–34 (see also time, lived experience); plurally thought—fractured, dispersed, irregular, 9; poetics of, 25–26; radical break with, 129; ravages of, 31; recast, refigure, relaunch, reorient, 15, 22, 53; representation of, 21, 106; scientific accounts, 13; serial, 29, 172, 206n8 (see also time, series of nows); series of nows, 13, 25, 41, 47, 191 (see also time, serial); simple predicate, 25; single intelligible coherent continuity, 12; social, 98; Spirit falls into, 141; structurally thought, 4, 35; subjective, 21, 41, 98; successive order-ability of all experience, 12, 19; synthetic powers, 24; teleological, 107; that a painting is, 189, 202; thinking about, 11, 26, 33, 42, 206n8; traditional models of, 5; ubiquity of, 25; unity of, 9, 12, 29, 34–35; unrepresentability of, 21; ways of inhabiting, 19–20; withdrawal of, 89

time after time, 1–3, 6, 191

time and: Being, 42; identity, 16; language, 30, 33

timeless forms, 28

timelessness, 85

time-shelters, 26, 28–30, 206n8, 207n10

time-space, 107, 111, 115, 196, 206n8

timetables, 172

time-wars, 15

to auto (the same), 73

to-come, 53, 96. See also democracy to-come

today, 18, 41

toilers, 123

totalitarian thought, slide into, 76

totalitarianism, 138

totality, 29, 123

tragedy, 30, 134; of false hope, 150. See also hope

transcend natural domain, 26

transcendence, 60, 66, 106, 197; within immanence, 87

transcendental, 63, 65; aesthetics, 123; causation, 147; dialectic, 13 (see also Kant, Immanuel); framework, 81; horizon, 68; imagination, 66; language, 148; phenomenology, 132; schema, 174; signified, 181

trancendentalize, 64

transformation, 2–3, 5, 27, 29, 55, 106, 124, 128, 130, 134; affective, 4, 21; deconstructive, 41; events as, 123; incomplete, 18–19; in the economy of time, 111

transformative: failure, 112; inhabiting of Heidegger, 111; reading of the tradition, 103; repetition, 102 (see also repetition)

transformatory intent, 106

transgression, 124, 127, 130. See also limits

transitions, 100, 109; inability to accept, 20

translation, 25; between languages, 27; risks of, 78

trauma, 16, 109, 114; traumatic transformations, 112
trial and error, 17. *See also* error
truth, 23–24, 76, 88, 99, 103, 126, 128, 150, 200; as (mere) accuracy, 115; as living in relation to disclosure, 115; as representation, 115; as teleological structure, 14; of Being, 81; illusion of, 151
tyrant, 138

ubermensch. See overman
ultramoderne, 198. *See also* modernist; postmodernist
unbound signification, 171, 173, 177, 179–180. *See also* Calvino, Italo
uncanny, 15, 101, 110, 169
uncertainties, 193
unconcealment, 45
unconscious, 19
understand, 49; ourselves, 11; understanding, 15
unexpected, 21
unity, 19, 65, 120–121; aesthetic, 35; of absolute distinctness, 82; of experience, 13; of history, 33; -through-continuity, 12; with the world, 26, 177
universalists, 14. *See also* relativism
universe, 26
unlock, 99
unrecognized, 16. *See also* recognition
unthinkable, 32
unthought, 69, 73; addressing a thinker's, 120
unwelcome, 112
upswing, 64
urgency, 109

values, 17
variation, 28
violence, 103, 104, 228n47
visions, 14
visual: images, 29, 173; relation to the world, 175; representation, 174

voice, 177
void, 197
vulnerability, 70, 159, 201; of beings, 36; of the writer, 156, 207n8

Wagner, Richard, 76, 184. *See also* Nietzsche, Friedrich
war, 9, 164, 187; of mass destruction, 80; world, 14
wasteland grows, 106
ways, 15, 100; of being, 5; of seeing, 100, 198; of thinking, 62, 65
welcome, 22–23
Weltanschauung, 71, 92
West, 22, 132, 134, 137
Wiederholung, 105, 133. *See also* repeat; repetition
Wilde, Oscar, 11
will, 32; -to-power, 87–88, 115; -to-truth, 125
win, 13, 76, 136, 149
wish-fulfillments, 19
withdrawal, 25
witness, 10, 16, 22
Wittgenstein, Ludwig, 93, 99–100, 204n6, 215n14
wonder, 10
words, 104, 121, 196. *See also* things
working, 198
world, 14, 23, 26, 29, 31, 97, 105, 109, 121–123, 134, 175, 177, 180, 187, 199. *See also* being-in-the-world; strife between earth and world
worldly: enclosures, 25; innocence, 2; time, 31
writer, 10, 198; writer's experience, 178
writing, 59, 72, 113, 144, 155, 157–159, 179; as a break with the metaphysics of presence and self-presence, 155; as transmission, 79; as the death of presence, 156; connection with death, 222n1; philosophy, 102; risks of, 78

Zeitlichkeit, 62–63, 66, 69–71. *See also Temporalität*

David Wood is Professor of Philosophy at Vanderbilt, and Honorary Professor of Philosophy at Warwick (UK). He teaches Continental philosophy, and co-directs a research group on ecology. His many books include *The Step Back; Truth: A Reader* (with José Medina); *Thinking After Heidegger;* and *The Deconstruction of Time.*